PHILOSOPHICAL FOUNDATION OF EDUCATION

PHILOSOPHICAL FOUNDATION OF EDUCATION

A Critical and Comprehensive Study

O.P. Dhiman

KALPAZ

Published by

Kalpaz Publications
C-30, Satyawati Nagar,
Delhi – 110052
Ph.: 011-47034999, 9811692060
www.kalpazpublications.com
E-mail: kalpaz@hotmail.com

Distribution Network
gyanbooks.com
India, USA, Canada, UK, Australia, France

ISBN: 978-93-5722-439-0 (PB)

First Published, 2024

Printed at: Gyan Press, Delhi.

Philosophical Foundations of Education: A Critical and Comprehensive Study

Author: O.P. Dhiman

Dedicated

To

Student-Teachers

and

Teacher-Educators

Contents

PART TWO: PHILOSOPHICAL FOUNDAIONS OF EDUCATION

PART THREE: EMINENT WESTEREN EDUCATORS

PART FOUR: EMINENT INDIAN EDUCATORS

Preface

It has been said that reading makes a full man, conference a ready man and writing an exact man. In the discharge of my duties related to teacher-education, I had to read a lot on education and also to lecture on it. As a natural sequence to these persuits, I started writing just after passing my M.Ed. from Govt. College of Education, Jalandhar and joining M.G.N. College of Education, Jalandhar as a lecturer in 1964. My first book 'A Text Book of Principles and Techniques of Education' was published by Punjab Kitab Ghar, Jalandhar in 1965.

This was my first attempt to write a book. Being very ambitions, the book became voluminous having 650 pages. It was a popular book, but it proved to be somwewhat above the level of B.Ed. and M.Ed. students, though it was recommanded as a Text Book for the B.Ed. class by the Punjab University, Chandigarh.

Later, when I joined Govt. College of Education, Patiala in 1965, I started teaching both B.Ed. and M.Ed. classes. After having taught this subject for about a decade, I felt it necessary to reshape the said book in the light of my experiences so as to make it more handy and useful for the students. The new book of 392 pages was published under the title "Principle and Technique of Education" by Sharda Brothers, Ludhians. This book was recommend as a text book for the B.Ed class by various universities. Three editions of this book were published. As there was a great demand for this book, my colleagues of different colleges and universities suggested me to get this book re-published. But, because of my various other engagements in the field of education, I could not do so. On my retirement from Govt. College of Education in 1991, I immediately joined Multani Mal Modi Post-Graduate College, Patiala as Principal. So I could not find time to reshape this book and get it published.

Still there was great demand for this book from the students-teachers, and teacher-educators and I had to bow these demands. So after teaching B.Ed and M.Ed classes for 27 years, I decided to reshape and get this book published under the title of 'Principles and Techniques of Education.' This book comprising 33 chapters and 410 pages was published by Kalpaz Publications, Delhi in the year 2007.

The book got wide circulation and appreciative comments from several authorities on the subject. Still there is a great demand for this book.

Now, on the persistent demand of teacher-educators of the colleages and universities wherever I went to deliver Extention lectures to write a comprehensive book on Philosophical and Sociological Foundations of Education, I wrote a comprehensive book on the subject. As the book became very voluminous, I have to divide it into two parts and publish it as two books under the titles—Philososphical Foundations of Education and Sociological Foundations of Education.

The present book 'Philosophical Foundations of Education' is the result of my 27 years teaching experience to M.Ed. and B.Ed. classes and 13 years to secondary classes. It is an endeavour to provide the readers with a deep study of the various aspects of Education.

The book of 20 chapters and 310 pages is divided into four parts—Part one: Understanding Education; Part Two: Philosophical Foundations of Education; Part Three: Eminent Westernm Educators; Part Four: Eminent Indian Educators.

I do not claim any originality in the selection of the suibject-matter for this book. I only seek to examine, analyse and present very analytically all the aspects of Educational Philosophy integrated into a logical sequence to give the readers thorough understanding of the subject.

The views and opinions expressed in this book, and whatgever inadequacies and shortcomings there might be, I alone an responsible for them.

I hope this comprehensive but comprehensible book, will be useful to the M.Ed., B.Ed., and M.A. (Education) students, teacher-educators and educational administrators and planner to understand Educational Philosophy in a better way.

I will be happy to receive comments and suggestions from the readers for the modification and improvement of the Second Edition of this book.

Ashiana,
49, Raghbir Nagar
Patiala-147001, India

O.P. Dhiman
professor.dhiman@yahoo.com

Acknowledgements

Any accomplishment requires inspiration, help and guidance of many people and this book is not an exception. During its preparation, I have been inspired, helped and guided by a number of well-wishers.

I cannot but remember with feeling of piety and gratitude my mother, Late Mrs. Maya Dhiman, my first teacher, friend and philosopher, a staunch democrat who created in me a burning passion for democratic ideals, critical objective thinking and positive attitude.

Formal, though it may look, I must acknowledge my grateful appreciation to my wife, Mrs. Manorama Dhiman, former Head, Department of Home Science, Govt. College for Women, Patiala for her inspiration and devotion but for which the present work would have been well nigh impossible.

I must appreciate my grand-children Shivam, Anish, Chahat, Muskaan and Ayush from whom I have learnt a lot to refresh my ideas on Education. They also helped me a lot working hard on computer.

I extend my thanks to my colleagues—Dr. C.P. Sharma, Former Head, Department of Economics and Dr. Harcharan Singh, Associate Professor, Punjabi, Multani Mal Post-Graduate College, Patiala for reading the manuscript of this book and giving valuable suggestions.

I must be thankful to all the authors on whose works I have drawn freely.

I take this opportunity to put on record my deep sense of gratitude to all the Principals of Govt. College of Education, Patiala with whom I have worked for 26 years and who always inspired me despite my habit of being critical and independent in my views.

I should not complete this preface without thanking my students who were instrumental in clarifying some of my thoughts and in stimulating me to think anew on Philosophy of Education. They taught me more than they realise.

Last though the least, I am grateful to my publishers, especially Kalpaz Publications for his enthusiasm in the publication of this book.

March 6, 2014 **O.P. Dhiman**

Part One

UNDERSTANDING EDUCATION

The Meaning Nature and Bases of Education

The Aims of Eduction

Educational Aims in India

1

Meaning, Nature and Bases of Education

What is education? This fundamental question has been exercising the minds of philosophers and thinkers from Socrates, and Plato to Gandhi and Dewey. The word 'Education' has a very wide connotation and it is very difficult to give its precise definition. A biologist, psychologist, priest, philosopher, statesman, teacher, merchant, shopkeeper and even an artisan will give widely different definitions. Definitions—whether naïve or serious—lead us nowhere. Those seldom reveal the real meaning and nature of Education.

Let us discuss, in this chapter, what education is or what it implies.

ETYMOLOGICAL EXPLANATION OF EDUCATION

The first step in any systematic attempt to understand the nature of education should be to trace its sources of derivation. Etymologically, the term 'Education' is traced to different sources.

Education as Bringing up Process

According to one view, 'education' has been derived from the Latin word 'educare' which means to *'to bring up'* or *'To raise'*.

According to this view, education is a process of imparting, to an individual, certain information and knowledge which society deems necessary. Education implies modification of the behaviour of the individual by imposing standards of society upon him. Thus, education is a process of external imposition rather than growth from within. This derivation gives us the concept of teacher-centred rather than child-centred education.

Education as a Drawing out Process

There is a group of thinkers who believe that the term 'education' has been derived from the Latin word *'educere'* which means to *'lead out'* or *'to draw out'*. Education, they think, means to draw out something and not to put in something.

These theorists who hold that education is a drawing out process, give a slightly different explanation of the word 'education'. They believe that the term 'education' has been derived from two Latin words, *'e'* meaning *'out of'* and *'duco'* meaning *'to lead'*. Education, therefore, means 'to lead out' or 'draw out' the best in man. It is the process of 'drawing out from within' rather than 'imposing from without.'

Education, from this point of view, is considered as a process of the development, of what is innate in the child. It is an agency of, or an instrument for, the transformation of the potential into the actual. This explanation presumes that all knowledge is inherent in children. Education, therefore, implies growth from within rather than imposition from without. Education is a process of the development of talent inborn in the individual and not conveying to an individual a body of information or knowledge. A large number of eminent educators and philosophers have endorsed this interpretation. "By education", says Gandhiji, "I mean an all-round drawing out of the best in the child and man—body, mind and spirit."

Education as a Bringing up as well as a Drawing out Process

The two viewpoints of education, discussed above, cannot be isolated from each other. The view that education is a drawing out process can be accepted with a pinch of salt. In this interpretation, an important aspect of education has been disregarded. Can it be possible that everything—which forms part of education was already inherent in the child's mind? Is it possible to draw out everything? Can it be established that everything—ideas, ideals, beliefs, opinions and attitudes—was potential in the mind of the child? It is true that certain inherent capacities do form part of the natural endowment of the child, but the factual knowledge acquired, skills learnt or the habits and sentiments developed, during life time, were not innate in the child's mind. Therefore, it can be said that in the absence of poured in knowledge or suitable foundation laid through learning under environmental influences, drawing out will be out of question. Unless knowledge or experience is given to the child, we cannot draw out the best in him. Education, therefore, is not only a drawing out, but also a bringing up process, whereby the educand is trained for certain types of social behaviour democratic living, worthy citizenship, international understanding and is developed into a full man or woman with a well integrated personality. "True education", says Gandhiji, "is that which draws out and stimulates the spiritual, intellectual and physical faculties of the children".

Indian Synonyms of Education

The word *'Shiksha'* (शिक्षा), and *'Vidya'* (विद्या) are the Indian synonyms of *'Education'*. Shiksha is derived from the Sanskrit verbal root (रूट) *'Shas'* (शास्) which means to 'discipline,' 'to control,' 'to instruct' or 'to teach'. Similarly the word Vidya is derived from the Sanskrit verbal root. *'Vid'* (विद्) which means 'to know'. Thus, it refers to acquisition of knowledge. Hence disciplining the mind and acquisition of knowledge has always been the dominant theme in Indian approach to understanding education.

NARROW AND BROAD MEANING OF EDUCATION

Narrow Meaning of Education

Education, in its narrow sense, is regarded as equivalent to instruction, imparted in a school or college. Education is believed to begin with the entrance of the child to a school and end with his departure from the school or university. The amount of education, thus received by the child, is measured in terms of the number and the grades of examinations passed by him. There is deliberate effort, on the part of the educator, to inculcate, certain habits, attitudes or influences in the learner, which by tradition are considered to be essential and useful to him.

In the narrow sense, therefore, education includes those specific influences which are brought to bear upon the child with a definite purpose, in pre-planned, suitable and methodical manner by parents, teachers and the community, and which are for the welfare of the younger generation and perpetual preservation of the cultural heritage. For the achievement of this end, in addition to home, a special institution, called the school, is created and a particular person, called the teacher, is appointed. According to this view, education is mostly limited to class-room teaching of ready-made materials.

"In the narrow and more definite (or specific) sense", says T. Raymont, "In which the term is used in common speech and in legal enactments, education does not include self-culture and the general influences of one's surroundings, but only those special influences which are consciously and designedly brought to bear upon the young by the adult portion of the community, whether through the family, the church, or the state." These influences or modes of influences are deliberately planned, chosen and employed by the community for the welfare of the members of the rising generation. The purpose of these influences is to modify the behavior of the child in such a way that he may become different from what he would have been without education. It is to affect change which makes possible a better adjustment of human nature to the surroundings and to change the surroundings so as to harmonies with human nature. It is restricted to that function of the community which consists of passing on traditions, its background, its knowledge and its attitudes to the members of the rising generation through specialised people, instruments, and methods.

Broad Meaning of Education

In its broad sense, education is a life-long process, which starts with the conception and ends with the death. Education, in its wider sense, includes all the influences which act upon an individual during his passage from the cradle to the grave. An individual goes on increasing his knowledge and learns through his experiences and contacts with environment. Education, as such, is not teaching or learning of 3 Rs'—Reading, Writing and Recurring. It consists of development of 4 Hs'—Head, Heart, Hand and Health.

Education, in the broad sense, includes all the knowledge and experiences, acquired during infancy, childhood, adolescence, youth, manhood or old age through any agency of education—the school, home, church, society etc. In this way, one's whole life and all life activities become a real source of education. Thus, education becomes the sum-total of all experiences that the child receives in the school or outside, through the study of different subjects, through various activities, through the library, the playground, the workshop or through other agencies. Lodge in his book *Philosophy and Education,* while explaining the nature of education in the wider sense, says, "In the wider sense, all experience is said to be educative. The bite of a mosquito, the taste of a watermelon, the experience of falling in love, of flying in an aeroplane, of being caught in a storm in a small boat— all such experiences have a directly educative effect on us. The child educates his parents, the pupil educates his teachers. Everything we say, think or do, educates us, no less than what is said or done to us by other beings, animate or inanimate. In this wider sense, life is education and education is life. Whatever broadens our horizon, deepens our insight, refines our reactions, and stimulates thought and feelings, educates us".

In the broad or non-specific sense, education means the process of development from infancy to maturity. In other words, it is the process, whereby a human being gradually adapts himself in various ways to his physical, social, and spiritual environments. Thus, education is a life-long process. "It is really life that educates," says T. Raymont. "One is educated by one's vocation, by home life, by friendship, by marriage, by parenthood, by recreation, by travel, and so forth."

Broadly viewed, education is life and life is education. Education, in the broader sense, is transmission of life by the living, to the living, through living and for living.

Synthesis of the two Meanings

Viewed separately, these meanings of education hardly serve the desired ends. There is a need of reconciling the two meanings. Education must include knowledge and skills along with the factors necessary for the modification of child's behaviour and development of his personality. Both the meaning have to play an appropriate and significant role in the education of the child.

Decidedly, education is more than schooling and instruction, although these are its significant features. We may say that education consists of acquiring knowledge, skills and attitudes which assist one in maintaining good health, a reasonable amount of economic security and genuine happiness in life. We can conclude with the remarks of Dr. S. Radhakrishnan, when he says, "Education, to be complete, must be human; it must include not only training of the intellect but also the refinement of the heart and the discipline of the spirit."

FORMAL AND INFORMAL EDUCATION

Education may be formal or informal. Informal education is incidental—the education which a person receives from living with others. It is important and natural, but it is not deliberately planned.

Formal Education is consciously and deliberately planned for the purpose of training the child. It consists in direct schooling or tuition. Let us now discuss these two types of education in detail.

Formal Education

Formal education is that which is consciously and deliberately planned for the modification of behaviour with a particular end in view. Formal education is undertaken in schools or institution specifically established and maintained for this purpose. It therefore, takes the form of schooling, tutition and instruction. As the child goes to a school, he has to be formal and act according to the discipline of that school. He is conscious of the fact that he goes to that school for getting education. He is aware of his presence in the school throughout the day. Similar is the case with the teacher. He is too, aware of all these things. Thus, both the pupil and the teacher deliberately engage themselves in the process of education with predetermined objective in view. In a school, not only the atmosphere is formal, but the curriculum and methods of teaching are also formal. These are fixed in advance with clear-cut ends in view. All teaching is a formal.

It may, however, be maintained that any process of teaching, which involves supervision, instruction, set plan, definite aim and principles, amount to formal education, no matter whether given in a school or a workshop. As such, it also includes vocational or general education imparted by parents in a formal way.

Informal Education

Informal education is not pre-planned or deliberate. It is incidental and takes place consciously as well as unconsciously. Child learns many habits, manners, and patterns while living with others or moving in different spheres like home, society and groups etc. Actually, such education is not given by any specialised agency or institution, although this forms the essential feature of all education.

In an informal way, child imitates the elder members of the community and thus imbibes certain virtues, most essential for life. He is in this way getting education. Such an education is gained through experiences and actual living in the family or community. There is no prescribed course, no fixed time-table and no formal means of education. The transmission of cultural heritage and life experiences takes place in a natural way. Such an education becomes life-long process and is called informal education.

Difference between Formal and Informal Education

Formal and informal eduction can be differentiated as follows:

Formal Education	*Informal Education*
1. Formal education has formal end.	1. Informal education has no. formal end.
2. It has formal means.	2. It has no formal means.
3. There are qualified. Teachers who impart education.	3. There are no specified. Teachers in informal education. Whosoever imparts knowledge is the teacher.
4. Both, the educator and the educand are conscious about the process.	4. Neither the educator nor the educand is conscious about the process.
5. It has some prescribed course and fixed time-table.	5. It has no prescribed course and no fixed time-table.
6. There is some organisation body behind it. It is given in school or college.	6. There is no organising body behind it. There is no fixed place for it.
7. In formal education, examinations are given and certificates or degree are awarded.	7. In informal education, there are no examinations. Such type of education is never completed.
8. Agencies of formal education are school, library, museum, art gallery, laboratory and books.	8. Agencies of informal education are family, community, religion, state and playground etc.
9. It starts and ends at a particular stage.	9. It continues throughout life. It is a life long continuous process.
10. It leads to mental strain because serious efforts are made.	10. Informal education, being natural does not strain the learner.

From Informal to Formal Education

During the primitive times, all education was informal. It was limited to activites like hunting, fishing, workshopping, protection from the natural calamities, and so on. The child could learn such life activities by direct participation in the day-to-day life of the community and in an informal way from the more experienced members of the community. At that time life was very simple. So was the social order and culture. A son was to follow the profession of his father, and the daughter of her mother. With the advancement of civilisation and growing complexity of social order and culture, education began to lose its informal nature. With the growth of civilisation and advancement in the field of science and technology, the accumulated knowledge and the skills became more and more complex, which created the need for formal education. It necessitated the selection of educational experiences and consequently, education progressed from the incidental and the informal aspects of life towards the conscious formality of school. Hence, formal education became differential from the informal, and school became a specialised agency of Education.

Synthesis of the Two Types

As we have already noted, both formal and informal types of education try to prepare the child for life. However, as teachers, we are mostly concerned with formal education and, therefore, consider this type of education to be more important. Whereas, the influences of formal education are systematic, definite and permanent, those of informal education tend to be vague and indefinite. That is why in the case of formal education, we can predict results to a certain extent which is not possible in the case of informal education. It is through formal education that we can train and educate the immature child according to the demands of society.

All this may be quite true; still we cannot ignore the important role played by informal education in the life of a child. For formal education, a child stays in the school for five or six hours while the rest of the day is spent in the home, community, church, playground, etc., outside the school. The environment where the child spends the major part of his day, must therefore, have much more effect upon him than the school. Therefore, the importance of informal education cannot be ignored.

Education in it's 'totality' includes both, formal and informal education. In the modern structure, both types of education play important roles. The difference may be of quality or quantity, but each is implied by the other. Both are independent, but inter-connected. We cannot minimise the essential virtues like social, moral, spiritual values etc. in human life that informal education imparts. Similarly, we cannot ignore the significance of schooling, instruction and training that the formal education provides. Granted, that education is modification of human behaviour, a process of social change and transmission of cultural heritage; it is evident that formal as well as informal education should essentially form the basis of all educational organisation and planning. The two types of education are complementary to each other.

FORMAL AND NON FORMAL EDUCATION

A new concept, which has developed recently after the publication of the report of International Commission on the Development of Education, entitled 'Learning to Be' is the Non-Formal Education. The Commission feels that inspite of the vast financial resources being spent on education, vast majority of the people do not get the desired education. Some of them find it difficult, due to their pre-occupation in earning, while others desirous of admission in Schools, Colleges and Universities fail to get admission, because of shortage of seats and a very large number of aspirants for admission.

The Commission, therefore, suggests that alternative arrangements should be made for those who cannot attend formal institutions, because of one reason or the other. As a result, Distance Education Departments have been started by many Universities and also a number of Open Universities have been started. Now, those who fail to get admission in Formal Educational Institutes can get education through correspondence programmes, contact programmes, vacation programmes, satellite instructional programmes, teaching machines, programmed lessons and the like, through Distance Education and Open Universities. Such education is known as Non-formal Education.

Formal, Informal and Non-formal are not three types of education, as it is mostly misunderstood. There are only two types of education. Formal and Informal from one angle, i.e., contents of education or 'what education' and Formal and Non-formal from another angle, i.e., method of education or 'how education'. Thus, formal education can be formal or non-formal. If a student passes an examination from some formal educational institution, it will be Formal Education. If he passed that examination through distance education programme, it will be to some extent Non-formal education because in this case, as compared to the former, somewhat less formalities will be there. But if he passes that examination as a private candidate, it will be still more Non-formal Education, as in this case very few formalities will be there.

Non-formal education, as a system, is supplementary or parallel to formal education. Open Schools, Open Universities and Correspondence or Distance Education departments of the Universities are coming to stay as important instruments of education. Whether they are capable of achieving educational excellence of the order of formal education system, is a big question? However, they are of unique importance in this modern world.

EDUCATION AND OTHER TERMS

Education is generally confused with literacy, instruction, schooling and training. In the interest of clarity, therefore, education should be distinguished from these terms, though a distinction line of demarcation is ruled out. A brief explanation of the meaning of each of these terms will, however, give us a better insight into the real nature of education.

Education and Literacy

We often hear the people saying, "He knows reading and writing." "My wife is not educated." In both of these sayings, education means reading and writing. Thus, we have not made distinction between reading, writing and education. A literate wife may be less educated than an illiterate wife. There is a difference between education and literacy. Knowledge of reading and writing is literacy. No doubt, literacy is a part of education, but it is not education. "Literacy," says Gandhiji, "is not the end of education, nor even the beginning. It is one of the means whereby man and woman can be educated. Literacy in itself is no education."

Literacy lays more emphasis on the subjects and tools rather than on the personality of the educand, which is the main concern of education. Education is an all-round harmonious development of all the aspects of human personality—body, mind and spirit.

The following tables will make the difference between Education and Literacy more clear:

Education	*Literacy*
1. Education has wider scope than literacy. Literacy is only a part of education.	1. Literacy means knowledge of 3 Rs' only i.e., reading, writing and recurring or arithmetic.
2. Education is the all-round development of personality i.e., body, mind and soul.	2. Literacy helps in development only and that is also to some extent.
3. Education humanises humanity. It makes the man social.	3. Literacy does not humanise humanity. A literate person may not be social.

Education	*Literacy*
4. Education is a life-long continuous process.	4. Literacy is not a life-long process.
5. Education means all-round drawing out of the best in child and man i.e., body, mind and spirit. Even the illiterate may be educated persons.	5. The person with the knowledge of 3 Rs' is literate person. A person knowledge of 3Rs' is not a literate person.
6. An educated person is competent to solve the complex problems of life.	6. A literate person may not be competent to solve various problems of life.
7. Education is not mere teaching. All formal and informal, active and passive agencies provide education to a person.	7. Literacy is the end product of teaching. Only formal and active agencies make a person literate.
8. Education is formal as well as informal, planned as well as unplanned, organised as well as unorganised.	8. Literacy is only formal, planned and organized enterprise.
9. Education is deliberate as well as incidental.	9. Literacy is always deliberate.

Education and Instruction

Sometimes the term *'education'* is used to indicate day-to-day teaching of lessons in school. The process of imparting knowledge and skills in the class-room or laboratory may be called instruction, but not education. Whereas instruction is the process of conveying to an individual a body of information or knowledge, education is a process of development of the powers which are inborn in the child, at a rate and in a manner, determined by the capacity of the child. Whereas instruction implies external imposition, education implies growth from within. Thus, instruction is only one of the means of education and not education. Education is the complete development of the student's personality.

The following table will make clear the difference between Education and Instruction.

Education	*Instruction*
1. The scope of education is very wide Education means all-round developments of innate potentialities of the individual. It helps in physical, intellectual, emotional, social, aesthetic, cultural, moral and spiritual development of the individual.	1. The scope of instruction is narrow. Instruction means to impart knowledge of specific subjects through teaching. Instruction is generally related to intellectual development only. It is always.
2. Education is a continuous and life-long process.	2. The period of imparting instruction is limited.
3. Education aims at many sided development of the individual i.e., physical, intellectual, emotional and social etc. It aims at preparing the individual for life.	3. Instruction aims at intellectual development of the individual which is one sided. The aim of instruction is to prepare the Individual for passing the school or college examination.
4. Education is imparted in home, educational instituteons, religious and political groups, libraries, cultural and social institutions.	4. Instruction is generally confined to the class-room. It is generally imparted in educational institutions, i.e., schools and colleges.
5. Both formal and informal agencies provide education.	5. Instruction are provided by Formal agencies of education.
6. Education, in the broadest sense, does not follow systematic and rigid approach.	6. Instructions are generally imparted in a systematic manner, in a certain framework of rules and regulations.
7. In education, child is more important than the educator. The place of child is central, pivotal and of prime importance. Teacher's role is subsidiary.	7. In instruction, teacher is more important than the child. Teacher occupies the central place.

Education	*Instruction*
8. In education, child's abilities, interest, aptitudes, developmental level and other potentialities are given special consideration.	8. In instruction, child's abilities, interests, aptitudes, developmental level and other potentialities are ignored. Readymade knowle-dge is forced into his mind.
9. Curriculum of education is very comprehensive. The person's entire life is the curriculum.	9. Curriculum of instruction is narrow and fixed. It is based upon various subjects.
10. The range of methods of imparting education is very wide.	10. Limited methods are used for imparting instructions. Instructions are generally imparted through lecture and notes-giving methods.
11. In education importance is attached to social discipline.	11. In instruction, discipline is through command.
12. In education all the members of society, depending upon the situation can play the role of teacher.	12. In instruction, teachers are professionally trained and fixed.
13. Knowledge acquired through education can be perma-nent. It can be applied to solve various problems of life.	13. In instruction, cramming is encouraged. It is soon for-gotten. It cannot be applied to meet the Challenges of life successfully.
14. Education is formal as well as informal, planned as well as unplanned, organised, as well as unorganized, deli-berate as well as incidental.	14. Instructions are always formal, planned and deli-berate.
15. In education, behaviour is more important. Degree or certificate may or may not be given.	15. In instructions good marks are the motivating factor. Degree or certificate is awarded after the successful completion of the course.
16. Education ends with life.	16. Instruction ends in class-room.

Education and Schooling

Education is sometimes confused with schooling. The concept of schooling is similar to that of instruction, but it is a wider concept. It includes academic activities and programmes, other than class-room instruction. Co-curricular activities, community work, hobbies, educational trips and social service camps form part of schooling, though they are excluded, from the limited sphere of instruction. The venue of schooling may be the school or its neighbourhood even environment taken as a whole. If education is considered as schooling it means that the child is educated only for five or six hours a day and not for the remaining time. Again, this means that he is educated only for six days a week and not on Sunday and other holidays. Perhaps he is educated more when he watches movies, listens to radio, chats with friends and members of his family. Education is more comprehensive than schooling which is confined to a certain functions only. Education is a life-long continuous process.

The following table will make clear the difference between Education and Schooling.

Education	*Schooling*
1. The scope of education is very wide. Education is a life-long process. It starts from the womb and ends with the tomb i.e., it starts when the child is born and continues up to his death.	1. The scope of schooling is narrow and limited. Schooling is confined to the period for which the child remains on the rolls of an institution. Schooling includes academic activities and programmes, other than classroom instruction of communicated information. Co-curricular activities form an important part of schooling, but they are not included in the scope of instruction.
2. Education is a life-long process.	2. Period of schooling is confined to childhood and adolescence.
3. There are formal as well as informal aspects of education.	3. School has only formal aspect.

Education	*Schooling*
4. The atmosphere in education is natural as is artificial.	4. The atmosphere in schooling is better than artificial.
5. The aim of education is all round development of personality, i.e., physical, intellectual, emotional, social, aesthetic and moral development of the individual.	5. The atmosphere in schooling is also all round development of personality of the individual, but major emphasis is on intellectual development.
6. The places of education are home, school, as well as social, cultural, political, religious and business institutions.	6. The place of schooling is confined to four walls of the school.
7. Agents of education are parents and other family members, friends, neighbours, teachers, preachers etc.	7. Agents of school are primarily teachers.
8. Agencies of education are family, school, peer group, places of worship, state, radio, television, press etc.	8. School is the only agency of schooling.
9. Curriculum is as wide as life. It includes the whole life.	9. Curriculum of schooling is limited to some specific subjects and activities.
10. The range of methods of imparting education is very wide.	10. Only fixed methods of teaching like lecture, notes-giving, demonstration, experimental, project and discussion methods are used.
11. There is social discipline and social control.	11. Emphasis is on strict discipline.
12. All members of the society, depending upon the situation can play the role of teacher.	12. There are specific teachers, for every subject and co-curricular activities.
13. Formality and informality between the teacher and pupil go side by side.	13. Formality is observed between the teacher-pupil Relations.

Education	*Schooling*
14. There is important place of practicality in education.	14. More emphasis is placed on theoretical aspect in schooling.
15. There may be no definite time of evaluation. It may continue throughout life.	15. There is definite time of evaluation. Evaluation is essentially done at the end It may be direct as well as of each class. Theoretical, indirect practical knowledge of the subjects and the activities are evaluated. It is direct and by fixed methods.
16. Certificate may or may not be given.	16. Certificate is given in schooling.

Education and Training

In the opinion of some thinkers, education is an act of training, meant to enable a person to take his proper place in the life of the community. Man is basically animal.

Hence, he needs training in emotional adjustment, in controlling his impulses and aspirations and in modifying his behaviour so that he may not face mal-adjustment when he participates in a group. Education, no doubt, provides training for adult life.

But, training itself is not education. Animals are also trained by imitating the action of others, but in their training the purpose is neither conscious nor well designed. In education, on the other side, the purpose is clear and well designed. Education is a conscious process to train the individual so that he should make correct responses to the problems of life. If a child bows automatically while he is in the company of others, his response is physical and he may be called a trained child. If the child bows out of respect, he may be called educated, because this is a mental response.

In training, the desired outer action is secured; in education, the desired inner attitude, the mental and emotional disposition of behaviour is secured. True education means training the individual to discriminate between good and evil, both on the level of physical response as well as mental response. However, in popular sense, training is associated with preparation for professional career, or technical education. Education is a comprehensive term and training is only a part of it. It is only because of this distinction between education and training that the names of 'All the Teachers' Training Colleges in India have been changed into Colleges of Education.

The following table will make clear the difference between Education and Training.

Education	*Training*
1. The scope of education is very wide. Education includes teaching and training. Education refers to overall growth and development. It takes care of man's development in cognitive, affective and psycho-motor domain.	1. The scope of training is limited. Training is cofined to teacher only. Training is only a part of education. It implies development and perfection of skills and competencies of the learner. It is primarily concerned with developing tricks of the trade and professional competencies; the psycho-motor dimension of man's personality.
2. Education is a life-long process. It continues from birth to death.	2. Period of training is fixed. It may be for a few days, few months or few years.
3. The aim of education is the all-round development of a person.	3. The aim of training is the development of one or more specific skills.
4. Places for imparting education are home, school, college or university, religious institutions, social centres, cultural centres, neighbourhood, political groups and community.	4. Training is imparted in training institutions, like school, college, hospital, workshop, factory, office or any other training centre.
5. Both formal and informal agencies provide education.	5. Training is provided only by formal agencies of education.
6. Education in the broadest sense does not follow rigid and systematic approach.	6. Training has rigid and systematic approach. It is given in a systematic manner, in a certain frame-work of rules and regulations.

Education	*Training*
7. Education is both, theoretical as well as practical.	7. In training, more emphasis is placed on practical aspect.
8. Curriculum of education is broad and indefinite as in informal education. It is definite, fixed or determined in formal education.	8. The curriculum of training is usually fixed or determined in conformity with the skills to be learnt.
9. In education, the range of methods used, is very wide.	9. In training, limited and fixed methods are used. Methods change only from one skill to another.
10. In education, importance is attached to social discipline. Education socialises an individual.	10. In training, discipline is usually strict and authoritarian. Training may not socialise an individual. Many intellectually trained persons are not social in their behaviour.
11. There is flexibility in the provision of teachers. There are no teachers in informal education.	11. There are fixed teachers or instructors.
12. Means of evaluation are very wide. Both direct and indirect means are used. Certificate or degree is awarded in formal education but not in informal education.	12. In training, proficiency in the skill of the profession or field is tested. Means of evaluation are direct. Certificate or degree is given on the successful completion of the training.
13. There are various sources of inspiration in education. Social frame is the important source of inspiration.	13. Economic aspect is the main source of inspiration in training.

Education and Indoctrination

Indoctrination means education by authority, imposition, strict discipline, regiment and controlled instructions. Authoritarianism is the hallmark of indoctrination.

Everything, including aims and objectives, content and subject-matter, activities and programmes of education of the pupil are selected and settled by authorities. Indoctrination is one-sided, with the sole purpose of forcing information, ideas and practices from outside, as part of education. There is no freedom to the pupil to learn by himself or to direct the process of learning according to his own needs, interests and aspirations. He is a passive recipient of learning experience. It kills his initiative, freedom and curiosity. It follows the technique of cramming and makes learning dull, mechanical and monotonous.

Indoctrination ensures that behaviour is changed in a specific direction without rational thought, reflection or even willingness. Indoctrination may be used for developing, in the students, a particular set of beliefs, values and moral principles. It should be noted that indoctrination is a part of education. Education is as broad as ocean, indoctrination is a tank.

The table given below will make clear the difference between Education and Indoctrination:

Education	*Indoctrination*
1. The scope of education is very wide.	1. The scope of indoctrination is limited and narrow.
2. Education is a continuous and life-long process. It continuous from birth to death. It is needed at every stage, i.e., childhood, adolescent and adulthood stage, including old age.	2. The time of indoctrination is fixed. Indoctrination is much needed in junior classes, because at this stage child's mind is not mature and he receives dogmas without arguments. As the brain of the child develops, he starts reasoning.
3. Education has formal, informal and formal, non-formal aspects.	3. Indoctrination is all formal.
4. Atmosphere in the process of education is natural as well as artificial.	4. Atmosphere in indoctrination is artificial and dominated by authority.
5. Education aims at all round development of the person.	5. Indoctrination aims at changing some beliefs and attitudes and developing, among the student, a particular set of values and principles. Indoctrination aims at emotional development of the child.

Education	*Indoctrination*
6. Education may be person-centred.	6. Indoctrination is dogma-centred, thought-centered, authority-centred or teacher-centred.
7. The activities of the whole life form curriculum in education.	7. Curriculum, in indoctrination is confined to belief, ideas and dogmas religious, political and moral.
8. Various methods are used to impart education.	8. Lecture Method is emphasised in indoctrination.
9. Education may provide freedom to a person.	9. There is no freedom to the child to learn by himself. Everything, including aims and objectives, curriculum, programmes and activities, are directed by the authority.
10. All the members of society can play the role of teachers in informal education.	10. Professional teachers impart knowledge.
11. Evaluation may be done by observing social adjustment of the person.	11. Evaluation of the person is done on the basis of the criteria of changes in his thoughts and beliefs.

The following table will throw more light on the terms—Schooling, Instruction, Training and Indoctrination.

The above table shows that the aim of education is all-round development of personality. Schooling helps in achieving the aim of formal education. Instruction helps in development of knowledge (i.e., cognitive aspect). Training helps in developing skills. Indoctrination helps in bringing about changes in affective aspect (feeling aspect) of behaviour, i.e., thoughts, beliefs and values. Schooling, instruction, training and indoctrination play an important role in achieving the aim of education.

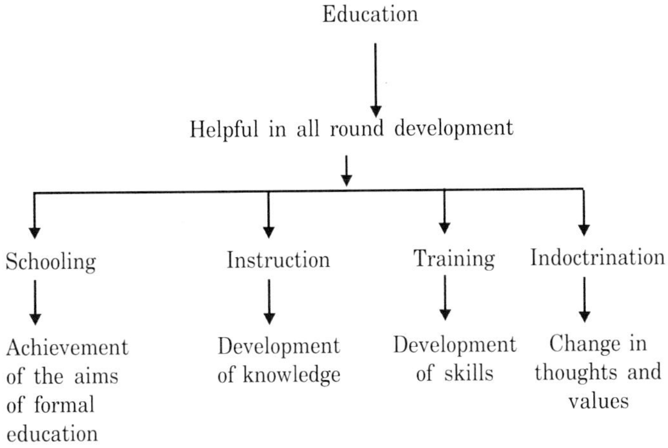

Education cannot be Equated with Literacy, Instruction, Schooling, Training or Indoctrination

In the light of above discussion; we can say that education cannot be equated with literacy, instruction, schooling or training. It is a comprehensive and continuous process. It is planned as well as unplanned, formal as well as informal. Literacy, instruction, schooling and training, however, are confined only to planned and organised enterprises. Education, no doubt, does include literacy, it does have instructional aspect, it implies schooling and it involves training of body and mind. However, education is growth from within rather than an imposition from without. Education is related to life, it is life itself.

IMPORTANT FEATURES OF EDUCATION

The best way to understand the nature of a thing consists in enumerating some of its important features. Let us now try to understand the nature of education by describing its salient features.

Education is a Human Enterprise

Education, it is clear, is for the human beings and not for the inanimate objects, plants, or animals. We may train a dog, but we cannot educate it. Educative capacity of man distinguishes him from other objects – animate or inanimate. It is only man who can be educated. Therefore, education is a human enterprise.

Education is a Process and not an Object

Education is not an object which persons possess or which is a part of them. One does not have education in the same way as one might have a thousand rupees or brown hair. Even knowledge or skill or good character is not in themselves education, but only evidence that one has been educated. Education is not an object; it is a process, a kind of activity in relation to human beings. To educate is to engage in a process and to 'have education' is to be someone who has undergone a process.

Education is a Purposeful Process

Education is a deliberate process, undertaken by the teacher and the taught, for reaching a definite destination. It is inspired both by immediate and remote goals. The central problem of education is educational aims. Methods and curriculum are determined in conformity with the educational aims. Aims are relative to a number of variables—socio-economic structure, political ideology, philosophy of life etc. The interpretation of aims of education by educational thinkers has varied from one thinker to another and from age to age. However, the individual and the social aims are the two broad categories under which the various aims can be subsumed. These aims are complementary to each other and not contradictory.

Education is a Continuous Process

Education is not a process which, after starting at one time, comes to an end at a definite time. We often say, "He has finished his education" or "He has now started education". In fact, education commences at birth and continues up to death. There is no end to this process. It goes on throughout life without any break or barrier. Education is not only the school, but the educand receives it by his participation in his environment—physical and social, specially through the informal agencies of home, the play group, the profession, the community, the church, the state, the press, the cinema, the radio, the television etc. Thus, education is a comprehensive, life-long and continuous process. Which starts from the womb and ends with the tomb.

Education is a Triangular Process

Education was considered a unit polar process in the past. It was Adams who first pointed out that education is a bid-polar process. "Education" says Adam, "is a conscious and deliberate process in which one personality acts upon another in order to modify the development of the other by the communication of knowledge." In the bi-polar process two persons are involved. At one pole we have the educator and at the other the educand. The one speaks, the other listens; the one teaches, the other learns; the one directs, the other follows. Their activities are inter-related and interdependent. If the educator does not come down to the level of the educand and if the educand is not stimulated to rise to the level of the educator, the work of imparting, and receiving education cannot proceed. Thus, it is a conscious and deliberate process in which there is subject-object relationship.

Unlike Adams, Dewey considers education as a triangular process. Dewey recognises the importance of psychological side of the process which includes the study of the child's needs, interests, capacities and talents, and which forms the basis of this process. Yet he lays a greater stress on the sociological side. "All education", he says, "Proceeds by the participation of the individual in social consciousness of the race." Thus, Dewey believes that society plays a very vital role in the process of imparting education.

Therefore, we can say that education is not a *bi-polar*, but a tri-angular process. It involves inter-play of three elements – the educator, the educand and the social forces. The social forces, provided by the social environment or society, supply the material to the teacher and it is taught in the form of curriculum. The curriculum is framed in the light of the needs and demands of the society. Hence, we can say that education is tri-angular process. It is a social process with social functions.

Education is Conservative as well as Dynamic

The social aspect of education includes cultural aspect. Education creates social order and it also stabilises it. It ensures and facilitiates the community of social life by preserving and transmitting the cultural heritage from generation to generation. Education is the instrument whereby culture is transmitted from the adult section of the community to the younger section, from one generation to another, and from one period of history to another.

Culture is not only transmitted but also preserved and developed further. Conservation and further development are implied in the process of transmission. We do not inherit culture in the way we inherit parent's property. Culture is not static, it is dynamic. It is in a state of constant flux. Thus, education, which acts as an agency for the transmission of culture, also serves as the means by which it is not only conserved, but also reconstructed, re-organised, transformed and expanded. Education is, thus, both conservative as well as a dynamic force.

Education is both—a Science and an Art

In the past, education was considered as an art. We thought that a man having perfect knowledge of his subject and interested in the process of teaching, turns out to be an efficient teacher by practice of teaching. This is true to some extent. It is said that teachers are born and not made. It is also said that doctors and engineers are born, and not made. But that does not mean medicine and engineering are arts. These are, undoubtedly, sciences. Education, is undoubtedly an art, but it is also a science. Education, like other sciences, undertakes a systematic study of certain facts and principles. It employs the usual scientific method of observation and experimentation. It classifies its data into certain categories, makes use of the analytic synthetic method, proceeds from particular to general, and tries to explain facts and discovers principles underlaying the various educational problems and finally establishes a number of generalisations about its methodology, motivation, learning, curriculum construction and evaluation. Education is a science in itself, and it has established its own existence, as an independent subject.

In 'education' we discuss subjects like Educational Principles, Educational Psychology, Educational Administration, Teaching Methods, Guidance, Evaluation etc. But, while we are saying that education is a science, we should not forget that education is an art also. In spite of the knowledge of educational science, one cannot become a successful teacher unless one puts it into practice. We have to put the principles into practice which is the artistic feature of education. Thus, education is both—a science as well as an art.

BASES OF EDUCATION

The process of education is based upon certain fundamental aspects of human life. It is actually man, who needs education and as such education is concerned with the various phases and stages of his life, right from his biological inheritance to social heritage. The whole process of education consists of transforming the animal being into social being, in the light of his instincts, urges, needs and temperament.

In order to realise this supreme aim of education, we require the study of man— his biological, psychological, social and ethical life.

Thus, it is clearly realised that education has its roots in human society, individual capacity and responsiveness and it looks upward for human excellence. Thereforc, thc form, process, content and objectives of education essentially have a base on which its theory and practice is to be erected. For systematic understanding of education, in it's entirety, we must understand its various bases.

Classification of Bases

The bases of education may broadly be classified as under:

1. Biological
2. Psychological
3. Social
4. Philosphical

Since education aims at something, it represents a learning process. Taking into consideration the nature of the learner, it tries to socialise the learner, enabling the learner to understand his social milieu and ultimately it leads the learner to realise his aspirations. This sort of involvement of man with education may be represented diagrammatically in the form of a triangle.

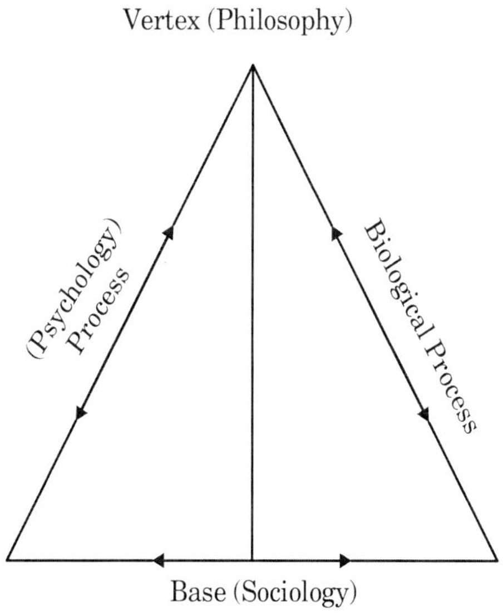

Thus, the major aspects of education are inter-linked and there takes place a two-way interaction amongst them. Each one is affected by the other and contributes to the formulations and intensity of the other. All such interactions will be elaborated in the succeeding pages.

Here it will be enough to make explicit that, education, as a social process, has its direction and content and all these are determined by its linkage with Biology, Psychology, Sociology and Philosophy which provide an adequate base for educational edifice.

Biological Basis of Education

Man often is looked upon as animal being. No doubt, he has affinities with the lower order, but he is superior to other creatures due to intelligence and mental powers. Man is a potential being and creates his own environment. He does not adapt himself to nature, but adapts nature according to his needs. He eats to live and lives to eat. Biological aspect of his life is the starting point. From biological existence man has to attain his sociological, cultural and ethical existence.

Biologically it is believed that man is the product of evolution. For the purpose of evolution, biological nature of man is human nature. Its conception of educational research is based upon the faith that the scientific study of human organism can give us all the essential knowledge about human nature and his behaviour. It also provides us the knowledge about his basic needs, urges, instincts and powers; his likes and dislikes. This whole approach to education is pervaded by the assumption that man is basically a biological creature. The essential characteristics of human beings are given in the structure and functioning of the biological organism.

In the case of man, life has been transferred from the instinctive to the rational basis and he becomes amenable to education. In the case of other animals, nature helps by adjusting them to the environment. But man has to acquire experiences which will later function in modifying action and it is possible because of the nervous constitution of the man that makes him an eminently educable being. His adjustment is on the mental plane.

As compared to other animals, the infancy period of human child is quite longer. During this period child needs care, nourishment and help. He is dependent on others. If we leave him unattended, bring him up in isolation, his future will not be better than Ramu, the wolf boy (died a few years ago). This prolonged period is meant to prepare the child for the complex human life. Without this, he is very much like a savage or a beast. All these factors provide essential bases to education.

Psychological Basis of Education

Every child is born with certain natural and inherited endowments. These endowments are modified and sublimated for making the individual child a useful member of society. The process of such modification of endowments or change of animal behaviour, is known as 'education'. For the ultimate success of this process, we have to base it on a scientific plan which depends upon the scientific study of the child's mind. This scientific study of the child's mind or behaviour is known as 'Psychology'. Thus, the psychological basis is an important basis of education.

A teacher has to deal with the child as material. Therefore, unless he thoroughly understands the natural inclinations of the child, his heredity, environment, desires, aptitudes, habits, feelings, likes and dislikes, he cannot succeed in imparting good education. All this is the knowledge of Psychology. It exhorts the teacher that 'when the rule of thumb fails, the laws of psychology can bring fruitful results'. With this knowledge, the teacher is saved from committing blunders and from learning at the cost of his pupils.

As we have already noted, education is a process of controlling and modifying behaviour and psychology seeks to discover the general laws which explain the behaviour of living organisms. It, therefore, follows that the theory of education must base itself, very largely, on the science of Psychology. The knowledge of human behaviour is of great help to the teacher in the formulation of the policy on education. Great educators like Rousseau and Pestalozzi had realised that teacher's primary concern is the over-all development of the child. With an accurate knowledge of the child's mental process a teacher can accomplish his task successfully. Later on, *Froebel* developed this idea in his Kindergarten scheme of child education.

'The teacher must know both Latin and John, in order to teach well.' While the knowledge of Latin is the mastery of the subject-matter, the knowledge of John is psychology. It, therefore follows that a teacher, to be a good and successful teacher, must know the subject-matter as well as the child or psychology.

The Sociological Basis of Education

"Man cannot be human, unless he learns to live, think, feel and behave like men." Great, individuals who have contributed a lot to the progress of mankind could not do so in a social vacuum, but only after assimilating the rich heritage of their society. Sociological factor, therefore, plays an important role in the education of an individual. According to *John Dewey*, "All education proceeds by the participation of the individual in the social consciousness of the race. This participation moulds his powers and personality to fit him in the society, for which and in which, he has to live."

Every individual child is a creature of the culture of his community or society. His personality, to a great extent, is a product of the cultural influences that his society brings to bear upon him. Aristotle says, that Man is a social animal. He is born physically, developed mentally and educated in society. Different social agencies react upon his individuality and then transform it into personality, enabling it to lead a useful and worthwhile life. As educators, therefore, it is essential for us to know how the individual lives and behaves in the society to which he belongs. Education must help the individual in his social adjustment to the total cultural milieu. It is only after we have gained this knowledge, we can plan his future education. Herein lays the importance of sociological basis of education.

The child is to live in and for the community to which he belongs. Hence true education comes through the stimulation of the child's power by the demands of the social situation in which he finds himself. *John Dewey* has also directed our attention to the social function of education which is carried through school, as a special environment. It is through and in the school that the development of desirable attitudes and dispositions, which is so essential for the continuous and progressive social life, takes place. Thus school is an important social institution which according to *John Dewey*, "Purifies and idealises the existing social institutions and customs and which is a living society for the children."

Philosophical Basis of Education

Education is a purposeful social process and it has its aims and objectives. It is not an undersigned process, mechanically operating on man. It has its why, what and how dimensions with clear-cut force of action. Priority-wise, what and how of Education take their inspiration from the why aspect. It makes quite evident that this 'why' is explained by philosophy alone and by no other human discipline. This normative dimension of education is a privilege of philosophy alone to determine. Therefore, a philosophic base of education is its first essentiality.

All the Bases of Education are Complementary to Each Other

After discussing all the bases of education separately, we can say that there is a need for synthesis among these bases. Education develops the whole man. All these bases have their distinctive features and the common factor of all the bases is the man—his total development. It is a truism that biological factors of human life discuss man only on the physical plane. Psychology studies an individual as a learner. All this keeps an individual in isolation. In the absence of sociological and ethical factors, human life is incomplete and education is only a half-way. Hence, for the complete development of human personality, there is a need to study these various factors. Man is essentially a social-being and a moral being. His biological heredity remains meaningless in the absence of social heredity. He can achieve social perfection only by cultivating ethical values approved by the society. To conclude, it may once again be emphasised that all these bases must be studied together in order to establish harmony between the individual and the society.

SOME DEFINITIONS OF EDUCATION

From the earlier times to the modern era, various thinkers and educators, in order to make the concept of education clear, have defined education in their own characteristic way. These definitions throw a flood of light on various aspects of education and its essential features. A general survey of some of the definitions by Western and Indian thinkers reveals to us a multiplicity of definitions of Education.

Definitions by Western Thinkers

Modern progressive education owes most to the West. The views of some of the Western thinkers are as under:

1. "I mean by education that training which is given by suitable habits to the first instincts of virtue in children." The end of education is "To develop in the body and the soul all the beauty and all the perfection of which they are capable." —Plato

2. "Education is the creation of a sound mind in a sound body". It is, "To develop man's faculties, especially his mind so that he may be able to enjoy the contemplation of the supreme truth, goodness and beauty in which perfect happiness essentially consists."

—Aristotle

3. "Education is enfoldment of what is already enfolded in the germ. It is the process through which the child makes the internal external." —Froebel

4. "Whatever helps to shape the human being, to make the human being, what he is, or to hinder him from what he is not—is part of his education." —J.S. Mill

5. "Education is a natural, harmonious and progressive development of man's innate powers". —Pestalozzi

6. "By Education, I mean the influence of the environment upon the individual to produce a permanent change in his habits of behaviour, of thought, and of attitude." —G.H. Thomson

7. "Education is the development of good moral character".

—Herbart

8. "Education is the complete development of individual so that he can make an original contribution to human life, according to his best capacity." —T.P. Nunn

9. "Education is a conscious and deliberate process in which one personality acts upon another in order to modify the development of the other, by the communication and manipulation of knowledge." —Adams

10. "Education is the development of all those capacities in the individual which will enable him to control his environment and fulfil his possibilities." —John Dewey

11. "Education is the influence of a person who holds the vital belief brought to bear on another person, with the object of making him also hold that belief." —Ross

12. "Education is the deliberate and systematic influence exerted by the mature person upon the immature, through interaction, discipline, and harmonious development of physical, intellectual, aesthetic, social and spiritual powers of the human being, according to individual and social needs and directed towards the union of the educand with his creator, as the final end."

—Redden

Definitions by Indian Thinkers

Education, being an important social activity, its meanings have been changing through the ages, due to change in social and physical conditions. Different educationists, therefore, interpret it differently, at different times. Some of the most popular definitions, given by Indian educational thinkers, are given below:

1. "Education is something which makes a man self-reliant and self-less". —Rig Veda

2. "Education is that whose end-product is salvation." —Upanishads

3. "Education is that which makes a man of good character and useful to the society". —Yajnavalkya

4. "Human education means the training which one gets from nature." —Panini

5. "Education means training for the country and love for the nation." —Kautilya

6. "Education means development of self-contentment." —Kannada

7. "Education is the realisation of the self." —Shankaracharya

8. "Education is the manifestation of perfection already in man." —Vivekananda

9. "The highest education is that which does not merely give us information but makes our life in harmony with all existence." —Tagore

10. "By education, I mean an all-round drawing out of the best in child and man—body, mind and spirit". —Gandhiji

Various Features emphasised by Different Educators

The scope of this chapter on 'Understanding Education' does not permit any detailed discussion, explanation and comment upon the definitions enumerated above. What seems to be possible or expedient under the present limitations, is to indicate and stress various features that have been emphasised in these definitions. These are:

1. It's unilateral, bi-polar or tri-angular in nature.
2. It's a drawing out or a bringing up process.
3. It's being knowledge or experience.

4. It's the development of some particular aspect of human personality or a harmonious integrated growth.

5. It's being conducive for the good of the individual or the welfare of the society.

6. It's being a liberal discipline or a vocational course.

7. It's being stabiliser of social order and conservator of culture or an instrument of change and social reconstruction.

CONCLUSION

Although comparisons are often arbitrary, the conclusion seems to be irresistible that education, it is universally admitted, whatever else it may be, is a means for the development of full man or woman —a balanced all-round harmonious development of personality, but the precise analysis of personality is unfortunately, controversial in nature. Educators have some-how, been victims of 'this' or 'that' philosophy. Many of them have been influenced by a partial view of human nature. No definition can be adjudged satisfactory, if it is not determined by the proper synthesis of the two main factors of human personality— the animal and the spiritual or the rational self.

It is generally admitted in the West that personality constitutes body and mind, and it is the function of education, therefore, to bring about a harmonious development of all these aspects of human personality. This explanation is perhaps based upon an inadequate understanding of human nature, because it neglects the most important aspect of human personality— namely the spirit. Personality constitutes body, mind and spirit or soul. Any definition or concept of education that puts exclusive emphasis on one of these aspects of human personality militates against the basic principle. Most of the ills of our educational system from the dawn of civilisation can be traced to undue emphasis laid on the one or more of these aspects and indifference to the others. An evil of the present day education, all over the world, is the neglect of the spiritual aspect of human personality. Gandhiji revolts against this evil of the modern education and emphasises on all the aspects of human personality. Thus, his concept of education tends to remove the inadequacies of modern education and his definition of education seems to be more suitable than any other, when he says, "By education, I mean an all-round drawing out the best in child and man – body, mind and spirit". In other words, "true education is that which draws out and stimulates the spiritual, intellectual and physical faculties of the children."

2

The Aims of Education

Education, as we have already discussed in the previous chapter, is a purposeful activity. It is undertaken both by the educator and the educand for the sake of a clear-cut objective. Therefore, every system and process of education, in order to be worth anything, must have some aim which should reflect the philosophical aim of human life. If there is education without an aim, the educator does not know where he has to lead his pupil to and what the learner has to become as a result of his education. Unless there is a clear-cut aim before education, it would be impossible to measure the achievement of the educand. Therefore, the first consideration in any discussion on education must be a statement of its aims.

NATURE OF THE AIMS OF EDUCATION

In order to know the aims of education, it is necessary to understand the nature of these aims. Are the aims of education fixed, final, eternal and universal or are they flexible, adaptable, changeable and relative? Let us discuss this problem in the light of two distinct philosophies of education—Idealism and Pragmatism.

Idealism on Aims of Education

Idealism stands for superiority of mind over matter and it conceives the nature of ultimate reality in terms of mind or spirit rather than in terms of matter. The idealist believes in the existence of absolute, eternal and unchanging values and consequently defines the ultimate aims of education in terms of these values. According to Idealism, the aims of education are spiritual in nature and they are pre-determined, absolute, unchanging and universal. The values of life are not man-made, but pre-existing. The aim of education is realisation of these pre-existing, absolute and universal values.

According to some idealists, there are two types of educational aims —immediate and ultimate. Whereas the immediate aims are changing, flexible and adaptable, the ultimate aims are eternal, absolute and unchanging. In determining any hierarchy of values the immediate objectives must occupy a subordinate position.

Pragmatism on Aims of Education

Pragmatism believes that the nature of reality is not fixed. What is true today may not be true tomorrow. Pragmatism, therefore, does not believe in absolute and eternal values. Values are man-made and constant experimentation is needed to test their validity. Thus, pragmatism requires an individual to be creative so that he should formulate values of life on the basis of his experiences.

Unlike Idealism, Pragmatiosm believes that aims of education are man-made, relative and changing.

THE DETERMINANTS OF EDUCATIONAL AIMS

Even a casual survey of the history of education will reveal that there have been different aims of education in different countries in the past. Event in the same country the aims of education have been different at different times. For example, in India the aims of education during Ancient Period were not the same which were during British Period. Again, the aims of education in the Modern India are different from those which were prevalent in British India. The aims of education in a democratic country like England or America are not the same as they are in Communist countries like USSR and China. The important determinants of the educational aims which have led to their diversity are discussed below.

The Philosophies of life

The philosophy of life in which the people of a particular society or time believe, goes a long way in determining the aims of education. In a materialistic society educational aims are based on the materialistic outlook of the people. In such a society there is no place for moral ideals and spiritual values and the aim of education is self-gratification or self-expression. On the contrary, for the idealists who believe in the spiritual basis of the universe, the aim of education is self-realisation or exaltation of personality. A pessimistic attitude towards life fashions pessimistic aims of education, whereas an optimistic philosophy of life determines optimistic aims of education. In short, the different philosophies of life give rise to different aims of education.

The Socio-political Ideologies

Socio-political ideologies, too, determine educational aims. For example, different social philosophies views about the Individual-society or Individual-state relationship had led to different concepts of educational aims. According to totalitarianism, the state is considered as an end in itself. The individual is regarded only as a means for the good of the state. Evidently, the educational aim under such a regime is to train the individual for blind obedience to the state and there is a rigid, state-controlled and stereotyped system of education. On the contrary, according to the individualism or pluralism the individual is regarded as an end in himself and the state as a means to the good of the individual. Accordingly, the aim of education is considered as self-expression or self-gratification and the state adopts "Hands off" policy in the sphere of education. Democracy strikes a balance between individual freedom and social obligations. The authoritarian and dictatorial attitude of the state is replaced by parental one. The aim of education under democratic regimes is considered to be social efficiency or citizenship.

Again, education in any country and at all periods reflects values of the ruling class. All forms of governments—democratic, fascist or communist—formulate their own aims of education to serve their purposes. In a democracy educational aims are not fixed, absolute or eternal. They change with the changing aspirations and demands of the society. Man, in a democracy, is considered as an end in himself and not as a means to an end. Therefore, educational institutions cater to the diverse abilities and aptitudes of children. The child is educated for a life of freedom, for the fullest possible realisation of his capacities and their service to the community. In a Fascist regime, the Individual exists for the state. Thus, in a Fascist state the individual must bow to the demands of the state and the aim of education is to inculcate values like service, sacrifice, duty and obedience. The educational aims in a communist state are formulated quite differently from those in a fascist or democrate state. As labour is the cardinal ideal of the communist society, it forms the central pivot of the educational aims. The student must feel himself a worker in a labouring society. Educational institutions are considered as deliberate instruments of State Policy. To ensure the victory of communist ideals, educational aims stress the need of virtues like bravery, loyalty, steadfastness and discipline.

Hence, we can say that different socio-political ideologies give rise to different educational aims.

The Socio-economic Problems

Sometimes social and economic problems of a country also influence the educational aims of that country. For example, India is a country of various castes, creeds and religions. Social stratification has been rigid. This has created special social problems. Education, therefore, must fight the caste-barriers. Similarly, in determining its educational objectives every country has to take into consideration its economic conditions. We can take the example of Denmark. About half a century back the country faced economic crises. Traditional occupations did not yield income to support all the people of the country. A survey of national resources and man-power was made. The country had meager resources, but it was close to a steady market for certain food articles. For the economic advancement of the country, it was advised to start dairy products, even though the food for the cattle was to be imported from other countries. Denmark educated its generation to meet the new requirements. The result was that Denmark not only increased the per capita income and her national wealth, but also captured the markets of England and several other countries.

Similarly, India of today has low economic standards of living. As a large majority of the people in India have to live at an economically sub-human level, one of the most important functions of educations is to improve productive efficiency, to increase national wealth, and to bridge the gulf between the rich and the poor so that the dream of socialist society may become reality. Thus, we can say that social and economic conditions of a country also determine the educational aims of that country.

Exploration of Knowledge

Educational aims are also influenced by exploration of knowledge. Because of rapid exploration in sciences, education today has become science-oriented all-over the world. In India also educationists are stressing the need for science oriented education in the schools, colleges and universities. More and more stress is being laid on the study of modern sciences. The government is giving liberal grants and scholarships by way of providing incentive for the study of science. This clearly shows that the spreading of new knowledge is an important factor in determining aims of education.

DIFFERENT AIMS OF EDUCATION

We have already discussed the important determinants of educational aims which have led to their diversity. We shall confine our attention to some important ones and discuss them here.

The Knowledge Aim

Since, the time of Sophists (400 B.C.) down to the present day, knowledge has almost been universally considered as the aim of education. There are some educators who hold the acquisition of knowledge to be the only aim of education. They emphasise the cognitive or the intellectual side of personality. Forgetting that knowledge is merely an instrument for achieving other ends, they exalt it into an end by identifying it with education. The acquisition of knowledge of different subjects is regarded as the test of successful schooling and success in examination is regarded as the criterion of such acquisition. The only aim of education is 'complete knowledge' or 'knowledge, more knowledge and yet more knowledge.'

Those philosophers and educationists, who hold the knowledge aim of education, offer a justification for their view. They argue that knowledge is indispensable for all right action and it alone is the source of all power and happiness. Before one could feel either pleasure or pain in respect of any object, or could make any response with regard to it, one has to know what it is. Thus, knowledge is not an idle or merely ornamental possession; it is a source of complete living and progress. For example, if education is intended to help individual for adjustment to the environment, the individual must have knowledge of his environment, before he can think of adjusting himself to it. Again, if education is to help the child to realise moral values, he must first have knowledge of those values. Thus, knowledge alone is power; knowledge alone is happiness; knowledge alone is virtue; knowledge alone is progress.

Criticism of Knowledge Aim: The knowledge aim of education has been criticised by many educators who put forward number of arguments against this aim. They argue that over-emphasis on the knowledge is likely to reduce all schools to mere 'knowledge-shops' and the teacher to the mere information monger'. Schools are infact agencies to bring about the all-round, not merely intellectual development of pupils. They believe that knowledge is not the only aim of education. They argue that no amount of factual knowledge can make a person truly educated. True, we cannot be wise without some basis of knowledge; but at the same time we may remain devoid of wisdom, even after acquiring much knowledge. True, we should have knowledge of moral values to become virtuous, but we may remain immoral, even after having knowledge of all moral values. Education is partly information and partly formation. The knowledge aim ignores the latter part. The knowledge aim is unpsychological because it emphasises the study of subject matter rather than the child. It reduces the child to the position of a passive learner and places the teacher on a very high level.

Conclusion: If we weigh the arguments advanced for and against the knowledge aim, we arrive at the conclusion that knowledge, though, is not the only or supreme aim of education, yet it is one of the important aims of education. Knowledge is an indispensable means for any suitable and comprehensive aim of education. But knowledge should be a 'means to an end' and not an 'end in itself'. It should be acquired for human happiness and social welfare.

The Vocational Aim

Whenever we ask any parent the question: "Why do you send your children to schools and universities?" The answer will always be, "So that they may get some good vocation in life." No one can deny this concern of parents for their children. Man has three basic needs – food, shelter and clothing. If education does not fulfill these, it does not fulfill its aims. The long stride taken by industrialisation and mechanisation in the modern age of science gives priority to vocational aim over all other aims. Every man, unless he is born with a silver spoon in his mouth, has to search out a living for himself. It is this aim which enables an individual to solve the problem of his livelihood. If education fails to do this, it is not worth its name. Therefore, the main aim of education should be to train the child for a vocation, profession, business, calling or trade. This aim is also called as, "bread and butter aim" or 'utilitarian aim' of education.

The supporters of this aim maintain that education for vocation makes use of the habits and instincts of the educand: appeals to his interest and aptitude: stimulates his thought, skill and observation; and trains him for social efficiency. They argue that man cannot live without means of subsistence: his economic needs will have to be satisfied. If an individual is not able to earn his own living and that of the children dependent upon him, he is a parasite upon others. He misses for himself one of the most educative experiences of life. Therefore, no scheme of education can afford to neglect such basic consideration. Moreover, the vocational aim is an integral part of the general aim of education. For example, from the idealistic point of view 'Exaltation of Personality' is regarded as the aim of education.

Criticism of the Vocational Aim: The vocational aim in education has not been spared criticism. It is argued that man, after all, is born not only to eat and drink but also to gain knowledge, acquire culture and develop personality. Therefore, the vocational aim is not a complete aim by itself. Earning one's bread is only one part of man's life not the whole of it. Moreover, if vocational aim is over-emphasised, education is reduced to nothing but commercialism. It ceases to be a refining and enabling influence. It may make an individual a good doctor, a good teacher, or a good engineer, but it does not necessarily make him a good man. It does make him rich, but does not inspire him for the ideals of life. It does not prepare him for complete living.

Conclusion: In the light of above discussion it may be said that there is a considerable justification for the vocational aim of education. But the fact remains, that most of the evils that have crept into the life of the modern man because of an over-emphasis on this aim.

The Moral Aim

There are some educationists, generally belonging to the idealistic school, who think that the ultimate aim of education should be character-building or moral development. Character means an inner consistency or unity of personality. It means consistency, steadfastness, dependability and stability. A man of character acts as he does because of principles or ideals within rather than from expediency or because of pressure from without. They believe that a man of character— a man endowed with a strong will, virtuous conduct, and noble ideals— is the only man who can be said to be really educated. On the contrary, one who lacks these qualities however learned or cultured otherwise, is a person on whom education has been completely lost. Therefore, knowledge, culture, physical development, vocational efficiency, all are secondary to moral training. The formation of sound moral character should be the primary and only aim of education. Education is the process of modifying the child's original behaviour.

Criticism of Moral Aim: True, character—building is a very laudable aim of education, but it has its other side also. Morality, as pragmatists believe, is never fixed, absolute or predetermined. It is relative. Moral ideals change with a change in time and social values. Ideals valued today may not be given any importance after the lapes of a hundred years. As such, it is not possible to interpret and trace moral ideals which can be considered effective in a particular situation. Moreover, undue emphasis on moral aim throws the other aims of education to a lower level. The physical and intellectual development of the child is as necessary as his moral progress.

Conclusion: Therefore, we can conclude that only character building cannot be the aim of education. Not only good moral qualities, but qualities like intelligence, creativeness, health and vigour are also needed for the welfare of man and society.

The Complete Living Aim

Some educational theorists insist upon the need of an aim in education which will be all-comprehensive. This view point has led to the emergence of two aims —'the complete living aim' and the harmonious development aim'. The former has been formulated and brilliantly expounded by Spencer. Education, according to this great thinker, should acquaint us with the laws and ways of complete living. He has given a list of activities and suitable subjects. According to Spencer, training of activities of self-preservation, indirect preservation of life, rearing of off-springs, social preservation and leisure can be imparted through Hygiene, Physics, Language, Mathematics, Geography, History, Child Psychology, Home Science, Music etc.

Criticism of the Complete Living Aim: The emptiness of this aim can be shown with the help of certain questions. What can determine the completeness of life? Is the aim completeness of life an unchanging thing? It should be noted that no mention has been made of art, literature and religion in the above list. Therefore, it can be said that the aim of complete living put forth by Spencer is too vague to be held and carried out by any educator.

The Harmonious Development Aim

One serious objection to the various aims of education discussed above, is that they all are one sided or incomplete. In the opinion of some thinkers harmonious development of mental, physical and aesthetic powers is the aim of education. According to them every child is born with certain powers and capacities – physical, mental and intellectual powers, spiritual moral and aesthetic capacities and social tendencies. The aim of education is to help the development of all these powers and all these powers and capacities hidden in the child. If some of these capacities are developed while others are neglected, the result would be an unsystematic and irregular development of personality. Therefore, the advocates of harmonious development aim urge that education should aim at the development of all capacities and powers of the child, rather than that of only a few of them and neglect others.

Gandhiji is a strong advocate of the harmonious development aim. For him, the aim of education is the development of full man and woman. However, since the essential nature of man is spiritual, Gandhiji advocates the aim of all-round development of the physical, intellectual and emotional aspects of personality under the guidance of spiritual self. Lop-sided development of personality is the product of modern education which neglects the spiritual aspect of human personality.

Conclusion: The harmonious development aim deserves credit for its comprehensiveness. This aim embraces all other aims discussed above, because all these together aim at the harmonious development of personality. In fact, no aim is worth persuing unless it contributes towards such development. But the critics of this aim maintain that man is a unit and this division of his personality in different aspects is impossible. And, even if we take this division to be true, what would be the measure of definite quantities of harmonious development. In their opinion this harmonious development is an imaginary ideal which cannot be applicable in life.

The Leisure Aim

Science has revolutionised human life. It has shown us how we can do a greater volume of work in shorter time and with less physical labour. It has placed at our disposal innumerable labour-saving devices. The type-writer, the computing machine, the telephone, the motor-cars, the electric fan and light, the refrigerator all these and many others show how much work we can do with minimum labour. They save us from the mechanical drudgery of manual work. At the same time, they create plenty of leisure. Hence, the aim of education in the modern time should be to teach people a proper utilisation of leisure so that they add to the achievements of man in art, architecture and literature, and thus, develop their culture. Teachers and organisers should pay their attention to education for leisure. For doing so, reasons are not far to seek.

Education for leisure brings out the hidden talents of children and thus helps them to find their proper place in life. It trains them to participate in creative activities leading to their development and the progress of society. It makes their life richer, their tastes refined, their minds occupied. Hence, schools must make a provision of co-curricular activities, hobbies, games, sports, music, painting, dancing etc.

All this sounds well.

Synthesis of Different Aims

Since, the aims of education discussed above are epigrams rather than real definitions, they do not take us very far and quite naturally leave us unsatisfied. They are half-truths, one sided or incomplete statements, for obviously it is impossible to compress in one small sentence the whole meaning and aim of an important human activity as education. But, inspite of their lack of agreement and their inadequacy, one-sideness or incompleteness, the various aims are complementary rather than contradictory. Instead of contradicting each other, they supply each other's deficiencies. There is no real antithesis between them, but merely a difference of stress. They overlap, although they do not in coincide. Since, they are complementary and overlapping in nature, they can be reconciled with one another.

INDIVIDUAL VERSUS SOCIAL AIMS

We have discussed in brief some of the important aims of education. The main emphasis of each of them is either on the individual or on the social aim. Thus, they are ultimately reducible to only two major aims—individual and social—which appear to be opposed to each other. Before we see whether they are opposed or compatible, let us discuss in brief the nature of these two main aims.

The Individual Aim

The exponents of the individual aim in education assert that the individual should be in the fore-front of the picture. This concept is based on the socio-political philosophy that social institutions, such as the family, the church, the school and the state, exist only for bettering and improving the life of the individual. The individual is the end and these social institutions are the means. Therefore, they justify their existence only if they are conducive to the promotion of the individual's welfare. The school as one of the important social institutions exists for the educand, and not the educand for the school. Therefore, the school should offer an environment and atmosphere which will be conducive to each child's development. Rousseau, the father of naturalism is the greatest supporter of individual aim in education.

Some of the supporters of the individual aim in education are extremists. They are against all sorts of restrictions and they advocate untrammelled and unrestricted freedom for the educand. According to them, the aim of education is self-expression. It implies unrestricted freedom for the individual to act according to his own nature, even if that action is objectionable to others. They are against discipline, religion or morality. The purpose of educational efforts, according to Sir Percy Nunn, is to secure conditions conducive to the complete development of individuality and to help him to make his original contribution to the variegated whole of human life as fully and as truly characteristic as his nature permits. Although Nunn supports his contention by an appeal to biology, his conception of individuality is a philosophic one. It is an ideal which has to be yet attained, "a spiritual perfection that is possible to each individual." In other words, Nunn's conception of individuality is synonymous with what self-realisation stands for.

Self-realisation is not the same thing as self-expression. Self-expression as a meaning of development of individuality emphasises the play of self-assertion. It implies unrestricted freedom to act as nature prompts, even if that action is objectionable and undesirable. No doubt, self-realisation does necessarily imply a certain amount of self-assertion, but only if it is not undersirable for society. Moreover, in self-expression, the self is taken as ready-made, merely waiting to express itself. The self in the ideal of self-realisation is not the undisciplined self which is ready-made, but one that is a bundle of possibilities and potentialities. Self-realisation does not always need freedom from restraint. According to Adams, the self in the ideal of self-realisation cannot realise itself against society, it realises itself in society through social interaction.

Narrow Meaning of Individual Aim

In the narrow sense individual aim of education is given names like Self-expression, All Round Development of Child's Power and Natural Development. In this sense this aim of education is based on naturalistic philosophy. According to this philosophy, the child should be given complete freedom to develop according to his instincts.

Wider Meaning of Individual Aim

In the wider sense, development of individual as an aim of education can be described as 'Self-realisation'. According to this meaning, while keeping in view needs, interests and abilities, the child should be given all those opportunities which may help him in the total development of all of his potentialities and in making him an excellent individual.

Factors Influencing Individual Aim

The following factors influence the Individual Aim of Education.

1. Effect of Biological Sciences: The biological sciences suggest that every living being is different from every other living being. Every individual has certain unique characteristics. Natural development means the development of only these unique characteristics of the individual. Thus education aims at development of the individual abilities of each child. *Sir Percy Nunn,* who takes the biological point of view, holds that the central aim of education is the autonomous development of the individual. Hence individual and not the society should be the centre of all educational efforts.

2. Effect of Naturalism: Naturalists like Rousseau, Comenius, Pestalozzi suggest that education which aims at the development of individuality is the only education 'according to nature.' They assume that the child's nature is good and any interference with its evolution would be harmful. They believe that the child is born with "trailing clouds of glory" as *Wordsworth* says, "And society Simply corrupts him, for its influence is as heavy as frost." According to *Rousseau,* "Everything is good as it comes from the hands of Author of Nature, but everything degenerates in the hands of man. God makes all things good. Man meddles with them and they become evil."

3. Effect of Psychology: Modern psychology places a lot of emphasis on individual differences. All individuals differ from one another in respect of their interests, abilities, attitudes and personality. The aim of education is to develop each child in conformity with his special abilities. Consequently, education has become individual (child) oriented.

4. Influence of Progressivists: Progressivists are of the view that the progress of mankind is due to great individuals.

The world has progressed only because some individuals have contributed to it according to their special abilities. They include great educationists, philosophers, scientists, inventors, social reformers, religious leaders and the like. Had such gifted individuals not existed, progress in any sphere of activity would have been impossible. Hence education should aim at individual development if it seeks to contribute to social development. According to *T.P. Nunn,* "Nothing good enters into the human world except in and through the free activities of the individual men and women and education practice must be shaped to accord with this truth."

Nunn, further says that education must secure conditions under which individuality is most completely developed and should help the individual "To make his original contribution to the variegated whole of human life as full and as truly characteristic as his nature permits." If an individual is fully developed, the society is automatically developed. Hence the aim of education is to develop the abilities of men and women as individuals. This alone will produce leaders in various walks of life and make the world progressive.

5. Influence of Spiritualists: The spiritualists are of the view that the good of the society lies in the good, the "Infinite value of the individual person." Since the spiritual development, of the man is individual, education should produce such conditions as would be conducive to the highest development of an individual's innate powers... In other words, education should lead the individual to self-realisation.

6. Effect of Democratic Ideals: Democracy emphasises the freedom of an individual. Democratic state' should provide facilities for all individuals to develop in any direction they conceive to be useful to themselves. *Bertrand Russell* has suggested, "Education of the individual is a finer thing than the education of the citizen."

Education must not only seek to produce fine citizens but also fine individuals. The educational system should be so designed that it helps to develop the individuality of the child. All educational efforts should bring into focus the individual and not the society.

Criticism of Individual Aim: Individual aim of Education has been criticised on the following grounds:

1. Encouragement of Individualism: Individual aim of education supports individualism. The opponents of this aim of education hold that if education aims at development of individuality, then it will lead to spread of anarchy. The individual may begin to exert to the extent 'Ahm-Brahmo-Asmi.' (I am God) and then believe "Life exists for me; clear of my way. I must have what I want, and so on." It may produce persons like *Hitler* and *Mussolini*, and society will have to face harmful consequences of individualism. Thus individual aim of education is the enemy of socialism. Hence individual aim of education cannot be accepted in the socialistic state.

2. Disregard of Man's Social Nature: The supporters of individual aim of education ignore the fact that man is a social animal and his individuality or self is realised through social interaction. Raymont says, "An isolated individual is a figment of imagination." It means that only in society and because of society, he acquires a personality—otherwise he remains an animal.

3. Disregard of Environment: Criticising Nunn's autonomous development of individuality, *Rusk* says that this idea is biological and therefore, defective. Biological development is determined by the past. It ignores the influence of socio-cultural environment and stresses only heredity. Psychology has proved that environment plays a very significant role in the development of the individuality of the child. *Ross* beautifully remarks, "Individuality is of no value and personality is a meaningless term apart from social environment."

4. Difficulty in Making Social Adjustment: Under all circumstances man has to live with other individuals in the society. For leading a successful life, it is essential for him to make adjustment with others. Too much emphasis on individual aim will cause difficulty in making social adjustment.

5. Not Practicable: Theoretically individual aim of education may be accepted but it is not practicable. It is not possible at any stage to fix different types of curriculum for each student.

In the light of above discussion, we can say that the extreme individual aim is not desirable. We must admit that individual cannot develop his individuality in vacuum. He can develop his maximum potentialities in the social context alone. Self-expression is essential for the development of the individual, but it does not mean that the individual should have absolute freedom. Absolute freedom enjoyed by the individual will disintegrate society. Self-expression is desirable only when it integrates rather than disintegrates society. Similarly, self-realisation is good, but it should not be achieved in isolation from the society; it should be realised while living in the society. Thus the emphasis that is now-a-days being placed on the individual aims of education does not imply total neglect of the social aims. It is in fact a synthesis of the individual and social aims. It is impossible to conceive of one in the total absence of the other. There is no human being outside society and society is made up of human beings. Hence, even if education is designed to aim at social service, it implicitly promotes the interests and the individuality of the human being.

From the above discussion of' Individual Aims of Education, it is clear that there are narrow and wider meanings of Individual Aims of Education which can be summed up as below:

Individual Aim

- Narrow Meaning
  - Self-expression
    or
    All round development of child's power
    or
    Natural development
- Wider Meaning
  - Self-realisation

The Social Aim

The supporters of the social aim of education believe that society or state alone is the real, and the individual is only a means. They hold that an individual should be educated for the good of the society. The social aim of education, they believe, will produce social cohesion and a sense of co-operation which is necessary for enjoying the amenities of life. Its supporters cannot conceive of an individual living and developing in isolation from society. As Raymont says, "The isolated individual is a figment of the imagination." As long as a human individual is a social animal, living in society and developing through social contacts, there will be some subordination of individuality to public or social needs of society and the curbing of individuality will go on consciously or unconsciously.

The social aim, "However, is not as simple as it seems. It has two meanings. In the first sense, by social aim we mean purposes of the state. The function of education in relation to that aim is to cater consistently for the welfare of the state, subordinating the welfare of the individual to that of the state. This is a narrow interpretation which is given by certain extremists. They think that the state is an "Idealised metaphysical entity over and above the individual citizen, superior in every way." The state or society alone is the reality and the individual is only "A throb in the social pulse." The state is the embodiment of reason, justice and morality and the individual is inferior to it in all respects. Hence, the state is to control and direct every affair in life including education which is but a means of shaping its citizens to a certain mould. It is the state which is to decide the mode and type of education or training which an individual is to receive. The curriculum and methods of education are also the complete monopoly of the state and the individual has no choice to develop his powers in his own way. He is only to obey what the authorities dictate. His needs, urges and nature are completely ignored. The exponents of this school of thought believe in imparting education through social control and their watch-words in the educational process, are discipline, obedience, regimentation and authority. The interpretation is best illustrated in the Spartan system of education in ancient times and by the more recent *Japanese* and *Nazi* systems of education. These systems crushed individual initiative and enterprise and brought for the misery of man such cataclysms as those of 1914 and the world war of 1939-1945.

Another interpretation given to social aim' in education is the one which is applauded in Great Britain, America and other democratic countries. It finds expression in such slogans as 'education for social service' or education for citizenship', and aim at the good of the community laying stress on teaching citizenship in schools directly and indirectly, through various subjects in the curriculum and through various social activities. Such virtues as co-operation and self-abnegation are to be cultivated. It is true that the demands of society are to be given priority against the inclination and wishes of an individual but the dictatorial or authoritarian attitude of state will be replaced by paternal attitude. The function of education according to this ideal is to enable the individual to develop himself fully according to means compatible with the interests of society.

Professor Bagley and Dewey think that social aim in education attempts to bring about 'social efficiency'. According to Professor Bagley, social efficiency stands for:

1. 'Economic efficiency' or ability 'to put his own weight' in economic life;

2. 'Negative morality' or willingness to sacrifice those of his desires the gratification of which would interfere with the economic efficiency of others;

3. 'Positive morality' or the willingness to sacrifice his own desires when gratification would not contribute directly or indirectly to social progress.

In a broad sense social efficiency means cultivation of one's powers and capacities to join freely, intelligently, and fully in the shared activities of the community as a whole. Education should make each individual socially efficient and must secure social efficiency by the positive use of individual powers and capacities in social occupations and 'not by negative constraint' or imposition from without. A socially efficient individual is able to earn his livelihood. He is not a drag or parasite on any other member of society. He is a good citizen and as such possesses knowledge and intelligence enough to understand and appreciate the world. He is ready to sacrifice his own desires if their satisfaction is harmful for others or if their gratification does not contribute, directly or indirectly, to social progress. 'A socially efficient individual conforms to a certain standard of conduct known as the moral standard.

From the above discussion of Social Aims of Education; it is clear that there are narrow and wider meaniongs of Social Aims of Education which can be summed up as below:

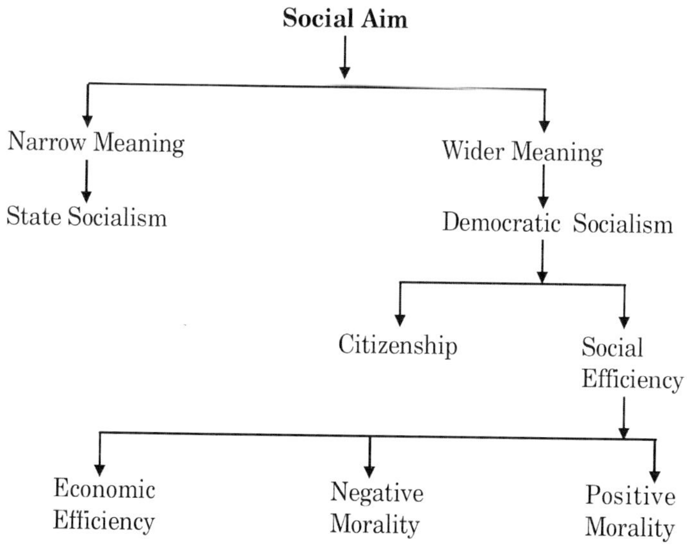

Narrow Meaning of Social Aim

In the extreme form of socialism, narrow meaning of social aim is emphasised. The advocates of the social aim in its extreme form conceive that society or state is an idealised super-human entity over and above the individual. The individual is subordinated to the state. The state is the embodiment of reason, justice and morality and the individual is inferior to it in all respects. The state or society alone is the reality and the individual is only "A throb in the social pulse." It has a mission and destiny to fulfil, which is the good and greater glory of itself. Individuals of a particular state will have to sacrifice their own interests for the welfare of the state. The good of society and the state comes to be the *summum bonum* (ultimate aim) of life and particularly of education.

Education seems to be the most powerful means for the achievement of this end. It is the state which is expected to devise and enforce a rigid system of education. The state is supreme to lay down the curriculum and even to dictate the methods. In the words of *Ross,* "The watch-words are always discipline, organisation, a willing acceptance of authority, a damping down of individuality." The slogan is "Everything of the state, everything for the state, and everything by the state."

The concept of state socialism arid subordinating the individual to the state is not a modern concept. Such concept was held in ancient times by Sparta and the other city states of Greece. Italy was its exponent in the medieval times. *Hegel* revived the same in his political theory and philosophy in the eighteenth century. *Hitler*, *Mussolini*, *Stalin*, *Khrushchev* and *Mao* have been its recent subscribers.

Wider Meaning of Social Aim

In democratic socialism wider meaning of social aim is emphasised. The supporters of this aim contend that the purpose of education is to prepare the individual for successful participation in activities. The development of the individual should be secured to promote the welfare of the society. Individual development, in no case, should interfere with, or restrict the welfare of the society, of which he is a component. In other words, democratic view of the social aim of education is to make the individual socially efficient for a democratic society. A socially efficient individual is one who is physically strong, intellectually enlightened, culturally refined, vocationally self-sufficient and morally well disciplined. A socially efficient individual, according to *John Dewey,* would be able to control his environment and fulfil his possibilities. He further adds, "All education proceeds by participation of the individual in the social consciousness of the race." Social efficiency becomes the measure of man's success in life. It has come to stay as the' be-all and end-all of education.

Bagley and *John Dewey*, who are the chief exponents of this aim of education have given it the names like "Social service" and "Social efficiency".

John Dewey states, "In the broad sense, social efficiency indirectly means cultivation of one's powers and capacities to join freely, intelligently and fully in the shared activities of the community as a whole. It implies socialisation of mind which is actively concerned with making experiences more communicable, in breaking down the barriers of social stratification which make individuals impervious to the interests of others."

In short, wider meaning of social aim of education finds expression in such rallying cries as "Education for social service," and aims at the good of the community, laying stress on teaching citizenship in school, through various subjects in the curriculum and through various social activities. This democratic view of social aim of education is applauded in India, Great Britain, America and other democratic countries.

Why Social Aim?

Following arguments are given in favour of Social Aims of Education.

Social Nature of Man: Man is a social animal. He cannot live without society. Hence he should give top priority to the welfare of society and should sacrifice everything if need arises.

Socialised Individual: Individual is born with certain animal tendencies. It is society which makes", him cultured and civilised. Qualities like sympathy, social service, obedience, kindness, love and brotherhood are developed in the society, Social environment makes him human. He is socialised through society; hence welfare of society should be emphasised in education.

Development of Individual: Development of individual is possible only in society. Hence every individual should be ready to sacrifice his greatest interest for the betterment of society. According to Ross "Individuality is of no value and personality, is a meaningless term apart from the social environment." Similarly

J.B. Baldwin opines, "Personality cannot be expressed in any but social terms."

Peace, Justice and Security: Man cannot have peace, justice and security without social organisation. Hence society or state is a basic necessity. Thus, education should prepare the individual for the state.

Salvation: Some philosophers believe that salvation lies in social service.

Criticism Against Social Aim

The social aim has been criticised on the following grounds:

Unpsychological: The social aim of education, in its narrow meaning, is unpsychological. In this form, personal interests, instincts and abilities of the children are ignored. Individuals are asked to sacrifice their own interests for the welfare of the state. So their natural development is blocked.

Man is only a Means to an End: In its extreme form, social aim stresses the fact that individual should sacrifice even his life for the betterment of the state. In this way, man is only a means to an end, end being the betterment of the state. Thus, the social aim reduces the individual to a non-entity.

Suppression of Individual Freedom: Social aim opposes individual freedom. There is a complete regimentation of ideas and feelings. Under a totalitarian form of government, this aim makes the individual a mere puppet in the hands of unscrupulous statesmen. Thus his individuality will be crushed. It is felt that education should not stand for the superssion of individuality. It should rather work for its exartation.

Hindrance in the Development of Art and Literature: Development of art and literature depends upon individual's devoted efforts. As we have stated that under social aim there is no place for individual freedom. Hence according to this aim of education there will be hindrance in the development of art and literature.

Hindrance in Intellectual and Character Development: Over emphasis on this aim will stand as an obstacle in the way of intellectual and character development as well as emotional integration. Home is also of this view.

Development of Narrow Nationalism: This aim of education will develop narrow nationalism. The idea or the belief of "My country, right or wrong" will take place. Such a frame of mind will block the progress and lead to narrow-mindedness, blunt thinking and unscientific understanding. The idea of my country right or wrong, has brought about two world wars.

Synthesis of the Individual and the Social Aims

How far is it possible to strike a balance between individual and social aims in education? At one glance it seems that they are poles apart and that no synthesis is possible. If social aim in education means education for 'good of the state' and individual aim in education means 'self expression', there cannot be any synthesis between the social and individual aims in education.

However, a synthesis is possible if the, social aim in education implies the encouragement of social service, social efficiency, ideals of good citizenships and the individual aim in education means 'self-realisation' rather than 'self-expression'. As a matter of fact, there is no real antagonism between the rival claims of the state and the individual. The interests of the state can be promoted by the development of good qualities in the individual, and the individuals can make the best of themselves in and through state. The individual has no meaning apart from society. Man by nature is not self-sufficing; and he is a social creature. He must live in a social environment, and have social contacts if individuality is to be fostered and personality is to be elevated. *Ross* has summed up the whole controversy as follows: "Thus individuality is of no value and personality is a meaningless term apart from the social environment in which they are developed and made manifest. Self realisation can be achieved only through social service, and social ideals of real value can come into being only through free individuals who have developed valuable individuality. The circle cannot be broken." Gandhiji also believes that self-realisation can be achieved only through social service. He says, "Willing submission to social control and restraint for the sake of the well-being of the whole society enriches both the individual and the society of which the former is a member."

To sum up we can say that there is, in fact, no conflict between the individual and social aims of education. Individual as well as society has the same claim on education. Hence, a synthesis of the two aims is essential. And the real aim of Education is good of the individual as well as the welfare of society.

CONCLUSION

There is no conflict between self-realisation and social service therefore individual and social aim of education are not contradictory. They are rather one and the same. They are the suitable ideal of life and education. We can make this world a richer, nobler and happier place only by promoting both. Both are complementary and can be pursued at the same time.

3

Educational Aims in India

We have already discussed in the previous chapter, the nature and determinants of educational aims in general. In this chapter, we propose to discuss the same with reference to Indian conditions. Every society evolves its own system of education meant to prepare individuals for particular end. In India the aims of education have been changing with changing philosophies of the people from time to time. Let us have a brief historical retrospect of educational aims in India.

A HISTORICAL RETROSPECT

In the Brahmanic system of education, the religious and moral aims dominated. Education was regarded as a means of inculcating such moral habits as strict obedience to elders, truthfulness, honesty and temperance. It enjoined on the pupils the tenets of the all comprehensive Dharma which included the ideals of sacred law and duty, justice, religious and moral rectitude and the established practices and customs of caste and community. Later on, when the caste system became rigid, a vocational aim in education also came into being. Each caste was to be given a certain type of education which would fit its members for a certain profession or vocation in life.

Buddhistic education was primarily monastic in its outlook and contents. It aimed at the religious development of the individual. Late on, Buddhistic education underwent change in ideology and practice. It became secular in content and was given a vocational bias. Education was to pave for royal appointments and other lucrative jobs.

Early Mohammedan education did not depart from the ancient religious ideal. The chief function of the '*Maktabs*' which were invariably attached to some mosque, was to instruct the boys in those portions of the *Holy Quarban* which were to be memorised and was to be used by them in performing their daily devotions and at other religious functions and ceremonies.

During the *Mughal* period, educational aims were reshaped for the better. The emphasis was shifted from the religious aims in education as such to moral aims. Such moral virtues as equanimity in the face of success or failure, the ability to adjust to the surroundings and the ability to earn one's livelihood were looked up in an educated person.

The educational system implanted by the British in India, was designed only to prepare Indians, for taking certain subordinate positions, in government offices; it was not intended to develop among the people capacity to take leadership and initiative in different walks of life. The aims of education were not based on the broad foundations of national culture and did not derive their inspiration from the achievements of the past or the pre-occupation of the present or the hopes of the future. Hence, after her independence when India transformed herself into secular democratic republic and declared the establishment of the socialistic pattern of society, it was inevitable that the existing education system should be reviewed and a new comprehensive system of education responding to the challenging needs of the country be devised.

To evolve such a national system of education, the government of India appointed from time to time three commissions, namely (a) the University Commission (1948-49), (b) the Secondary Education Commission (1952-53) and (c) the Indian Education Commission (1964-66). The Secondary Education Commission has formulated the aims of Secondary Education. The Indian Education Commission has also given a list of national objectives, of education.

Now let us discuss the aims of education as given by these two Commissions.

SECONDARY EDUCATION COMMISSION ON EDUCATIONAL AIMS

From a careful analysis of the dominant needs of India, the commission formulated the following aims of Secondary Education:

Developing Democratic Citizenship

The adoption of the goals of Democracy and Socialism necessitates the development of habits, attitudes and qualities of character which will enable its citizens to bear worthily the responsibilities of democratic citizenship. Among these qualities which are to be fostered through curricular and co-curricular activities in secondary schools are:

1. The capacity for clear thinking (allied to which is the capacity for clearness in speech and writing).
2. The scientific attitude of mind.
3. A receptivity to new ideas.
4. A respect for the dignity and worth of every individual.
5. The ability to live harmoniously with one's fellow-men through the cultivation of discipline, co-operation, social sensitiveness and tolerance; and
6. A sense of true patriotism.

Vocational Efficiency

India is rich in potential resources, but at present she is actually a poor country. Therefore, one of the urgent needs of the country is to improve productive efficiency and to increase the national wealth and thereby to raise the standard of living. In this respect the Commission recommends fostering dignity of manual labour and promotion of technical skill for the advancement of industry and technology. Thus, our Secondary Education must be ridden off the purely theoretical instruction, and must lay greater emphasis on craft, productive-work and diversification of courses. This will certainly result in equipping educated youngmen psychologically and practically result with better vocational efficiency, whereby they will help in increasing the national wealth and in improving the general standards of living.

Education for Leadership

Since, the youth of today will assume leadership in different walks of life tomorrow, special function of the secondary education is to train persons who will be able to assume the responsibility of leadership in social, political, industrial and cultural fields in their own small group of community or locality. To achieve success in this work, the qualities of justice, courage, discipline, tolerance, wisdom, sacrifice, initiative, resourcefulness, understanding of social issues, civic as well as vocational efficiency should be developed in the youngmen and women of our land.

Development of Personality

An important aim of democratic education is the all-round development of every individual's personality. This requires that education should take into account all his needs—psychological, social, emotional, and practical—and cater to all of them. It should release in him the sources of creative energy so that he may be able to appreciate his cultural heritage, to cultivate rich interests, which he can pursue in his leisure, and contribute in later life, to the development of this heritage. Hence, education should be so organised that subjects like art, craft, music, dancing, and the development of hobbies should find a place of honour in the curriculum. Only when education is organised on the basis of freedom and its scope is widened to include new subjects and new activities, the pupils will go out with more sensitive and quickened minds and will respond readily to the numerous stimuli in the world of Art and Nature. At the same time, they will be able not only to enjoy their cultural heritage more keenly but also help in its enrichment.

THE INDIAN EDUCATION COMMISSION ON EDUCATIONAL AIMS

The latest and the most authentic report on Indian Education has also given a four-fold aim of our national education. According to it education should aim at:

1. Increasing productivity.
2. Achieving social and national integration.
3. Accelerating the process of modernisation.
4. Cultivating social, moral and spiritual values.

The Commission has also given suggestions for the achievement of these aims. Let us now discuss those suggestions.

Increasing Productivity

For the promotion of productivity the Commission emphasises that:

1. Science education should become an integral part of school courses.

2. Work-experience should be introduced as an integral part of all education.

3. Every attempt should be made to orient work-experience to productive processes including agriculture, technology and industrialisation.

4. Secondary education should be increasingly and largely, vacationalised.

Achieving Social and National Integration

It is an important objective of education. The following steps should be taken to strengthen national consciousness and unity.

1. The common school system of public education should be adopted as a national goal and effectively implemented in a phased programme spread over twenty years.

2. Social and national service should be made obligatory for all students at all stages. It will prove an effective instrument for building character, improving discipline, inculcating a faith in the dignity of labour and developing a sense of social responsibility, if it is organised concurrently with academic studies in schools and colleges.

3. The development of an appropriate language policy can materially assist in social and national integration.

4. A re-evaluation of our cultural heritage is needed. For this, there should be well organised teaching of language, literature, philosophy, religion, history of India, Indian architecture, sculpture, painting, music, dance and drama. Inter-state camps, summer schools etc. should be organised without any barrier.

5. The educational programme in schools and colleges should be designed to inculcate democratic values.

Accelerating the Process of Modernisation

There has been a great explosion of knowledge during the last few decades. Education in a modern society, is no longer concerned with the imparting of knowledge or the preparation of finished product, but with the awakening of curiosity, the development of proper interests, attitudes and values and the building up of such essential skills, as independent study and capacity to think and judge for oneself, without which it is not possible to become a responsible member of democratic society. The progress of modernisation will be directly related to the pace of educational advance. And the one sure way to modernise quickly is to spread education, to produce educated and skilled citizens and to train an adequate and competent intelligentsia, coming from all strata of society, whose loyalties and aspirations are deeply rooted in the Indian soil. This also involves a radical change in the methods of teaching and in the training of teachers.

Cultivating Social, Moral and Spiritual Values

The expanding knowledge and the growing power which it placed at the disposal of modern society must be combined with the strengthening and deepening of the sense of social responsibility and a keener appreciation of moral and spiritual values. For this puropose, active measures should be adopted to give a value-orientation to education.

1. The Central and the State Governments should adopt measures to introduce moral, social and spiritual values in all institutions under their control (or under local authority) on the lines recommended by the University Education Commission and the Committee on Religious and Moral Instruction. The privately managed institutions should also follow suit.

2. Departments of Comparative religions and philosophies of the Universities should be specially concerned with the ways in which these values can be taught widely and effectively and should undertake preparation of special literature for use by students and teachers.

3. The Commission observed that a multi-religions democratic state like ours, should also promote a tolerant study of all religious so that its citizens can understand each other better and live amicably together. For this purpose a syllabus, giving well chosen information about each of the major religions, should be included as a part of the course in citizenship or as a part of general education to be introduced in schools and colleges upto the first degree. It would be of great advantage if common text books are prepared at the national level by competent experts in each religion.

CHALLENGE OF EDUCATION — A POLICY PERSPECTIVE ON EDUCATIONAL AIMS

The document, 'Challenge of Education — A Policy Perspective' released in August, 1985 by the Union Ministry of Human Resources Development for a nation-wide debate for evolving a new education policy, over the 1968 education policy, states that education is a complex subject with wide ranging ramifications. A definitive view on a new policy for education has to be finalised in consultation with the decision makers in the State and Central Governments, the parliamentarians, educationists, intellectuals, teachers, parents, students, entrepreneurs etc. The document states various viewpoints in a forthright manner. It has also given Aims of Education.

Goal Orientation for Educational Planning

A recapitulation of the goals of education, emphasised by the Indian Constitutions and enunciated, from time to time, by thinkers, planners, policy-makers and educationists indicates that this basic issue should be considered from three interrelated approaches.

First of all, it is necessary to define the role of the educational system in totality, since it has an institutional character of its own which goes beyond its main function of imparting education to the pupils. The system is expected to generate new knowledge in all fields within the reach of the human mind. In addition, it has to evolve principles, methodologies and guidelines for the application of knowledge for benefiting society. It is also expected to provide knowledge and skills for solving the problems of development. It must also enable the students to develop an understanding and perspective of the physical and social environment. Research and development and extension, therefore, have to be accepted as essential ingredients of the educational process.

Secondly, emphasis has to be laid on the socio-economic well-being, competence and creativity of the individual, which encompasses:

(i) physical, intellectual and aesthetic development of personality;

(ii) inculcation of a scientific temper and democratic, moral and spiritual values;

(iii) development of self-confidence to innovate and face unfamiliar situations;

(iv) creation of an awareness of the physical, social, technological, economic and cultural environment;

(v) fostering a healthy attitude to dignity of labour and hard work;

(vi) a commitment to principles of secularism and social justice;

(vii) dedication to uphold the integrity and honour as well as foster the development of the country; and

(viii) promotion of international understanding.

In addition to develop the personal attributes listed above, education has to assume the responsibility for imparting knowledge about concepts and facts relating to different subjects and for developing skills in the area of languages and communication, as also interest in hobbies, games and sports.

Besides, in relation to economic development and employment, education has to equip the pupils with competence, in terms of knowledge and skills, in various combinations at different levels of understanding, relating to the opportunities of employment in the context of a particular pattern and the rate of development.

Education has to play an important role in integrating the individual into the social system. It is meant to inculcate suitable habits for health care, mental application, management of time and conservation of physical, mental and emotional energy.

Thus perceived, education can be the most effective means for equalising opportunities and reducing disparities between human beings. In a democratic society, it is considered a fundamental right of the citizens. In the ultimate analysis, therefore, the aim must be to enlarge the coverage and improve the quality of education in our institutions so that a person, belonging to any region, caste, creed, sex or economic strata, would have the chance of developing his or her potentials to the full.

It seems relevant to underline the fact that the goals of education listed above do not envisage the laying down of omnibus objectives for all levels of education on, a priori basis. Adult education would have different goals from those of school and university education. In different age groups relevant to elementary, secondary, vocational and higher education, the need as well as capacity for acquiring knowledge and skill s varies considerably. Moreover, the process of learning itself is a hierarchical process and therefore, envisages different levels of inputs and outputs. Another point which needs consideration is that many students do not pursue formal education beyond a certain stage. This necessitates that, for each stage of education, discrete objectives and competence would have to be spelt out and for achieving these, integrated and holistic packages of formal and non-formal learning will have to be developed.

THE RAMA MURTI REPORT (1990) ON AIMS OF EDUCATION

The Rama Murti Report (1990) laid down the following goals and aims in education.

1. Education must provide a techno-informative or a sound knowledge base, empowering a person through knowledge and one on which he can build later on.

2. Education should also provide opportunities to acquire skills through engaging the students in a variety of processes and situations. These skills would be basic life skills, such as foundational skills in computation, communication, social skills, and manual skills, skills which would enable a student to develop specific job oriented skills later on.

3. Education must further provide a climate for the nurture of values, both as a personalised set of values forming one's character and including necessarily social, cultural and national values, so as to have a context and meaning for actions and decisions, and in order to enable a person to act with conviction and commitment.

4. Education must play an interventionist and catalyst role for promoting national cohesion and unity by empowering the students to become agents of social change.

INDIAN SOCIO-POLITICO-ECONOMIC SITUATIONS AND EDUCATIONAL AIMS

We have achieved freedom after centuries of slavery. This freedom can not be preserved and the vision of a socialistic pattern of society that we have held before us cannot be built unless we improve the quality of our education.

We have adopted Democracy, Socialism and Secularism as our national ideals. We should keep in our mind that democracy in India has evolved in a society which, to a very great degree, is rural and agrarian, also in a society in which vast majority of the people are ignorant, where many superstitious and rigid ways of behaviour prevail; where people are victims of many prejudices, and social maladies; where there are wide diversities in their modes of living, in their methods of speaking, in their customs and manners, and loyalties; where people have got political freedom without having necessary resource to defend it. Therefore, no system of education borrowed from other countries can be grafted to flourish in the Indian soil. No doubt, there has been a marked progress in education in many states; the literacy figure has risen, many more schools have been opened, the number of technical and professional schools and colleges has increased, there has been a rapid growth of University Education and much has been done to promote scientific research, many plans—both at the union as well as states level—have been carried into execution and many of them are still on. Yet it seems that things have not progressed in the way and in the direction in which they were intended.

What is needed now? We need a system of education which is geared to the needs of the country, which is practicable within the resources in men and material which we have; which is based on country's traditions and social behaviour and; which assures all those efficiencies to the youth.

To achieve these national goals our education must inculcate among the pupils such qualities as respect for the opposed views, respect for freedom, respect for the dignity of man, respect for rule of law, and respect for constitutional change. It must develop among them optimistic outlook, positive attitude towards work and dignity of labour, scientific and objective thinking and critical judgment. It must teach them to utilise their leisure time in a proper manner, and above all it must promote among them Emotional and National Integration, National Pride and International Understanding.

Part Two

PHILOSOPHICAL FOUNDATIONS OF EDUCATION

What is Philosophy
Value of Philosophy
Philosophy and Education
Idealism in Education
Naturalism in Education
Pragmatism in Education
Realism in Education
Existentialism in Education

4

What is Philosophy

A little girl stood looking out the window, very thoughtful. Presently she turned and said, "Mother, what I don't understand is how there came to be any world". With this reflection she became a philosopher. Most children just take the world for granted; most men and women do also. But some children and some grown-ups are very thoughtful and reflective; they wonder what the world is, how it came to life, what it is made of, and what it is for. When their wonder begins to be serious and systematic inquiry, they are philosophers. Plato said that philosophy begins in wonder. But what is Philosophy.

MEANING OF PHILOSOPHY

Let us first see what are Etymological meaning of Philosophy

Etymological Meaning of Philosophy

The term 'Philosophy' has been derived from two Greeks, words — *'Philos'* and *'Sophia'*. *'Philos'* means love and *'Sophia'* means *'wisdom'*. Thus, an etymologically speaking philosophy is love of wisdom. Plato accepts this meaning of Philosophy.

It is rather difficult to define philosophy in a way that is universally acceptable. There are different meanings for philosophy. The following meanings of philosophy have been useful for a systematic understanding of education.

Philosophy as Love of Knowledge

This is the etymological meaning of philosophy. The ancient Greeks believed that a person becomes wise by knowledge and understanding. There is an observation by Plato in his 'Republic' which reflects the belief that philosophy is that love of knowledge which makes a man wise and to live wisely. He says, "He who has a taste for every sort of knowledge and who is curious to learn and is never satisfied may be justly termed a philosopher." It is to be noted in the above definition that a philosopher is to be interested in 'all types' of knowledge. A physicist is interested in the physical processes of the universe, a biologist in the biological universe, a sociologist in the social life and likewise persons of different disciplines have their focus of interest. It is quite possible for them to limit their interest in such a way. But when it is said that to become a philosopher one must get interested in all these disciplines, it may be wondered whether such multi-dimensional interest is possible at all. But a great scope of philosophers of the world have provided an answer through their life and works. To illustrate, Aristotle who was one of the great philosophers of Greek culture was a repository of contemporary knowledge. His works such as De Anima (meaning 'of the soul' and a book on psychology), Politics (a book useful to students of politics and education), Poetics (a book on literary criticism), Ethics and other works of Science reflect his breadth of interest and depth of scholarship. A few centuries earlier, that is till recently, a number of disciplines which enjoy an independent status in the present universities were considered as a part of philosophy. Physics, Chemistry, etc., were called as Natural Philosophy; Politics, Economics, Sociology, etc., were called as Moral Philosophy and Psychology was included under Mental Philosophy. Even now there has been no shift from the focus of interest in Philosophy. Philosopher is interested in the first principles and final conclusions of all branches of knowledge. As the greatest educational philosopher of America, John Dewey has said : "The primary aim of philosophy is knowledge of 'Being' or 'Reality' which is more comprehensive, fundamental and ultimate than the knowledge which can be provided by the organs and methods at the disposal of the special sciences." For this kind of an ultimate, comprehensive knowledge the first principles of physical, natural and social sciences must be the basis.

Philosophy as an Activity

Studying philosophy is just as good as engaging in an activity. Many have considered philosophy as primarily an activity or a process; secondly as a subject-matter for teaching and learning. As Levisohn defines it: "Philosophy is first of all an activity of a certain kind and only secondarily a subject-matter consisting of a definite body of literature." We are engaged in numerous activities every day. Should we call them philosophy? If not, then in what way can we say that philosophy is an activity. Philosophy is a mental activity; thinking about the problems of mankind. For example it is a mental activity of thinking about life, its nature and purposes; the mind and its occupations, birth, death and other phenomena of world; feelings, ideas, values of social life, etc. This activity must not be limited to a study and discussion among a few persons but be able to stimulate the interest of humanity at large. As Russell puts it: "Philosophy deals with matters of interest to the general educated public and loses much of its value if only a few professional understand it. Henderson also has expressed himself in a similar way while defining philosophy : "Philosophy is a rigorous, disciplined, guarded analysis of some of the most difficult problems which man has ever faced." If the life and works of the great philosophers is studied in the light of these definitions it can be perceived that philosophy right from the earliest times has interested itself in the common problems of mankind. The title of one of the many books by John Dewey and written purely about philosophy is 'Problems of Men'. However, Dewey argues that philosophy is not a panacea for the problems of men but is that which emerges out of the methods employed by them to solve their problems. Philosophy must emerge out of life, rather than life being guided by dictates of philosophy. For Socrates, philosophy was a daily activity. He used to invite the Athenian citizens into arguments and discuss with them the problems of life and the world around without himself getting bored. That is how he was referred to as the gadfly of Athens. Therefore, philosophy can be conceived of as an activity of criticism, clarification, and interpretation of life. D. J. O'Connor has defined philosophy as 'an activity of criticism or clarification. There has emerged a distinct and well known school of philosophy in the present century which has kept this meaning of philosophy as basic to their distinctiveness. This school is represented by great scholars such as Wittgenstein,

Israel Scheffler, D.J. O'Connor, A.J. Ayer, P.H. Hirst and is called as "Language Analysis".

Philosophy as a 'Comprehensive Picture of the Universe'

Philosophers have attributed this meaning to philosophy right from the beginning. The Greek Philosopher Sophocles had said that a philosopher had to see life steadily and see it as a whole. He must have a holistic and self-contained view of the universe. As Henderson puts it: "Philosophy gives a synoptic view of universe". It gives a total picture, a synthetic understanding, a synoptic vision and an integrated view. Keeping this meaning in his mind, Dr. Radhakrishnan has defined the aim of philosophy thus: "The aim of philosophy is to give an integrated view of the universe". The physical, natural and social sciences might provide an integral understanding of the physical, natural and human world, but fail to offer a holistic vision of the universe. The philosopher would study generalisations of all the above sciences and on the basis of his accumulated understanding would offer an organised and systematic knowledge of the universe. As Dewey has viewed it: "With respect to subject–matter, philosophy is an attempt to comprehend—that is, gather together the varied details of the world and of life into a single inclusive whole." As such philosophy does not involve in the creation and publication of knowledge; it implies a study and re-organisation of the knowledge that is already available. It involves the organisation, interpretation, clarification and criticism of what is already within the realm of the known and experienced. It is a way of looking at knowledge which we already have. If science is defined as a systematised and organised body of knowledge, it is for this reason that Brubacher has called philosophy as the sciences of sciences. It has been called as the mother of sciences because the independent disciplines of today were an integral part of philosophy at one or the other times of yester-years. Plato also conceived of the philosopher as a spectator of all time and all existence.

P.G. Smith has suggested three dimensions for philosophical thinking. They are comprehensiveness, penetration and flexibility. 'Flexibility' is a noteworthy dimension of philosophy. Philosophy does not offer a panacea for all problems of mankind or an eternal truth about the organisation of the universe. It will also change as the truths, view points and knowledge in the sciences, on which philosophy is based, go on changing and expanding. Philosophy does not preach an eternal and all pervasive permanent knowledge. As Kilpatrick describes it: "Philosophy is a point of view, outlook on life. The test of a good philosophy is that it should stand the test of scrutiny, re-examination and revision in the light of new problems and new insights." Therefore, in this way, the philosopher must possess an integrated, self-contained but flexible view of the universe.

Philosophy as a Guide to a Way of Life

Philosophy is a view of life. It gives a direction to life, offers a design for living. *Dr. Radhakrishnan* has suggested this meaning to philosophy through the titles of two of his works; they are 'The Hindu view of life' and 'The Idealist view of life.' Philosophy directs life and gets refined on the basis of experiences of life. When man is caught in ambiguous situations, he thinks about morality, duty, justice, right, goodness, world and its management, etc., and reaches his own conclusions. Philosophy is created out of life's experiences and life through the light of such philosophy. As Arnold Reid, formerly Director of the Institute of Education, London and Professor of educational philosophy has put it, "I repeat that philosophy is, in the end, about life, and not only about reported statements concerning life, and that one must live richly in order to think and talk sense." Even among Indian philosophers there was not much divergence between the philosophy and the way of life. For them life was the laboratory of philosophy. Gandhiji has titled his autobiography as 'My Experiments with Truth'. Once when he was asked to give a message for the world he is reported to have answered thus: 'My life is my message' (Humanistic Idealism). It is said that philosophy in the West was born out of wonder, (Thales of Miletus has been considered by the historians of Western philosophic thought as the father of Western Philosophy as he was the first to wonder about the phenomena of the world around him). But philosophy in India emerged as a result of reflection over the experiences and problems of everyday living. Prof. Hiriyanna has also suggested the same meaning for philosophy in his writings.

Philosophy as Analysis

The critical and analytical function of philosophy is much less appreciated by people than the activity of synthesis. Philosophy is concerned only with the problem and method of knowledge. Philosophy is not the study of ultimate reality as a whole. The function of philosophy is wholly critical and to provide us with definitions for use as it is a special branch of knowledge. Most philosophers in the history of philosophy were not metaphysicians, rather they were anaylsists, e.g., *Locke, Berkley, Hume, Mill, Moore, Hegel*, etc. Propositions of philosophy are not factual but is linguistic in character.

Philosophy as Synthesis

The other main function of philosophy is the more traditional one. It attempts to synthesise all knowledge and man's total experience. Here the emphasis is upon the anticipated result, rather than upon the tools and methods employed. In this synthesising activity, philosophies seek the most inclusive view possible regarding the nature of reality, the meaning and purpose of life, the origin, the status and the destiny of consciousness and other such ultimate questions. This view was held by some early philosophers who did not claim to be wisemen, but merely lovers of wisdom. They claimed that their role was to help others in their search for wisdom. Yet, there were certain other teachers, i.e., Sophists, meaning thereby one who is wise. Such teachers delivered information to the students after charging a fee. This information formed the content of the education of a wise man. This is, in fact, the tradition, even now maintained in our campuses.

In the second sense, philosophy is a man's attempt to give meaning to his existence through the continued search for comprehensive and consistent answer to basic problems. This sense makes philosophers as active persons, Socrates himself took philosophy as an activity. In the words of Plutarch: Socrates neither set up benches for his students, nor set on a platform, nor set house for his teachers. He was philosophising all the time—while he was joking, while he was drinking, while he was soldiering"

Wherever he met you, on the street and met the end when he was in prison and drinking the Poison. He was the first to start that all your life, all the time, in everything you do, whatever you are doing is the time for philosophy.

However, it has not always been a fact that all philosophers philosophised, rather many of them developed themselves by undertaking the endless study of the work of other philosophers. The result was that the title philosopher was more frequently used for those who knew philosophy, even when they did little philosophising. In the recent past, especially in U.K. emphasis has been on activity rather than only on theory. In the words of Bertrand Russell, "Philosophy proper deals with matter of interest to the general educated public and loses much of its value if only a few professionals can understand what is social."

Philosophy and Science

There is an unique relation between philosophy and science. Philosophy takes over from the end-point of science. Philosophy grows on the base of the detailed knowledge of science. As Butler has put it: "Both are interested in knowledge. But there is a difference in the kind of knowledge. Science seeks knowledge of facts. Philosophy seeks ultimate knowledge." This fundamental knowledge though beyond the facts of science. Still is based on them. The following description helps in understanding the relation between the two:

Phenix: "Science attempts only at the discovery of facts. Philosophy is not just interested in facts in so far to provide an attitude towards them. It tries to organise, interpret, clarify and criticise the already discovered facts of science."

Dewey: "When science denotes not simply a report of the particular facts discovered about the world but a general attitude towards it — as distinct from special things to do it merges into philosophy."

G.T.W. Patrick: "Between science and philosophy the very close relationship exists. They spring from the same root, the love of knowledge, and they aspire to the same end, the knowledge of reality. While science describes the facts, philosophy interprets them."

Brubacher: "Science is interested in the proximate or efficient causes of facts, while philosophy is concerned with its ultimate or final causes."

The foregone statements suggest that if the outlook of the scientist is partial, narrow in scope and details, the outlook of a philosopher is holistic and comprehensive. But to enrich life, for the world to trace the path of progress, philosophy and science must be complementary. For instance, science would supply the technical knowledge and skills required to generate atomic energy. There is a need for a healthy and desirable philosophy to put this energy into creative and constructive use. An unhealthy philosophy would tempt one to misuse the same energy for destructive purposes. If discovery of knowledge is the task of science, the task of philosophy is to direct the use of such knowledge. As such there is no contradiction between science and philosophy; rather there is a harmony between the two.

PHILOSOPHY AND RELIGION

Those who are not aware of the nature and methods of philosophy often confuse it for religion. Though there are a few similarities between the two, still there are some prominent differences. The objective of both religion and philosophy is the same; discovery of truth. The difference between the two lie in the method of investigation of Truth. Faith is the basis of the method in religion. Religion begins with a faith in a few priori beliefs. These beliefs should not be questioned. Commitment to these beliefs on the part of the individual is a primary requisite. But the method of philosophy is an independent, objective and impartial enquiry. If philosophy is speculative and contemplative, religion is action-oriented and ritualistic. Religion is an approach to realise the given ultimate realities of life. Philosophy is an attempt to understand the ultimate realities of life. Though these distinctions apply fully in the context of Western philosophies and religions, still they do not perfectly fit in, in the context of Indian culture. This is because; the religions of India are more speculative and philosophical. As Bertrand Russell and Albert Schweitzer have opined, it is difficult to draw a clear line of demarcation between the religions and philosophies of India.

Though, the original meaning of the term philosophy is the love of wisdom. The modern point of view might prefer to call it as the search for or pursuit of wisdom. The important point is that it is the desire for wisdom that arouses the philosopher to activity, rather than the more usual things which men strive for. Philosophical wisdom implies some genuine understanding of the universe and of all human experience. One definition holds that philosophy is a persistent and organised attempt to see life steadily and see it whole. Sometimes, it is taken in the sense of a systematic search for meanings and values and sometimes as suggesting a profound probing into the nature of reality. However, philosophy is a systematic and thorough attempt to relate the universe and human life to each other in a meaningful way. Someone has said that the aim of philosophy is to discover the nature of universe and our relationship to it. Thus, philosophy represents the efforts to combine into an integrated system all knowledge and all experiences both individual and racial. It seeks to organise all truths into a unified whole.

It is an organised search for knowledge carried on by means of scientific reflections upon the discoveries of the scientists the findings of the historians the insight of the artists the poets and the mystics. A basic part of philosophical activity consist of the study of the sources of the methods and the limitations of human knowledge. It has two important functions to do analysis and synthesis.

BRANCHES OF PHILOSOPHY

Following are the main branches of Philosophy:

Ontology

Very early in the history of philosophy, thinker began to ask about the stuff the world is made of. Can everything in the universe be resolved into some elementary form of being, some ultimate reality, such for instance as matter, or energy, or mind? This is the ancient problem of Reality, or the problem of Being. The technical term for it is Ontology, from two Greeks words meaning the science of being? It represents the search for the "First Principle". We love to reduce everything to some final unity or elementary "stuff", and if we believe that we have found such a final unity, we call our theory of reality a monistic view, or just Monism, from a Greek word signifying alone or single. If now we believe that there is only one ultimate reality and that this reality is matter, we may call this view Materialistic Monism, or just Materialism. On the other hand, if we come to the conclusion that the one ultimate reality is not matter, but Mind, or Spirit, we may call this view Spiritualistic Monism, or Spiritualism. Sometimes it has been called Idealism.

But perhaps we shall not succeed in resolving the whole world into one elementary substance and shall find that in the very last analysis there are two ultimate forms of Being, such as Mind and Matter. If so, we may call this theory Dualism, from the Latin word for two.

Or, finally, it is just possible that reality cannot be reduced even to two ultimate forms, but that there are more than two, possibly many. Then our theory of reality will be called Pluralism. These Ontological problems we shall find difficult to solve and the various answers not quite satisfactory; but men have always wondered about ultimate reality and we can at least study the various views of the philosophers. This second class of inquiries may be put in tabular form as fallows:

Ontological Inquiries	Monism	Materialism Spiritualism or Idealism
	Dualism	
	Pluralism	

Epistemology

Even before we reach this point in our philosophising, we shall encounter so many difficulties and find our doubts so hard to resolve that we shall begin to wonder whether the human mind is capable of real knowledge and whether the best avenues of knowledge are through the sense organs or through some "faculty" or reason. So we shall be forced into the study of the Theory of Knowledge, or Epistemology, as it is called. Perhaps some readers will think that we should have begun with this — and that, no doubt, would be the logical order. But the Theory of Knowledge is a difficult subject, and if presented first might frighten us away from the study of philosophy and we may assume tentatively that the human mind does have the power of real knowledge, and that such real knowledge is offered us in the special sciences. In general, faith is better than skepticism as a point of departure. Later we may ask about the sources and the validity of human knowledge. This inquiry will cover the following special subjects:

The Theory of Knowledge or Epistemology	The sources of Knowledge - discussing the rival theories called Rationalism and Empiricism.
	The Validity of Knowledge — as seen from the standpoint of Realism and Idealism.
	Pragmatism—its theory of knowledge and of truth.

Axiology

A quite distinctive field of philosophy is that of values. What are values and how do they differ from facts? Are they objective in nature or subjective in the human mind? There are three kinds of values which might be studied in philosophy, namely, religious values, moral values and aesthetic values. Preliminary to the study of religious values, we shall wish to inquire about God —the meaning of God in human experience. If God is good and created the world, how shall we explain the presence of evil in the world? Then the study of moral values will open a subject of the most extreme interest, and especially at the present time, when there is so much confusion about morals. Finally, aesthetic values, or the study of Beauty, as exhibited in nature and the fine arts, should engage our attention.

So our fifth division will be as follows :

Axiology	Religious values
The higher values of life	Moral values
	Aesthetic values

Cosmology

The study of Cosmology, inquiring first about the Cosmos, or the Universe, and about the nature of Space and Time. Then we may ask about the Earth and the first beginnings of Life upon its surface. Then will follow easily the study of the Evolution of life, and this will suggest the problem of its Purposiveness, if it has any. Teleology is the name given to the study of purpose or design in nature.

Branches of Philosophy in Tabular Form

To sum up the branches of Philosophy may be put in tabular form as follows:

Ontological Inquiries	Monism	Materialism
		Spiritualism or Idealism
	Dualism	
	Pluralism	

The Theory of Knowledge or Epistemology	The Sources of knowledge - discussing The rival theories called Rationalism and Empiricism
	The Validity of Knowledge — as seen from the standpoint of Realism and Idealism
	Pragmatism — its theory of knowledge and of truth

The Higher Values of Life	Religious of Values
	Moral Values
	Aesthetic Values

Cosmological Inquiries	The Universe, Space, Time
	The origin and Nature of Life
	The Philosophy of Evolution
	Is there Purpose or Design in Nature?

5

Value of Philosophy

Philosophy influences both the personal and social aspects of human life. Most of the Western philosophers have considered the goal of philosophy to be the achievement of knowledge, but the aim of philosophy in not merely intellectual. It is true that philosophy gives us knowledge but, as Sri Aurobindo has pointed out, "Still the truth once discovered must be realisable in our inner being and our outer activities; if it is not, it may have an intellectual but not an integral importance; a truth for the intellect, for our life, it would be no more than the solution of a thought, puzzle or an abstract reality or a dead letter." The existentialist school of our time has emphasised the life of the individual, his feelings, expectations and frustrations, in philosophical thinking. It is a revolt against logical and naturalistic system building, analytic intellect and dead thought which make philosophy a useless search for the ideas which are entirely unconnected with our practical life. Therefore the contemporary school of pragmatism emphasises the pragmatic value of truth. Humanism lays emphasis upon the Protagorian principle of Homo-Mensura. The instrumentalism of John Dewey explains knowledge and intelligence as instruments for success in life. Hence philosophy and life are closely connected. This can be seen particularly in the following points:

Value of Philosophy on Personal Life

In our personal life we daily come across the problems when we have to decide between right and wrong. This decision requires criterion of right and wrong or good and ultimate good. To present such a criterion is the job of moral philosophy. Thus, it is clear that we are in need of philosophy at every step of our life. Man cannot live a thoughtful life. He has to always think over many types of problems. Is it not strange that though many people think, few know those laws of thought and the ways of thinking? The laws of thought and the ways of thinking form the subject-matter of an important branch of philosophy known as Logic. A man may sometimes think properly event without any knowledge of logic but knowledge of logic will definitely make his thinking better and more valid. In the modern times, everywhere in urban areas one hears talk about art. Many want to refine their lives. Many want to live amidst beautiful things and beautify their surroundings. But how many persons think about the basic questions as to what in beauty? What is art? These questions are raised by an important branch of philosophy known as aesthetics. Many people are prepared to sacrifice their lives for the sake of their values. What is this value? What are the ultimate values? These questions are answered by Axiology. Every man, sometime or the other, tries to know what will happen to him after death? Is there a world other than our own? What happens to the man when he dies? These questions are raised in Eschatology, an important branch of philosophy. Again, some thoughtful persons, when they reach at some crossing in life, thinks as to where they have to go? Why have they come to this world? What is the aim of life? Who am I? These questions are philosophy of self. When the man looks at the towering tops of the mountains, murmuring sounds of the forests, pitch-dark nights, roaring oceans and ferocious earthquakes and other peculiar natural phenomena a question arises in his mind as to what is this world? What is its nature? All these questions are discussed in Cosmology and Cosmogony. Thus, numerous types of questions that are raised in our everyday life fall beyond the scope of common sense or science because they are basically philosophical questions. The value of philosophy in a man's life is, therefore, quite clear.

Value in Behaviour Towards Others

Whereas philosophy influences personal life, it influences social life as well. Our behaviour towards others is determined by our philosophy. If a man consider others as ends in themselves, his behaviour will be different from that of those persons who consider others is determined by our philosophy. If a man considers others as mere instruments to achieve their own selfish ends. Everyman has divine element in him, this is a philosophical attitude. Everybody is a thief; this is a different philosophical attitude. It can be easily understood that these different philosophical attitudes will lead to different types of behaviour towards others. In fact, it will not be an exaggeration to say that at the root of the behaviour of different persons, there are some philosophical difficulties. For example, the hatred of a Communist towards capitalists is the result of Marxist philosophy.

Value in Political Life

Philosophy also influences political life. Various types of political philosophies such as democracy democratic socialism, communism, totalitarianism, anarchism etc., lead to different types of government and state and to a lot of difference concerning human rights and the aspects of political life.

Value in Economic Life

Everyone has to earn money in order to earn his livelihood. The question is as to what is the aim of life? Is money an end or merely a means to it? This is a philosophical question and the answer to it, depend not only the economic activities of the individuals but also those of nations. The form of production, consumption and exchange very much depends on the answer to this philosophical question. According to M.K. Gandhi, capitalists are the trustees of the capital of society. On the other hand, according to Karl Marx, the capitalists are the exploiters of the proletariat. These two different philosophical attitudes have widely influenced economic life.

Value in Social Life

Society is a web of social relationships. These relationships are found in different institutions such a family, marriage, business etc., in thousands of associations. All these are influenced by philosophy. For example, whether the wedlock between male and female is a religious sacrament, this is a philosophical question on the answer to which depends the form, stability and result of marriage in a particular society. Similarly, the relationships between parents and their children in a family do not depend on the biological and psychological attachments alone but also on their philosophical attitude towards life. Whether the children should be brought up as ends in themselves or whether they are mere instruments for the progress of the family, this is a philosophical question the answer to which determines many important issues in a joint family. Similarly, what are the rights of society over the individual and do these rights have a limit? How far should the individual accept social control and how far can he evade it? All these are philosophical questions which have important social influence.

Value in Culture Life

The philosophy of a nation is the index of its cultural progress. Thus philosophy influences each aspect of culture. The forms of dance, music, art, literature, etc., are very much influenced by philosophy. A healthy philosophy will lead to a healthy attitude towards all these. To illustrate, Indian philosophy is mainly spiritual, therefore, one finds the stamp of spirituality on Indian dance, music, art, literature, etc. On the other hand, Western philosophy is materialistic. To quote John Dewey, "Thus philosophy makes a change of culture. In forming patterns to be conferred to in future thought and action it is addictive and transforming in its role in future thought and action it is additive and transforming in its role in history of civilisation. This is expressed in even more clear terms by Archie. J. Bahm, when he says, "Without philosophy then there would to be no civilisation, and civilisations differ from one another as romantic, rationalistic, pacific, aggressive, mystical and mundane, partly because of their philosophical differences."

The philosophy of a nation represents the infancy, adolescence and maturity of a nation's culture. Philosophical progress manifests cultural progress. In a nation where there is no philosophical progress, its culture is dead. Cultural revolutions have also coincided with philosophical crises. In Greece when Socrates was made to drink hemlock, it was not because of the enmity of people against him only but also because of his opposition to philosophy of the community of his time. Similarly, many other great men have sacrificed their lives by challenging the philosophies of their contemporary philosophers and thus changing it through their blood.

Vale in Educational Field

Though now-a-days, the number of students of philosophy and departments of its teaching in Indian universities is gradually becoming less and less, no thoughtful person denies the value of philosophy in educational field. In the words of Blanshard and others. "The function of philosophy in universities in properly the same as its function in the cultural development of a society, to be the intellectual conscience of the community". The most fundamental question in the field of education is concerning its aim? This question raises another question as to what is man, because what he is not, he cannot become. He can become only that what is already implicit in him. Man's nature is, therefore, a philosophical question on the answer to which have developed so many philosophies of education which are the foundations of different modern methods of teaching.

Value in the Field of Knowledge

In the modern times, many educate persons, who swear by science, consider philosophy to be useless in the age of science because they are ignorant of the function of philosophy in the field of science. It can be said without exaggeration that without a philosophical basis, any knowledge is imperfect, because no total picture can be presented without the synthetic function of philosophy. Without this total picture there will always be tension in the field of knowledge which leads to philosophical activities. As Aristotle has said, "Whether we philosophies or not, we must philosophies." This has been expressed by Perry in somewhat different terms when he says, "Philosophy is neither accidental nor supernatural, but inevitable and normal".

Besides its synthetic function, another important function of philosophy is the criticism of the postulates and conclusions of different sciences. Whenever a scientist delves deeper in his own particular field, he reaches a depth where the process of his thinking is not scientific but philosophical. This can be seen in the thinking of many a great scientists of the world. The importance of philosophy in the field of knowledge is, therefore, quite clear.

CONCLUSION

From the point of view of different aspects of the individual and social life, and in different fields of knowledge, the discussion of the value of philosophy shows the utility of its study. In the words of J. W. Cunningham, "Philosophy thus grows directly out of life and its needs". Everyone who lives, "If he lives, at all reflectively, is in some degree a philosopher." In the words of Chesteran, "The most practical and important thing about a man is his view of universe — his philosophy. The employee is at the mercy of the philosophy of his employer and the employer stakes his business on the philosophy of his employees."

6

Philosophy and Education

Fichte in his 'Address to the German People' observed that the art of education would never attain clearness in itself without philosophy, there is an interaction between the two, and either without the other is incomplete and unserviceable. Fichte's contention will become clear if we examine the meaning of philosophy.

THE MEANING OF PHILOSOPHY

Etymologically, the word Philosophy is derived from two Greek words Philo (love) and *Sophia (wisdom),* means love of wisdom, Wisdom is not the same thing as knowledge. It includes knowledge, but goes beyond it to find relationship and to discover implications. Philosophy means 'mature reflection' about any problem in its complete perspective.

In the ordinary sense of the term 'philosophy' means the sum of man's beliefs. Technically it is 'the sum of man's reasoned-out beliefs.' What are these beliefs about? They are about the most fundamental question, the nature of reality. What is this universe? What is Man and what is his relation to the universe? Philosophy is a search for a comprehensive view of nature, an attempt at a universal explanation of the nature of things. It is a continuous seeking of insight into basic realities—the physical world, life, mind, society, knowledge and values. According to Dr. Radhakrishanan "It is a logical inquiry into the nature of reality." It explores the basic sources and aims of life. Thus, philosophy means beliefs or points-of-view concerning purposes and values according to which man tries to live. He raises questions about reality, universe, and nature of man, his origin and his destiny. He tries to answer these questions and forms a reasoned-out point of view on these fundamental matters. These answers come from his philosophic attitude towards life or his philosophy according to which be lives, "Men live," says Huxley, "in accordance with their philosophy of life, their conception of the world." It is impossible to live without metaphysics. If this metaphysics is vital enough, it is bound to urge it's possessor to live in accordance with it. A philosophy always results in a certain way of life. According to Dewey, philosophy signifies "A wisdom that would influence the conduct of life."

The three great religious teachers of the world — Buddha, Christ and Mohammed — had their own philosophy resulting in different ways of life. So was the case with *Gandhiji*, *Hitler* and *Omar Khayyam*. *Buddha* preached the philosophy of renunciation and personal salvation; Christ advocated the philosophy of love and charity; *Mohammed* upheld the doctrine of brotherhood; *Gandhiji* believed in the philosophy of non-violence; Hitler supported a militant philosophy; *Omar Khyyam* extolled the *Epicurean philosophy*. All these philosophies, based on different beliefs, resulted in different ways of life.

Thus, every philosophy of life is based on a certain belief. And a belief, if it is vital must lead to an educative effort. As such philosophy is inseparable from education.

RELATION BETWEEN PHILOSOPHY AND EDUCATION

The common subject for both philosophy and education is 'man'. Education, concerned with the modification of the natural man, looks to philosophy for the ideal to which to lead him. The two notions — philosophy and education like the two sides of a coin present different views of the same thing, and one is implied by the other. Education is the dynamic side of philosophy or its active aspect while philosophy is the contemplative side of it. In other words, education is the practical means of realising the ideals of life.

It is impossible to come across a philosopher without a blazing urge to propagate his beliefs and metaphysics among others and educate them to follow his way of thinking and living. It is equally impossible to imagine a system of education completely divorced from any philosophy. Philosophy provides the aim of life and thereby the aim of education and education provides the vehicle for carrying out that philosophic aim in practical life.

Education means a planned modification of the natural behaviour of the child. At birth the child is not what his community would ultimately wish him to be. Therefore, he has to be shaped and reshaped into a socially desirable individual. He has to be changed accordingly. Change presupposes a direction which is chosen consciously and deliberately, and along which the change has to be effected in the child. Before, the child's native behaviour begins to be modified, the agency attempting the change has to be clear regarding the direction along which change has to be made, and this direction of modification is to be defined by the aim or purpose of the change. The aim and direction of the modification to be attempted in the child's behaviour through education are supplied by philosophy. This is what education owes to philosophy.

Dependence of education on philosophy is clearly seen by the fact that great philosophers of all times have also been great educators and their philosophy finds reflection in their educational schemes. In the words of Rusk, "We need only cite Plato's Idealism and his cultural scheme of education; Rationalism and formal training; Empiricism in philosophy and Encyclopaedism in education; Rousseau's anti-society philosophy and his negative or natural education; Spencer's Hedonism and his discipline by natural consequences; and American Pragmatism and Project Method in education."

Dependence of education on philosophy is further realised by the fact that in view of modern developments in the field of education, we need a 'co-ordinating if not determining principle,' which will give meaning to our whole educational endeavour. Only the philosophy of the subject can furnish us with such a principle. We need an ideal life to which education should aspire.

The relation between philosophy and education is proved still more clearly by the relation between education and politics. No political system can do without evolving a suitable educational policy and practice. For instance, the educational system in a democratic country cannot escape the influence of democracy; its educational methods and institutions cannot but be democratic to a large or to a small extent. Infact, every philosophy has both a political and an educational system following closely in its wake. The educational system has to find its guiding principles in the aims of social order for which it prepares. Education is a sustaining, progressive and purposive endeavour, and its strength comes only from the moral and political values of the community, the only source of which is philosophy.

Therefore, we can say that without philosophy, education would be nothing but a blind effort; and without education philosophy would be no better than a cripple. In the words of Adams, "Education is the dynamic side of philosophy, the practical means of realising ideals of life." Divorced from philosophy, education would become an aimless endeavour, a hopeless waste of time and energy; philosophy gives its point, its target and its goal. This is how philosophy and education are inter-related.

IMPACT OF PHILOSOPHY ON THE THEORY AND PRACTICE OF EDUCATION

Having established the fact of a fundamental relation between Philosophy and Education, we should now discover what concrete form this connection takes with reference to different aspects of education. Philosophy exercises its influence on education in all its aspects. "From every angle of the educational problem," say Rusk, "There is comes the demand for a philosophical basis of the subject." "There no escape from a philosophy of life and of education." Philosophy determines the practical aim of educational effort; it determines the content of curriculum; it influences the discipline in the school; it exercises an effective influence on the methods of teaching and it defines the place of the teacher in the educational set-up. Let us now discuss the impact of philosophy on these different aspects of education.

Philosophy and Aims of Education

Philosophy has an effective bearing on the aims of education. It is philosophy which determines whether the aims of education are universal or relative; whether the aims of education should be intellectual development or moral perfection; whether education should be vocational or liberal; whether education should be for the development and happiness of the individual or for the good of the society? Such conflicting opinions regarding the aims of education are reconciled in the light of philosophy.

The aims of education have a reference to the aims of life. The aim of life is determined by the philosophy that prevails at a certain time. Thus, educational aims depend on the philosophy that prevails among the people living at a particular time. That is why aims of education have been changing with the changing philosophy of life. They have varied in different countries in accordance with their respective philosophy of life.

In ancient Sparta, for example, the ideal was understood as dedication of the life and property of the individual to the cause of the state. It was ingrained in the mind of educand's that the country's honour must be vindicated at all costs. Hence, the aim of the Spartan system of education was to prepare citizens to be soldiers and patriots. On the other hand, the Athenian system of education aimed at the cultural development of each individual in conformity with the Athenian philosophy of that time. Rousseau learnt much from nature and received hard rebuff from society. In due course of time he developed a philosophy of education which was anti-social, negative and naturalistic. The British Public Schools, the Folk High Schools of Denmark, the American High Schools — all aim at producing good citizens in accordance with their democratic philosophy of life. The German system of education illustrates effectively how philosophy determines the aims of education. In pre-war Germany, the philosophy of life that prevailed 'was based on the idea of Kultur — the great achievements and creations of the German mind; its language, literature, art, science, history — the nation was regarded as the chief factor for determining the aim of life. This philosophy which emerged in accordance with the needs of times created an ideal of education that deliberately instilled the spirit of national egoism, crushed individuality ruthlessly, and cultivated in individual citizens unquestioning loyalty and obedience to the Nazi regime by means of a rigid, militarised system of education deliberately planned for the purpose. Thus, we can conclude that philosophy is the determining force for laying down the aims of education.

Philosophy and Curriculum

Choice of means depends on the ends which they are required to realise. Ends determine the means. Curriculum is only a means for realising the aims of education. So it is bound to be determined by educational objectives. The objectives of education, as has already been discussed, are derived from the general aim of life which is determined by Philosophy. Thus, the curriculum to be followed in schools has to conform to the prevailing philosophy. For instance, if the philosophy of life accepted by the people of a country is Naturalism, the curriculum followed in her schools cannot allow any place to humanities subjects that have only a cultural value. The curriculum naturally will consist only of those subjects which would enable the pupils to secure a better adjustment with their environment. Natural sciences are, therefore, bound to form an integral part of the naturalistic curriculum. According to the naturalists the present experience, activities and interests should be the guiding factor in framing the curriculum; while to the idealists, the experiences of the human race as epitomed in science and humanities, should provide the primary consideration in deciding a curriculum. In fact, the idealists attach great importance to the spiritual perfection to which some subjects are abundantly conducive. The pragmatists emphasise the principle of utility as the main criterion for determining the nature of the curriculum. The realists think that a bookish, abstract or sophisticated curriculum is useless. They want to concentrate on realities of life and emphasise the importance of subjects that fall within the range of natural science.

The above discussion indicates that the problem of curriculum construction is tackled and solved in terms of the philosophical beliefs held by a group of people. The same is true of text book as well.

Philosophy and Methods of Teaching

Even the choice of methods is ultimately a question of philosophy. Kilpatric, realising the ultimate relation between philosophy and methods of education, introduced the significant term' philosophy of method. It is through this method that the teacher is going to establish and maintain contact between the child and the subject-matter. The nature of the method of teaching is determined by the aim, which is sought to be realised by the method in question. Since, the aim of education is determined by philosophy, the method of teaching is also determined by the prevailing philosophy. If the philosophy prevailing at the time is that of Rousseau and the system of education is naturalistic the method naturally would be to follow nature, and 'learn by experience'. The child's nature being basically good, he must be left entirely to his natural inclinations and all external impositions and interference must be avoided. In the naturalistic scheme of teaching, the method of teaching has to be the "Method of experience, and not the method of telling. On the other hand when the prevailing philosophy is idealism, the child has to understand and realise certain ultimate values and ideals, the method of teaching will be teacher-centred. Pragmatism holds that the most effective and lasting learning is possible only around a problematic situation of practical life. Consequently, method of education consists in the creation of a practical problem or a project and in inducing many-sided learning through it.

Philosophy and Discipline

The nature of discipline is always determined by the philosophy one holds. Naturalism stands of unhampered freedom for the child. It emphasises self-assertion of the individual, as against blind obedience to authority. Idealism relies much on the personality of the teacher for the maintenance of discipline. With the help of such a discipline, idealism advocates the development of a transcendental or a spiritual self which is liberated from the fetters of a merely physical, reality. Pragmatism does not believe in the employment of external discipline as a means for the adequate performance of educational functions. It gives complete freedom to the child and stresses the educational value of interest. We, thus, see that the problem of discipline is closely related with philosophy and the conception of discipline as held by a teacher or educator will always be influenced by his philosophical beliefs.

Philosophy and the Teacher

Lastly, let us consider the teacher himself. He must have a definite outlook on life, optimistic or pessimistic; positive or negative, materialistic or idealistic. This vital belief of his will effect the various problems of education — the educand, the aims and its realisation, the type or nature of discipline to be maintained, social organisation in school, its general tone, the method he employs, the matter he emphasises in each subject and the conclusion he cherishes as his ideal.

A typical Indian teacher with a negative, fatalistic and other worldly philosophy cannot possibly help the child in the realisation of such an aim as 'complete living' or 'harmonious development'. He cannot but place the virtues as self-denial, self-sacrifice, and renunciation on a high, but false pedestal imbued with ideas of other worldliness or personal salvation, he can not cultivate a social sense. On the contrary, he is likely to create in the young minds an attitude of pathetic indifference to the real problems of everyday life.

CONCLUSION

We have looked at the problem of relation between philosophy and education from several angles and have found education to be completely in the grip of philosophy. From every angle of the educational problem comes the demand for a philosophical basis of education. The determination and formulation of aims, the choice of suitable curriculum or even text books, the employment of proper methods and devices, the decision about the type of discipline to be maintained and how to maintain it, the creation of a general tone in school by school organisation: nay, even the problem of examination and mental testing are ultimately questions of philosophy. "Education," as says Adams, "Is the dynamic side of philosophy. It is the active aspect of philosophical belief, the practical means of realising and the ideals of life." There is no escape from a philosophy of life, and of education. In the words of Ross, "Philosophy and education are like the two sides of a coin; the one is implied by the other; the former is contemplative side of life, while the latter is the active side, "Philosophy is wisdom that education transmits and disseminates it. Philosophy represents a system of thought which education embraces in the content of instruction; Philosophy offers an outlook on life; which is fostered or developed through education in the young. Philosophy presents a way of life, education is an understanding of and a preparation for it. Both of them go together. They are allied in origin, inter-dependent and work jointly. Hence, we would end the chapter with Fichte's words with which we began it, that the art of education would never attain clearness in itself without philosophy. The next few chapters dealing with the different schools of philosophy in education will further support our contention.

7

Idealism in Education

Idealism takes many and varied forms, but the underlaying principle is that "Ultimate reality" is spiritual in nature rather than physical, mental rather than material. Idealism does not deny the existence of world around us—the physical world which science and ours senses acquaint with us. It maintains that real as it is, it is not ultimately real. It is manifestation of some more fundamental reality, a universal mind, which is all-embracing, all-knowing, all-rational. This spiritual reality may be either personal or impersonal.

Since, the ultimate reality is spiritual in nature, it is to be found in man's mind rather than in his material nature. Therefore, all knowledge is from within rather than from without. Idealism attaches more importance to knowledge that is acquired through the activity of mind than to the knowledge that is acquired through the senses. It contends that the material universe known to science is only an incomplete manifestation of reality; it is subordinate to a higher type of reality—a spiritual universe of ideas and values. Ideas are of ultimate cosmic significance. They are the ideals, moulds, patterns or standards by which things of senses are to be judged. These ideals or values are eternal, unchanging, and absolute in nature. These values are not man–made, they pre-exist, the chief of them being Truth, Beauty and Goodness.

BASIC PRINCIPLES OF IDEALISM

Below are given some of the basic principles of Idealism, which will make the concept of Idealism clear.

(i) Ultimate reality is mental or spiritual in nature. The material world is nothing more than an outward manifestation of ultimate reality.

(ii) The material world is mortal and changing. Ultimate reality which consist of ideals, purposes and values is eternal and unchanging.

(iii) On this basis, body is false as it is mortal; soul is true as it is immortal.

(iv) Man is essentially a spiritual being and his spirituality alone distinguishes him from animals. His spirit alone enables him to control his environment.

(v) Man is a free agent, free in the choice of his ends and means to realise them.

(vi) Values are pre-existing, ultimate, eternal and unchanging. Man cannot create values, but the aim of his life is realisation of ultimate values—Truth, Beauty and Goodness—for their own sake.

IDEALISM IN EDUCATION

The idealistic school in education is represented by such thinkers as *Plato*, *Comenius*, *Pestalozzi* and *Froebel* and others. We are indebted to idealism more for the aims and objectives of education than for its devices and methods. In as much as idealism believes that reality is spiritual rather than material in nature, that the world of ideas and experience is more important than the physical world, it lays more emphasis on the study of the humanities than on the positive sciences. Man, it asserts, is an important subject of study while the human personality and its dignified expression is the important function of education.

Some general principles of idealism have been mentioned above. Now we shall discuss the aims of education, curriculum, methods of teaching, concept of discipline and the role of teacher in the light of these principles.

Idealism and Aims of Education

Idealism believes that man has two natures—original and spiritual. The aim of education is to convert the original nature into spiritual nature. It must make him a man in the true sense of the word. It has been rightly remarked that man can become man by education only. In other words, we can say that the divine in man is to be unfolded and brought to his consciousness by means of education.

Rusk as well as *Ross* have given us the aims of education associated with Idealism. "The aim of education", says Rusk, "is the enhancement or enrichment of personality, the differentiating feature of which is the embodiment of universal values." "The aim of education specially associated with Idealism" says *Ross*, "is the exaltation of personality or self-realisation, the making actual or real the highest potentialities of the self."

Since idealism believes human personality to be the most important, it wants education to aim at the development of human personality culminating in self-realisation. In the words of *Horne*, "The end of ends, the goal of goals, according to Idealism, is the increasing realissation of the Absolute Idea for the individual, society and the race". Further explaining this aim of education, Rusk has commented, "We may accept that the aim of education is the enhancement or enrichment of personality, the differentiating feature of which is the embodiment of universal values". These universal values are expressed as the Beauty, Goodness and Truth, and the aim of education is to concretise these values in the child's life. Thus, the idealists cherish the following aims and ideals of education.

1. Development of personality: As has been already pointed out, the most important aim of education, according to the idealist thinkers, both ancient and modern, Eastern and Western, is the development of personality. This has been called man-making by Vivekananda.

The idealists believe that man is God's finest and ultimate creation. That is why development of the human personality has been accepted as the aim of education, and stress has been laid on the teaching of humanitarian subjects such a literature, art, religion, ethics, etc. Through education the cultural and social heritage of the community must be maintained and transmitted to the following generations. Some other idealist believe that the aim of education is to guide the individual to self-realisation, for this also includes the development of the personality. Such development, in fact, is the development of those divine qualities which are inherent in human being but which are dormant at his birth. The educator's task is to manifest these qualities. And for this reason every human being has an equal right to education.

2. Self-realisation: As has been already pointed out, according to idealists the aim of education is self-realisation. This is the individualist aim of education emphasised by the idealists.

3. Cultural Development: Greatest significance is attached to the cultural environment created by religion, morality, art, literature, mathematics, science, etc. That is why the idealist tendency is to stress the teaching of humanities so that the cultural and social heritage is maintained intact and allowed to grow. Education is also concerned with enabling the individual to make his own contribution to the cultural development of the community. The ideals of Beauty, Goodness and Truth are the spiritual ideals of the human race, and the child has to be trained to achieve them in reality. Education must transform the child into a true human-being by educating him to manifest the divine qualities which are invested in him. The idealists argue that there is system in every part of the universe, and to hence the individual must also be taught to create some system in his life through intellectual and spiritual guidance. For this it is essential to develop every aspect of his life—the physical, moral, ethical, intellectual, spiritual and the aesthetic. Failure to develop any one of these would create an imbalance in the individual's personality. In the words of *Froebel*, "The object of education is the realisation of a faithful, pure, inviolable and hence holy life. Education should lead and guide man to clearness concerning himself, and in himself, to face with nature, and to unity with God."

4. Exploration of Universal Values: Idealism places more emphasis upon more universal objects of education. Ross puts it thus, "The function of education is to help us in our exploration of the ultimate universal values so that the truth of the universe may become our truth and give power to our life. Education must aim at adapting not only to the physical environment but to every kind of environment." *Rusk* points out, "The purpose of education is to enable the child to reconcile himself to reality in all its manifestations, not merely to adapt himself to a natural environment". From among all these various kinds of environment, the cultural environment is considered to be the most important because man's cultural characteristics are his most distinctive qualities.

Hence, according to Idealism the foremost aim of education is to exalt personality. The exaltation of personality implies the realisation of the highest potentialities of the self in a social and cultural environment. The education has to be provided with suitable environment and conditions that will be conductive to the realisation of his self.

Idealism and Curriculum

Idealism believes that goal of human life is exaltation of man's personality. Education has to achieve this aim. The school curriculum accordingly, consists of those subjects which are conducive to this goal. The curriculum must reflect the capitalised knowledge and experience of the race. So it must primarily consist of 'humantities' or 'cultural studies'.

Plato, a great exponent of Idealism, conceives of the curriculum from the point of view of ideas. He believes that the highest idea of life was the attainment of the highest good or God, hence, the curriculum ought to impart inherent values in order to enable the educand to attain his highest good. The inherent or spiritual values, according to him are Truth, Beauty and Goodness. These three values determine to three type of activities, intellectual, aesthetic and moral. Each type of activity is represented by studies and should form a part of the curriculum. Intellectual activities are represented by subjects as languages, literature, science, mathematics, history and geography; aesthetic activities will be possible through the study of art and poetry and moral activities through the study of religion, ethics and metaphysics.

Interpreting the idealistic conception of the curriculum, *Ross* talks of two types of activities which would be represented by it. On the one hand, we have physical activities, and on the other spiritual activities. Physical activities draws our attention to such subjects as health and hygiene and to subjects that foster bodily skills such as gymnastic, and athletics. These subjects will lead to good health and fitness, thus making the pursuit of spiritual values possible. Spiritual pursuits imply the intellectual, aesthetic, moral and religious studies.

Hence, such subjects as history, geography, languages, fine arts, morality, ethics, religion, sciences, mathematics and others should be included in the curriculum.

The idealistic scheme of curriculum may be represented, with Rusk, by means of the following table:

Education
- **Physics activities**
  1. Care of body
  2. Skills
- **Spiritual activities**
  1. Intellectual
  2. Moral
  3. Aesthetic
  4. Religious

Sir Percy Nunn, recommends that the school should make a provision for these activities that are of greatest and most permanent significance in the wider world and are the grandest expression of the human spirit—those that are essential for maintaining the standard of individual and social life and those that represent the lofty attainment of civilisation.

Idealists insist on emphasis being placed on the study of humanities such as literature, art, religion, morality, etc., along with the teaching of science. All the elements necessary for attaining God are included in the curriculum suggested by idealistic followers of *Plato*, who laid down that education must aim to realise the ideals of Truth, Beauty and Goodness. Hence, he has suggested the inclusion of all those subjects or disciplines which help in the realisation of these ideals. Most significant among man's activities are the intellectual, the aesthetic and the moral. The teaching of language, literature, history, geography, mathematics and science will encourage intellectual activity while the aesthetic impulse can be reinforced through art and poetry. Moral activities can be taught and instilled in the education through the teaching of religion, ethics, etc. This curriculum is determined on the basis of the goals to be realised through education and by the criterion that it must reflect the experience, culture and glory of the human race. Man's experiences relate not only to his physical or natural environment but also to his social experiences, knowledge of which can be obtained through a study of the natural and the social sciences.

T.P. Nunn, another educationist, has glanced at the idealistic conception of the educational curriculum, and has remarked, "The school is to consolidate the nation's spiritual strength, to maintain its historic continuity, to secure its achievements, and to guarantee its future". In order to achieve all these goals, education in the school should consider two kinds of activities. In the first group fall such activities which create conditions by which the individual and social life is ensured and maintained, and this can be done through physical health, customs, social organisations, ethical conduct, etiquette, religion, etc. Education must provide opportunities, therefore, for physical training, ethics, religion, etc. The second group of activities is the one which is more important outside the sphere of the school. In this group lie those activities which maintain the cultural life of the community because they are creative. In order to evolve skills for such activities, educationists advocate teaching of literature, art, music, various kinds of handicrafts and manual skills, sciences, mathematics, history, etc. Hence the curriculum must be so designed that it can help to acquaint the individual with his social and cultural heritage and also to enable him to make some positive contribution to this heritage. *Nunn* writes, "In the school curriculum all these activities should be represented. For these are the grand expression of the human spirit, and theirs are the forms in which the creative energies of every generation must be disciplined if the movement of civilisation is to be worthily maintained."

Idealism and Methods of Training

Idealism has exercised more influence on the aims and objectives of education rather than on methods of teaching. It speaks of general nature of teaching methods. It does not specify any method to be adopted. The great Greek Idealist Plato, however, advocated the Socratic method, i.e., Dialectics. Many educational philosophers advocated many other methods—the didactic method, and so on. Idealism is not much concerned with the choice of methods and so long its essential objective is fulfilled, which is the enrichment of personality of the pupil. To educate a child as to lead him to discover and develop what is within him rather than that which is beyond him is the real goal of education and with a good teacher any method can work well to realise that objective.

Idealism lays stress on instruction, activity and experience. The word instruction has been used in the wider sense, meaning "Educative instruction," not 'order' or 'repression'. It implies sympathetic guidance by the teacher. Emphasing the need of such instruction, *Herbart* says, "I have no conception of education without instruction and do not acknowledge any instruction which does not educate." Instruction does not let the mind become a store-house of vague and undesirable ideas. It chisels and chastens them.

Another factor which Idealism emphasises in the methods of teaching is activity or learning by doing. The normal child should learn through activity. Idealism does not decry questioning, discussion, and lecture method of teaching but it extols the method of creative and spontaneous mental activity. It does so because creative activity leads to self-expression and realisation of the highest potentialities of the child. Mental activity leads the child to learn with pleasure and love and this love exalts his personality and introduces him systematically and deliberately into a wholly new order to things.

Experience has a significant place in the Idealistic Method of teaching. The truly educative acts are those which go on within the private experiences of the learner and are comprised of the student's own self-activity, never of the artifices of the clever teacher. The duty of the teacher is to develop in him an insight into deeper experiences than he already possesses. In addition to it, the teacher should endeavor to unfold his potentialities 'by providing him stimulating experiences. Turning to methodology in education, idealists suggest that the method must be oriented to achieving the complete development of all the innate abilities of the child and to train him for self-realisation. In *Rivers*' words, "The process of education in childhood consists, or should consist, in the direction of innate or instinctive tendencies towards an end in harmony with the highest good of society of which the child is an active member. Idealists believe in a harmony between individual and social objectives. The child must be provided with a liberal environment for his development and his education should be related to present experience. One finds, therefore, that many elements of the idealist methodology are common with those of the naturalist, realist and pragamatist methodology.

The idealist methodology in education lays special stress on the following three processes:

1. Instruction: The term instruction as used here implies educational instruction which is believed by *Herbart* to be essential to education. But instruction does not mean that the child's mind should be stuffed with various scraps of information. It implies a modification and a refinement of the child's mind. For this it is essential that the educator must provide sympathetic guidance. The idealists believe that training of all kinds must be provided in the schools.

2. Activity: Like the naturalist methodology, the educational methods recommended by the idealist also are based on activity. The child must learn through doing. Although the child can learn much by asking questions after lectures in the school, creative activity is much more important. This creative activity should be natural, continuous and progressive. This helps in moving towards self-realistation, because it encourages the child to manifest his innate tendencies. Through mental activity the child learns cheerfully and happily and this also helps in the development of his personality. Besides, by these means the child learns rapidly. Hence, idealists also stress that instruction should be active.

3. Experience: Idealist methodology also places considerable stress on experience. Every educand must base all his education on his own experience. The educator's task is not to stuff his own experience in the educand's mind. The guidance given by the educator helps to manifest many frustrated and repressed tendencies and drives of the educand. Independence is an essential pre-requisite for experience. For this reason idealists believe freedom to be an essential part of education but it must be remembered that this freedom is not absolute, but controlled and guided.

It is evident from the foregoing account that idealists believe the experiences of both the educator and the educand to be of great importance. Both of them should be active and they should indulge in the mutual exchange of experience so that they can progress. The teaching method should be such that the child should recognise it as a mode of self-instruction.

In short, the essence of Idealistic method of teaching is activity and freedom, freedom which is regulated and guided.

Idealism and Teacher

The naturalist would do without the teacher at times, he positively resents his interference in the development of the child and would like this development to be unchecked, unrestricted and unmodified by any sort of suggestion, guidance or direction. According to him, there is no place for the teacher in his natural, autonomous process of development towards perfection. The idealists does not be-little the importance of the teacher. In the Idealistic system of education, the teacher is indispensable.

The immature pupil cannot be expected to be able to understand by his own intelligence the real nature of the eternal values he has to realise in his life. It is only under the enlightened advice and able guidance of some individual of mature understanding and seasoned experience that the child can have such a knowledge. Thus, according to Idealism, there can be no teaching without a teacher. The immature learner can never be able to perfect his personality unless there is someone to teach him the methods of becoming perfect.

The universe is a rational system of which the teacher forms one part and the pupil another. The two are related to each other by the bond of a common purpose—the purpose of perfecting the personality of the child. This purpose is known clearly to the teacher but only vaguely to the pupil. The teacher has to make this purpose clear to the immature pupil. He has to explain it and also devise methods of enabling him to realise this purpose. The teacher is thus necessary for advising, directing, and events controlling the conduct of the pupil in order that he may be able to ensure the perfection of his personality.

The Idealist teacher can guide and help his pupils in three ways. Firstly, he can influence them by his personality i.e. by associating with them personally. Secondly, he can suggest questions and problems to them and encourage them to think for themselves. Thirdly, he can enable them to understand the problems by following the scientific methods of analysis and synthesis.

According to *Ross*, in the Idealistic scheme of studies the teacher is needed "To assist the educand, who is developing according to the laws of nature, to attain levels that would otherwise be denied him." The teacher is needed to draw the attention of the pupil to the 'formative' side of his education as much as a garden requires a gardener to tend the tiny and young.

According to idealism, education is a process in which "The educator as well as the educand is working out his salvation", and both are achieving self-realisation by inter-action with one another. The pupil is as much a necessity for the teacher as the teacher for the pupil. The teacher needs the pupil for his own spiritual growth and salvation.

Idealistic pattern of education grants the highest place to the educator, and conceives of the educator and educand as two parts of an organic plan. The educator creates a specific environment for the educand's development and provides guidance so that the latter may progress towards perfection and a rounded personality. The most precise explanation of the educator's role is manifested in *Froebel's* Kindergarten pattern of education, in which the school is treated as a garden, the educand as a delicate plant which requires nurturing and the educator as the cautious gardener. Although even in the absence of the gardener the plant will continue to grow and will inevitably follow the laws governing its nature, the gardener has a certain significance in that he has the skill to develop plants. He may be unable to change a rose into a cabbage, but he certainly can contribute his mite to the plant's development. His efforts help in achieving perfection in this development, a level of perfection which would otherwise have been impossible.

The educator plays a parallel role in the school. He can guide the educand appropriately because he knows the rules which govern the latter's development. Through his guidance he can make this natural development into a process leading to perfection and beauty. Ross explains, "The naturalist may be content with briars, but the idealist wants fine developing according to the laws of nature, to attain levels that would otherwise be denied to him". Clearly, the idealists attach much more value to the educator than do the naturalists. *Adams* opined that both the educator and the educand are two parts of the intellectual universe both of which should be considered equally important. The educator inspires the educand to realise the ideals of Truth, Goodness and Beauty, and Guides him along the path to its realisation.

Idealism and Discipline

Discipline is a part of the question concerning educational methods and some people feel that idealists are in complete opposition to the naturalists for the latter believe in complete freedom while the former insist on discipline. Idealists interpret discipline as being based on independence and they try to harmonise the two. Rigorous discipline is never accepted by the idealists. Discipline must always take the shape of self-discipline, because only then can it guide the educand along the path of self-realisation. Education basically aims at training the child in true independence. It is argued that the child is not independent at birth. This independence is granted to him or acquired by him in the process of education because, in the absence of education, there is no self-realisation, and without self-realisation there is no independence. *Rousseau* believes that individual is born free but later on he is bound in chains. On the contrary, Froebel expressed the conviction that that man is born in chains, and that he has to steadily win this freedom for himself, for, no one can grant it to him. Independence is not divine gift, because even God cannot give independence. True independence can be owned only by oneself, by one's own acts. Through the medium of education the individual can break the chains which bind him at birth. The educator must develop in his educands the capability of reasoning and arriving at a decision by the use of which the educand can achieve his own development, naturally and by his own inspiration. Independence lies not in a revolt against the environment but in achieving harmony with it. Hence, the child must be trained for independence in the school. He should be taught to discipline himself and to contribute to the disciplined behaviour of others, besides himself. Through a steady development of this kind, the individual becomes the member of a group of self-disciplined individuals. It can thus be concluded that the idealists do not favour the notion of allowing the child to roam free of any restraint but prefer to guide his freedom. For this reason, the child's activities are controlled in the school. Physical punishment and external restraints are not the methods of achieving this. It is better realised through developing such qualities as self-resignation, obedience, humanity, politeness, etc. Once these qualities are evolved in the individual, he achieves a stage of self-discipline. *Froebel* denies any importance to any system of punishment. Instead, he believes that it is better to encourage self-control and self-guidance in the child through sympathy. He believes that the child should not be submitted to any external pressure. It is only through discipline that the child can realise the ideals of education, and once it has understood this, it can discipline itself. Idealists, therefore, believe in the efficacy of discipline through influence and impression, not through fear and coercion.

But, discipline can be created among the educand only when the educators themselves create and present good models of discipline. Their own conduct and behaviour should be conditioned by knowledge of the child's interests and inclinations. In their own behaviour, they must present the highest ideal of self-discipline, for only then can any discipline be expected from the educand. Idealist have criticised the establishment of discipline through threats, repression and punishment. They believe that the entire natural, social and spiritual environment in which the child lives should be fashioned in such a way that it should encourage the desire for self-discipline in the child. Plato believed that the child in the school is restrained with the intention that he may be granted greater liberty gradually as he develops higher. As the individual develops to a level of higher responsibility, he should be granted successively more liberty.

Freedom is the cry of the Naturalists, while discipline is that of the Idealists. The latter believe that the child cannot attain his complete development unless he submits himself to a process of discipline. It is only through this process that self-realisation and spiritual attainment can be made possible.

The idealists, however, do not favour rigid discipline. In fact, their theory of discipline is based on their concept of freedom. Their chief concern is "to harmonise freedom with subjection to authority and discipline, to unite submission to the necessary restraints with the child's capability of excercising his free-will". It is this process of discipline that will enable the educand to understand the great values of life—the inherent spiritual values. As such, the teacher's guidance is necessary. He will present ideals of conduct for the educand to follow and will see that his environment is conducive to the realisation of his spiritual potentialities. The idealists look askance at the free discipline, and at the same time they are against the discipline that amounts to external restraint and suppersson of spontaneous activity. *Froebel*, for example, advocated complete absence of physical constraint for the sake of developing the pupil's powers of self-expression through self-realisation. Self-realisation recognises the importance of teacher's guidance. Froebel, however, resented the imposition of the arbitracy.

IDEALISM IN CONTEMPORARY EDUCATION

Though idealism may have been very much left aside in the contemporary field of education, it is undoubtedly the most ancient school which has influenced education throughout its history. Even now the following points may be noted concerning the influence of idealism in the contemporary field of education.

1. Wider and higher aims: As the nationalist aims of education are giving place to humanist aim, idealism has become more relevant to the modern educationists. The idealists present the highest and the widest aims and ideals of education summed up in such terms as self-realisation, man-making, development of personality, harmony of man and nature, realisation of Truth, Goodness and Beauty and realisation of heaven upon earth. All these aims have beauty emphasised by contemporary philosophers of education in East and West.

2. The ideal teacher: In this age of science the model of ideal teacher is still presented by idealism. Whatever may be said about the need of practical education and the utilisation of scientific means, no teacher can influence the educands without some sort of idealism. Teaching involves communication which very much depends upon rapport between the teacher and the taught. This is possible only when the teacher considers the taught as a part of his self and thus becomes selfless in his profession. The ideal of character building can not be achieved unless the teacher himself presents the model of ideal character.

3. Integrated and multi-sided curriculum: While other systems of philosophy of education lay emphasis upon science and technology, the idealists point out the eternal value of humanities, social sciences, art and literature. In fact, they lay emphasis upon an integrated curriculum which may include every branch of knowledge. Thus the idealist curriculum is the most liberal, the most dynamic, the most multisided and therefore, most conducive to the cultural development of the individual and society.

4. Moral education: Thinkers everywhere today lament at the general loss of moral character. Everywhere development of moral character is being considered as an urgent need, to save the world from future catastrophe. The idealist explain the aims and means of moral education.

5. Self-discipline: The idealists concept of freedom as self-discipline has come to stay. It prescribes central place to the child in the system of education and lays emphasis upon natural development. Natural development requires freedom but freedom cannot be enjoyed without self-discipline. Contemporary educationists unanimously accept the need of freedom and discipline and agree that self-discipline is the only way for proper development.

6. Psychological methods: Event the pragmatist agree that some sort of idealism is necessary for teaching, particularly that of humanities, art and literature. The idealists include instruction, activity and experience in their methods of teaching. The idealist

CRITICISM OF IDEALISM

Some thinkers have criticised idealism in education on the following grounds:

1. Utopian aims: Plato, the first idealist philosopher of education, presented a scheme which was through and through utopian in spite of its deep insight into human life here and there. In fact, in his idealistic flight the thinker often leaves the solid ground and presents aims and ideals which can be neither realised nor cherished.

2. Theoretical methods: The idealist method of teaching makes too much of memory, personal contact and brain faculties. They lay less emphasis upon the development of various types of interests and abilities which help the educand in playing important role in society.

3. Lack of specialisation: The idealist curriculum is too wide and lacks specialisation which is a growing demand of modern education.

4. Neglect of science and technology: The idealist thinkers have laid emphasis upon culture in education and neglected science and technology. Therefore, today most of the educational institutions have rejected idealistic curriculum.

5. Teacher-centred: While modern education is child-centred or educand-centred, the idealist system is teacher-centred. By expecting too much from the teacher, it does not allow him to live as a human being with a multisided personality. Too much expectation from the teacher ultimately results in his criticism by the students and society. The role of teacher today is very much different from his role in ancient times. Education today is a life-long but limited part of life. It goes on even without the teacher. Various audio-visual means are replacing the all important role of the teacher. Therefore, neither the modern teacher nor the taught accept the ancient idealist concept and status of the teacher.

CONTRIBUTION OF IDEALISM

Idealism has excercised a great influence on education and has largely inspired educational thought in respect of the ultimate goals of education.

1. So far as aims of education are concerned, no other thought can stand the light of Idealism. It is the unique contribution of Idealism in its having given a clear definition of the goals and aims of education and having drawn a pointed attention to the cultural and spiritual side of man's life and education.

2. Idealism has laid an invaluable emphasis on the dignity of the individual and on the personality of the child. It has rightly stressed the importance of aiming at the training and perfection of the educand's personality. Character-building is the most laudable among the aims of education.

3. Idealism has rightly stressed the need and importance of discipline in education. The immature pupil can not be expected to be able to discriminate between good and evil. So there can be a danger of his committing blunders which may quite often involve a great risk for him. Thus, some set rules of conduct imposed by the experienced personality of the teacher are a necessity, at least

in the initial stages of the pupil's life and education. Method of teaching is most effective in religious and moral teaching. It is a solid ground for character building and realisation of intimate relations between the teacher and the taught.

CONCLUSION

From the perusal of the above mentioned advantages and disadvantages of the idealist philosophy of education it is clear that though some sort of idealism must stay in every field of education, the aims and ideals, the methods, the curriculum and the school management, etc., the ideal of education cannot be realised without the help of Naturalism, Pragmatism and Realism.

8

Naturalism in Education

Naturalism is a type of philosophy which takes Nature as the whole of reality. According to naturalism the material and physical world is the only real world. It denies the existence of spiritual universe — the universe of ideas and values. This material world which is the only reality is being governed by a system of natural laws. And man, who is the creation of the material world, must submit to it. Naturalism has regard for the observable facts, for the realities, and for the actual situations of life. It does not believe in spiritualism or supernaturalism. Therefore, it does not believe in any spiritual values or absolute truths. For it, nature is everything. It is the whole of reality. It denies the existence of anything beyond nature, behind nature, or other than nature. It believes that everything comes from nature and returns to nature. Nature, according to this philosophy, is a self-sufficient entity; it contains its cause within itself. It is self-determined; it has been created and is moved by natural forces only. Nature is governed by its own laws.

Naturalism does not believe in the spiritual nature of man. It takes recourse to such concepts as appetites and emotions which are regarded as the only motive of all our activities — biological, psychological or social. According to it, moral instinct, innate conscience, other world, and miracles, providence, power of prayer, freedom of will, are illusions and there is no absolute good or evil in the world. Values of life, according to it, are created by the human needs. Man creates them, when he reacts to, or interacts with his environment. He must adapt himself to environment.

Naturalism believes that mind is an accident in the process of evolution and it can be explained in terms of matter. Mind is the function of brain which is material in nature. Mind is not the source of knowledge; all knowledge is acquired from without and sense organs are the gate-ways of all knowledge.

BASIC PRINCIPLES OF NATURALISM

Below are given some of the basic principles of Naturalism. The understanding of these principles makes the concept of naturalism clear to us:

1. Nature is the final reality. All things have originated from matter and all are ultimately to be reduced to that. Matter combined in different proportions takes different forms.

2. Mind is the brain-functioning and brain is matter.

3. Experience, imagination, thinking, reasoning, etc., are all processes of mental activity, which is the function of the brain.

4. Laws of nature are unchangeable and the entire universe is governed by them. Science reveals the mysteries of nature; hence only that knowledge is true that is derived from science.

5. Real knowledge comes through our senses. All matter is within the ken of human senses and therefore, the final truth can be known through senses.

6. There is no God or Spirit. Therefore, there is no religion. There are no higher or eternal values. There is no spiritual ideal or aim or goal of human life. Man himself creates values in interaction with the environment in which he is placed.

7. Divine inspiration, revelation, strength of prayer, power of soul, other world—these are illusory conceptions and mislead human mind.

FORMS OF NATURALISM

Naturalism exists in many forms. The outstanding forms of naturalism are discussed below.

Naturalism of Physical Science

This type of naturalistic philosophy lays emphasis purely on physical nature. It believes, only in the reality of material objects and the laws of mass and motion. Mind, as something other than the body, has no existence at all. Man also is only one of the objects of physical nature, a creature of mass and motion. One is apt to agree with them, when they say that this universe of ours is governed by natural laws. However, their assertion that these very laws are applicable in their entirety to man and his experience—material or spiritual, is indeed a bitter pill to swallow. It believes that scientific laws govern not only the facts and events of external world but also the behaviour of animals and conduct of man. Too much emphasis is, thus laid upon the external nature and the inner and the spiritual nature of man is more or less neglected. These facts make it perfectly clear that this form of naturalism can have little bearing on education and has little to contribute to its theory or practice, because education is a mental rather than a physical activity.

Mechanistic Naturalism

Mechanistic Naturalism or Mechanicalism regards the whole universe as a big complicated machine, working according to the laws of Mechanics. Man, too, is a machine, only a little more complicated and intricate than other objects of nature. His life, too, is subject to the laws of mechanics; it is governed by mechanical laws of motion and causation. Though this form of Naturalism has made some contribution to education in the form of 'Behaviouristic Psychology', yet its contribution is not of much significance.

Biological Naturalism

Biological Naturalism believes that the nature and process of universe cannot be explained in terms of physical science or mechanical operation. In the realm of living creatures the sole basis of explanations is evolution. All creatures have an urge to live and life evolves from lower to higher levels. The process of evolution is continuous, and all life is involved in that process. The process of evaluation is, however, the same for all living creatures.

The basic standpoints of Biological Naturalism are two:

1. each creature has an urge to live and
2. he struggles to exist. In the struggle to existence those that

are fit, survive, and those that are not die. The theory is known by the comprehensive term, 'survival of the fittest'. According to Biological Naturalism self-preservation is the first law of nature.

Charles Darwin and Lamarck, were two great scholars who advocated and interpreted this theory. Let us take note of their views briefly:

1. The species of animal (and man, to *George Bernard Shaw*) are not unchanging. According to *Darwin* some sudden changes take place in germ cells, which create physical changes also. According to *Lamark*, "It is external environment that creates physical changes".

2. According to *Darwin*, "Only the changes, which are sudden, are transmitted according to the law of heredity". But to *Lamark* changes, instead of being sudden, are according to desire and need, and traits changed by efforts may be transmitted.

3. According to *Darwin*, "Organ is created first and used by activity afterwards whereas according to *Lamark* creation or attraction of need or activity comes first and then organ is created for its fulfilment".

Thus, according to Naturalism, there is a similarity between the instincts of man and animal. This school holds that man is continuous with animals; he has, infact, grown or 'evolved' out of his 'pre-historic' ancestors. Consequently, even now he has much which is common with animals and that common nature is the real man, and it is inherently good. Man's primitive impulses, instincts and emotions are an un-erring guide to his conduct. They are more dependable than reflection or capitalised experience of the race. This school emphasises the original nature of man and declines to place much faith in his spiritual nature. It believes that all forms of moral conduct and character can be evolved in man by a proper modification, training and sublimation of his instincts and emotions. MacDougall, the well-known psychologist, is the chief exponent of this view.

This form of Naturalism has a great bearing on the theory and practice of education. It maintains that real education lies in the modification and training of man's instincts and emotions. This is the view most acceptable to the modern educators.

NATURALISM IN EDUCATION

Naturalism as a philosophy of education was developed in 18th century. It exercised a great influence on the theory and practice of education. It decries all external restraint in education and it condemns all unnecessary formalities in education. In the naturalistic system of education there is no place for classrooms, text books, time-tables' curricula, formal lessons or examinations. The 'chalk and talk' method has no scope. The teacher has no significant role to play. External discipline is altogether out of place; the only discipline applied in this system is the discipline of natural consequences. Naturalism believes that formal education was the invention of society which was artificial and as such vicious. Good education can be had only by a direct contact with nature.

On the positive side, Naturalism in education stands for the doctrine of follow nature in education. It wants all education to be in strict conformity with the nature of the child. It stands for complete freedom to be given to the child in learning. He is to be left alone, absolutely free, face to face with nature, permitted to learn undisturbed anything he likes and by any method he likes. He is to be thrown into Nature as an explorer and discoverer, to make experiments with any objects of nature that appeal to him and to learn from them whatever he can. Even if he takes a wrong track, he is to be allowed to go on until his mistake is brought home to him by its unfavourable or unpleasant, consequences. Thus, the whole of the child's learning will come from his own experiences and their natural consequences. His whole education will be according to the natural laws of human development.

In the beginning, Bacon and Comenitics were associated with Naturalism. But much of the Naturalistic movement finds its root in the pages of Rousseau, who brought it to its zenith. He brought the child into the foreground of the educational arena and impressed on the people that educational material should be the facts and phenomena of nature.

Naturalism and Aims of Education: Of all the forms of Naturalism, it is the biological naturalism which has exercised the greatest influence on education. The influence of Physical and Mechanical Naturalism is practically nil in education, especially that of the former which seeks to interpret the entire universe in terms of physical science.

Views of Mechanical Naturalism: According to Mechanical Naturalism, the individual is also like a machine and consequently, the aim of education should be to make the machine work with as much perfection and efficiency as possible. According to this view, all activities of human beings originate on receiving some stimuli from the environment and hence they are functioning in the form of conditioned reflex actions. The process of education should be to improvise the stimuli in such a way that desired activities proceed from them. This form of Naturalism has given birth to Behaviouristic Psychology which has also influenced education.

Views of Biological Naturalism: Biological Naturalism interprets educational aims in several ways.

1. Spencer, affirms that preservation of the self is the main consideration and self-satisfaction constitutes the highest good in human life. It is self-satisfaction on which is based the present and future happiness of life. Hence, the aim of education should be to make an appeal to the primitive instincts and natural impulses of the child and assist him in securing self-preservation and self-satisfaction.

2. *MacDougall*, the famous exponent of the Naturalistic School of Psychology, does not accept the Hedonistic view (presented by Biological Naturalists) that all our actions spring from the pursuit of happiness and avoidance of pain. He believes that pleasure and unpleasure are not goals, but by-products of our activities: The aim of education is the sublimation of the native instincts and energies of the individual—the redirection, co-ordination and harmonious working of the native impulses.

3. The *Neo-Darwinians* base their aims of education on the notion of man's evolution from lower forms of life. They hold that the living-creature has to struggle continuously against the environment for existence, resulting in the survival of the fittest. The aim of education, therefore, should be to equip the individual for the struggle of life and thus ensure his survival.

4. Like the *Neo-Darwinians*, the *Neo-Lamarkians* believe in the theory of man's evolution from lower forms of life, but they offer another explanation. They maintain that evolution to higher forms of life is based on "The power of the living creature to adapt itself, its habits and its bodily structure to the circumstances in which it finds itself." As such they see education as the process of adjustment to environment. In other words, the aim of education should be to enable the individual to be in harmony with and well adapted to his surroundings. It will be through the process of adjustment that an individual will grow physically and mentally. The ideal is a well-adjusted, happy being, with no discontent, divine or otherwise.

5. Nunn regards the 'autonomous development of the individual' as the central aim of education and insists that an education which aims at fostering individuality is the only education according to nature. The term individuality is misinterpreted. It may be identified with mere self-assertion or selfishness. The individual may disobey all authority and may acknowledge only his own will and disparage all other individualities or wills. But Nunn does not imply all this form the use of the word; for him it means self-realisation. He seeks to establish a harmony between individual and social claims in education and does not believe that there is any dichotomy existing between the two.

Of all the Naturalists, Rousseau's statement of aims, in accordance with his Naturalistic Philosophy, is the most comprehensive and lucid. Education, he holds, should aim at the development of the child in conformity with his nature. Normal and natural development enjoins on the teacher and parents the need of the bodily health and vigour. It implies a respect for physical nobility and regard for individual differences among children. It impresses on the parents the need of observation of the child's natural tendencies, their origin, growth and decline.

Naturalism and the Curriculum

Naturalism emphasises scientific studies on a laboratory basis. For such studies, they recommend subjects like physics, chemistry, biology, etc. As regards language and mathematics they opine that only so much knowledge of these subjects should be acquired as is essential for scientific studies. It believes that the pupil should not be plunged into poetry and literature. Naturalism assumes that the nature of man is that which he shares to some extent with the animals that it consists of his instincts, appetites and primitive emotions; it therefore, damps down, it does not altogether ignore man's spiritual nature. As such, Naturalism gives a very insignificant place to spiritualism in the curriculum. At the same time it does not include classical music and painting in their curriculum. In its support, it says that children have no interest in them.

Almost all the Naturalist have expressed their views about the curriculum or the subjects to be taught. Let us make a brief mention of them.

Spencer, an extreme Naturalist, thought that human nature is strictly individualistic and that self-preservation is the first law of life. Accordingly, he advocated the inclusion of those subjects which would sub-serve self-preservation. He attaches no importance to cultural subjects or those which enhance the value of man's social and cultural inheritance. This was in strict conformity with his hedonistic philosophy.

Rousseau's curriculum for *Emile (*His imagined child) in the first two stages especially, and in the following stages generally, was illustrative of the principle of negative education which is typical of the naturalistic philosophy—the subordination of the child to the natural order and his freedom from the social order. The doctrine of negative education, as applied to physical education, demanded the greatest possible "Freedom for the child in his movements and exercises, simple diet, loose, scanty and light clothing, etc." Intellectual education would amount to absence of verbal lessons, books or any positive studies. The Naturalists in general, contend that the child's present experiences, interests and activities should determine the choice of studies.

The Naturalists, in general, contend that the child's present experiences, interests and activities should determine the choice of studies. He should be allowed to grow up in a free atmosphere, his natural inclinations finding a suitable outlet. Knowledge for its own sake is not an aim worthy of emulation or worth striving after.

Naturalism and Methods of Teaching

In methods of teaching, Naturalism is a revolt against the old, traditional and stereotyped methods. It condemns learning by rote and passive drill work, and emphasises activity and learning by doing. It advocates that education should provide real experiences to the child and help him to learn with his own personal experiences. He should take his lesson from nature, not from man. Hence, there should be no formal schools and text books. The best thing is to let him 'follow nature' because it supplies all the laws of learning. Direct experiences from nature, men, and things from the basis of instruction, according to naturalism. Rousseau's advice was, "Give your scholar no verbal lessons; he should be taught by experience alone. Teach by doing whenever you can; and only fall back on words when doing is out of question. Book knowledge should be as little as possible." *Emile*, for example, was to discover things for himself in learning science, he would make use of rough experiments performed with the help of self-made and self-invented apparatus. He was to adopt the heuristic attitude and to apply it in the first hand study of natural phenomena. The same principle is to work in learning mathematics, geography and history. Thus, the direct method of learning languages, the heuristic and laboratory methods of learning sciences and mathematics, the observational method in geography, etc.—all illustrate the naturalistic attitude.

The Naturalists believe that every child's ability to acquire knowledge and to benefit thereby is individual. Hence, those class methods which assume a uniform speed of learning for every child are discredited by them. The naturalistic methodology has been aptly described by *Ross* when he says, "The naturalist educator rightly thinks less of his own exposition much more of the learning experience of the pupil." In other words, they advocate the use of paedo-centric methods which stress the importance of educand in the process of education more than the subject-matter or the educand himself. To cut short, the Naturalists advocate such methods of teaching which offer the child an opportunity for self-education, self-expression, creative activity and integrated growth in an atmosphere of unrestrained freedom. In the words of *Ross*, "The Naturalists educator allows the child to follow the lines of his natural interests and to have free choice of activities with no interference or thwarting".

Naturalism and the Teacher

In an educational system based on the Naturalistic Philosophy, the teacher has a peculiar place and duty to perform. Neither is he to interfere with the activities of children, nor is he to provide any ideals or ideas in order to form their character. He must not impose himself on them and must see that their education is the free development of their interests and motives rather than an artificial effort made by him. He has to provide them with suitable opportunities for, and create conditions which are conducive to, natural development. He is not to expect any undue difference from the pupils he teaches, nor does he try to look superior. He tries to understand them, loves them and approves of their behaviour. He is on the side of the child. *Rousseau* and *Fichte* are in favour of such non-intervention of the teacher on account of the child's nature. It is contended by them that the child's nature is essentially good, and any intervention, is, therefore harmful. Montessori deems the teacher's interference as unjustifiable since the specially constructed environment through the use of the didactic apparatus can evoke the right type of response from the children and thereby perform the function of a teacher.

According to Ross, the teacher in a naturalistic set-up is only a setter of the stage, a supplier of materials and opportunities, a provider of an ideal environment, a creator of conditions under which natural development takes place. He has to be simply a non-interfering observer. He has only to understand the tendencies and capacities of the child, and arrange suitable conditions for their free development, and then he must retire into the back ground.

Naturalism and Discipline

Naturalists have no faith in discipline based on external force. They condemn corporal punishment as it represses the impulses, and instincts of the children and forms in them undesirable complexes. They uphold the theory that the child's conduct is based on impulses or instinct, which should not be repressed either by force or punishment.

Naturalism stands for a "hands-off" policy in education. The only discipline to be applied is the discipline of natural consequences. The child should be left perfectly free to act in any way he likes and then face the consequences of his actions. If the consequences of his action turn out to be pleasant and favourable, it would be repeated and therefore learnt. On the contrary, if the consequences of an action are found to be unpleasant, it shall be given up. Thus, the forces of pleasure and pain will effectively teach discipline to the child; his behaviour and moral conduct will ultimately be shaped by these forces.

Rousseau is of the opinion that children should never be punished. If they commit a fault its unpleasant natural consequences will inflict enough of punishment on them. Nature spares none. Every action is inevitably followed by its natural consequences. All immoral or undesirable actions will result in unpleasant consequences and these unfavourable results will make the individual avoid the repetition of such actions in future.

Herbart Spencer also supports the doctrine of natural discipline. He wishes the children to be left to suffer the natural unpleasant consequences of their wrong actions and learn from them. The punishment for their actions should come from their natural consequences rather than from the rod of any supervisory agency. *Spencer* writes, "When a child falls, or runs its head against the table, it suffers a pain, the rememberance of which lends to make it more careful; and by repetition of such experiences, it is eventually disciplined into proper guidance of its movement."

Spencer however admits that his principle does not apply without exception, and that during infancy it would be unwise to apply it. He says, "A three-year-old urchin playing with an open razor, cannot be allowed to learn by this discipline of natural consequences, for the consequences may be too serious."

CRITICISM OF NATURALISM

The Naturalistic Philosophy and its application in education is open to the following objections:

1. Naturalism altogether ignores the spiritual and moral sides of man's nature. While aiming at the natural development of the child, it omits the mention of his moral development—the development of his will, his conscience, his moral motives, his sense of good and evil and the moral law.

2. Naturalism pays attention only to the present needs of the child and ignores his future needs and the ultimate ideals and purposes of man's life.

3. Naturalism leaves the child purely to the 'discipline' of 'natural consequences.' But this discipline quite often involves grave risks, may be to his very existence. For instance, it would be extremely risky to allow the child to go near fire and burn himself in order to enable him to learn that fire should be avoided.

4. Naturalism throws the teacher completely into the background. He is not to impose either his knowledge or his personality on the child. This is bound to cause a serious loss to the pupil of the value which the teacher's knowledge and the seasoned experience of his mature personality can supply him. Every pupil shall begin with the scratch and a big zero.

5. Naturalism allows complete freedom to the child from the very start of his life, even when he has not yet learnt the right use of freedom. This is a very risky experiment. In some cases the pupil may completely lose himself in this freedom, lose himself beyond any recall or redemption. In the early stages, some guidance and authority are altogether necessary.

6. Naturalism attaches too much importance to the animal nature of man—his instincts, impulses and emotions, and completely ignores his spiritual and moral nature and cultural ideals.

7. Naturalism banks too much on the heredity of the child and ignores the influence of environment on 'raw' nature. This is a serious under-rating of the school environment.

CONTRIBUTION OF NATURALISM

Naturalism in education has resulted in the following educational principles:

1. Follow Nature: 'Follow nature' is the most significant slogan of Naturalism in education. The natural development of the child, the naturalist believes, takes place in the natural environment rather than in the artificially designed atmosphere of the school. In the domain of education, the term 'Nature' is used in two senses. It stands for 'physical nature' in one sense and the 'inner nature' of the child in the other sense.

2. Instincts as basis for Education: According to Naturalism there is animal in man, that is, his instincts and impulses, his appetites and primitive emotions are more valuable than his rational or spiritual nature. The Naturalists would even go so far as to assert that these very instincts. Which are not plastic or prone to any great modifying influence, are the chief dynamics behind the entire behaviour of the child. The instincts or life-urges of the child should constitute the basis of all education. Thus, according to the Naturalists, instincts should be the main instrument of education.

3. Paedo-Centricism: In the educative process the pivotal position is that of the child whose nature must be fully understood, before he can be helped to grow naturally, and harmoniously. As it, has been already stated above, "It is the child himself rather than the educator, the school, the book or the subjects of study that should be in the fore-ground of the educational picture." Unnecessary interference on the part of the parents or teachers should be avoided. Children should be treated as children and not as adults in miniature.

4. Freedom for the Child: The conviction of the Naturalist in the efficacy of self-activity and his bias for Hormic Psychology naturally Prompted him to advocate child's freedom as another important feature of naturalistic education. Freedom is indispensable, for only through the exercise of freedom can the child grow in a natural way. Freedom should be the pivot round which the educational programme should be planned. Education is merely the fostering of natural development, and true education takes place when the nature, powers, and inclinations of the child are allowed to develop freely with a minimum of guidance.

5. Senses the Gateway to Knowledge: According to Rousseau, "Education should prepare the way for reason by the proper exercise of the senses." He says that from the age of five to twelve, the child's senses are to be exercised. As such, naturalists consider the training of senses very important. They believe that senses are the gateway to knowledge. Hence, if effective learning is desired, the child must be provided sensory experiences.

CONCLUSION

To conclude, we can say that Naturalism has secured freedom for the child and has further succeeded in freeing the child from the tyranny and rigidity, interference and strict discipline. Naturalism has given an impetus to new Psychological Methods in education. Self-expression, follow nature, self-education, play-way, and self-discipline are some of the main characteristics of Naturalism in Education.

9

Pragmatism in Education

Pragmatism is a mid-way between Naturalism and Idealism. It criticises the impersonal interpretation of existence as forwarded by naturalism, and rebels against the academic and orthodox as forwarded by Idealism. Pragmatism holds that whatever fulfils one's purpose and develops his life, is true. Only those theories are true which work well in practical situations. There are no absolute ideas. All ideas are relative to the situations in which they arise and they are subject to continuous verification by consequences.

Pragmatism is a typical American school of philosophy. It represents the American life and mind and has arisen out of the history of the American nation. The Puritans who came to settle in the unknown land of America had to continually face difficulties and new problems of life. They had no ready-made solutions for such problems. They had to plan out an ideology that would help them to meet novel situations. They had to think of solutions that would enable them to make their headway in life. Consequently, they built up a philosophy of life through experiences instead of being guided any established theory. This philosophy denies the existence of any fixed eternal values and by revolts against absolutism. It is humanististic in as much as it is concerned more with human life and things of human interest than with any established tenets. It arises out of actual living.

The chief principle of this philosophy is that man creates his own values; there are no fixed, eternal truths. Truths, if any, are man-made. Reality is still in the making. It is never complete. Our judgement happens to be true if it gives satisfactory results in experience, i.e., by the way it works out. A judgment in itself is neither true nor false. There are no established systems of ideas which will be true for all times. All systems of ideas are relative to the situation in which they arise and the personalities they satisfy and are subject to continuous verifications by consequences. The Pragmatists lay emphasis on man's power to shape his environment to his own needs and to create by the successful solution of problems, fairer and better environment for himself. The chief exponents of pragmatism are *William James*, *Schiller* and *John Dewey*.

FORMS OF PRAGMATISM

There are three forms of Pragmatism—humanistic, Experimental and Biological. Humanistic pragmatism conceives of the true as that which best satisfies human nature and welfare as a whole. Whatever fulfills man's purposes, desires and develops his life, is true. According to Experimental Pragmatism, the true is that which can be experimentally verified or whatever works. Biological Pragmatism stresses the human ability of adaptation to the environment and that of adapting environment to human needs.

BASIC PRINCIPLES OF PRAGMATISM

Below are given some of the basic principles of Pragmatism, which will make the concept of Pragmatism more clear.

1. There is no ultimate unchanging reality. Reality is that which is 'experienced' by man. Since, the experience of man is constantly changing; truths and reality are also changing constantly.

2. Man's life is an unbroken series of experiments and through these experiments he creates values. He is constantly creating and recreating values of life. Therefore, values are man–made, changing and relative.

3. Man is a social creature. That is why, the quality of social efficiency in man is necessary. Man's life may be successful in a society. Man outside the society is a thing of imagination.

4. It is only in and through a democratic society that the individual can fulfil his purposes and perfect himself.

5. Thought is only a means to life. Man should think only to live. Action, not mere contemplation is the aim of life.

PRAGMATISM IN EDUCATION

William James and *John Dewey* are the two outstanding pragmatic educators. Education for them is not the pursuit of knowledge for its own sake. It may have its intellectual, aesthetic, moral, religious and physical aspects; but they are to be regarded as modes of activities through which the child has to create his values. These activities are to be produced by the child because they will satisfy aid subserve human needs or because they are useful. According to pragmatism education is not the dynamic side of philosophy as it is advocated by idealism. It is philosophy which emerges from educational practice. Education creates values and formulates ideas that constitute this philosophy. Philosophy is, thus, the theory of education in its most general phases.

Today this philosophy occupies the most dominant place in the United States of America. Those who build their educational theory on Pragmatism call themselves. Progressivsts and their education, progressivists education. Their approach to the theory and practice of education is based on two main principles, viz (i) education should have a social function, and (ii) education should provide real life experience to the child.

Pragmatism and Aims of Education

Pragmatism does not lay down any aims of education in advance. It believes that aims of education cannot be fixed. They must be revised with the changing times and needs. Aims towards which educative effort has to be directed or values which the educational practice has to realise are to be created by man himself in the light of his own experience. The only aim of education, according to pragmatism, is to enable the child to create values in his life. As stated by *Ross*, "The general aim of education is just the creation of new values; the main task of education is to put the educand into a position to develop values for himself."

Education is intended to direct the desires, impulses and interests of the child in such a way that he may be able to satisfy his wants in adjustment to his environment and solve his present-day problems. What pragmatism wants to achieve through education is the cultivation of a dynamic, adaptable mind which will be resourceful and enterprising in all situations—the mind which will have powers to create values in an unknown future. It is such minds that will reconstruct society in which the human wants will be fully satisfied through a social medium consisting of co-operative activities.

Pragmatism and Curriculum Construction

Pragmatists lay down the following principles for curriculum construction:

1. Principle of Utility: Practical utility is the only watch-word and the guiding principle of Pragmatism. Therefore, whatever is likely to help the pupil in his practical life deserves to be taught and what is not likely to serve any purpose in the day-to-day life of the child should be omitted from the curriculum. As such, language, hygiene, physical training, history and geography, mathematics, sciences, domestic science for girls and agriculture for boys, should be incorporated in the school curriculum. The utility criterion requires direct training for a vocation in the later stages. It also demands that different studies should be viewed from the stand-point of their usefulness in dealing with life situations rather than as a disinterested pursuit of knowledge. But the utility principle should not be adopted in the narrow sense. The main aim of knowledge i.e. human progress should not be over shadowed by it.

2. Principle of Child's Interest: According to the Pragmatic system of education, the only aim of education is to prepare the child for a successful and well-adjusted life. He must be fully adjusted to his environment. The school curriculum has therefore, to be guided by the natural tendencies, impulses and interests of the child at the various stages of his growth. So nature study, elementary arithmetic, drawing, reading and writing should be conspicuously present in the elementary school curriculum. This curriculum shall be expanded at the later stages according to the growing needs and interests of the child. According to Dewey, the child has four kinds of interests. Firstly, he is interested in conversation or communication. His second interest lies in inquiry or finding out things. In the third place he is interested in construction, or making of things. Lastly, he is interested in artististic expression. The curriculum should be constructed on the basis of these interests.

3. Principle of child's Experience: According to Pragmatism all education is 'learning by doing'. So it must be based on the child's experiences as well as occupations and activities. In addition to the school subjects, free, purposive, and socialised activities should be included in the curriculum. If these activities take the character of the activities of the community of which the school is an organ, they will develop moral virtues result in attitudes initiative and independence and will give training in citizenship and promote self-discipline.

4. Principle of Integration: This principle assumes the unity of knowledge and skills. Such an integration will be secured if the subjects are presented as modes of activities which are purposive and connected by a common end. The Pragmatist, it must be noted, does not want to abolish the division of curriculum into subjects. The scheme of dividing it into subjects is convenient and useful. Moreover, subjects are the capitalised experience of the race. But the pragmatist warns us against the water-tight compartments between one subject and another.

To sum up, we can say that Pragmatists have an idea of curriculum which is useful, flexible, dynamic, and well integrated. They offer an "Activity Curriculum", because they maintain that activities are necessary both to make education life-like and to make life yield the truth.

Pragmatism and Methods of Teaching

Pragmatism has to its credit an important contribution that it has made to the methods of teaching. While answering the question of the methods of teaching, Pragmatism places in the forefront the view-point of practical necessity and utility rather than logic. According to this Philosophy, it is the problem to be solved which determines the method rather than any dogmatic and predetermined concepts and views.

Pragmatism advocates the elimination of all formal aims, predetermined values, dogmatic principles, and stereotype practices employed in training. It only wants the child to be prepared for his practical life. Therefore, it gives the first place in school teaching to practical problems and real situations of man's life. The problem must come first and the learning should be incidental to its successful solution. The pupil should acquire principles, skills and methods as he experiences the need for them. Thus, the method employed by the pragmatist teacher is the experimental' method or the method of 'trial and error'.

The methods of teaching should be related to the practical life of the child — his desires, impulses and purposes. His learning should be thoroughly purposive. He should learn purely to fulfil the purposes of his life. He should be provided opportunities to indulge in purposeful activities. Action, rather than contemplation, is to figure conspicuously in the Pragmatic Education. Not books but practical activities, can and would provide knowledge of real value. Therefore, he should 'learn by doing' rather than by thinking. A child according to Dewey, learns not by reading books or listening to explanations, but by doing things himself.

The child has an inborn love for activity—action and construction. The Pragmatic system of education aims at providing opportunities for the development and free-play of this tendency of the child. He has to be placed in real situations which he has to tackle; he shall learn from the process of tackling these problems.

The pragmatist does not, however, fix up his methods once for all. His methods of handling his pupils vary from time to time according to the total situation—the situation regarding the teacher, the students, and the equipment.

The most general method of Educational Pragmatism, according to Ross, is "To put the child into situations with which he wants to grapple, and provide him, at the same time, with the means of dealing with them successfully". And these conditions are satisfied by the Project Method introduced by Kilpatrick, a follower of Dewey. The Project Method consists in initiating a "Whole-hearted, purposeful activity proceeding in a social environment."

Pragmatism and the Teacher

Pragmatism neither treats the teacher merely as an on-looker as Naturalism does, nor regards him as an indispensable necessity as Idealism does. It takes the middle course. According to Pragmatism, teacher is useful, even though not indispensable, for creating life-situations for the immature child and placing him in them to learn by making attempts to tackle them. He would make independent experiments to solve his problems and learn from them. The position of the teacher is of a guide and adviser. He has to make his pupils to think and act for themselves, to do rather than to know, to originate rather than repeat. He is considered a social environment. With his sympathetic and personal contact with the children, he is expected to develop in them social habits, social interests and social attitudes. His importance lies in the fact that he has to place his students in suitable problematic situations and to motivate their interests in such a way that they may solve the problems with tact, intelligence and co-operation.

The Pragmatist teacher is a Pragmatist first and a teacher afterwards. He is essentially an experimentalist, a trial and error man, who tackles and solves problems as they arise in the classroom and outside. He aims at teaching his pupils to do rather than to know, to originate rather than to repeat, to think and act for themselves.

Pragmatism and Discipline

Pragmatism does not believe in external discipline enforced by the superior authority of the teacher and the award of punishment. It advocates that discipline to be beneficial should be based on the principles of child's activities and interests. In fact, it deprecate all forms of individual and personal discipline. It uphold discipline based on social understanding. It believes in engaging the children in free and purposeful real activities. They are not only permitted but positively encouraged to undertake real activities of the human life and learn through their performance. This process is bound to inculcate in them permanent attitudes of initiative and independence. It gives him a discipline which is acquired in every kind of real and creative work, as a very natural consequence of the activity itself. Thus, the discipline in Pragmatic system of education is to be self-discipline—the discipline of the pupil's own work and activity.

In the pragmatic scheme of education the children are expected to work in co-operation with one another. They are to take up a "project", or a real problem, and to work at it as a team. These co-operative activities impart to them very useful qualities of social life — sympathy, give and take, fellow feeling, spirit of sacrifice and tolerance, which constitute an invaluable moral training for them.

The school of the Pragmatic conception is a reflex of the community to whom it belongs and whom it represents. Its pupils have ultimately to take their places in the community and live in accordance with its point of view. Therefore, the school has to provide for all those activities which constitute the normal life of the community. It has to provide for the socialised, free and purposive activities. These activities provide the pupils a very useful training in citizenship.

Since, in the Pragmatic system of education, external restraint and imposition are altogether absent, the entire discipline that the pupils are to learn, will come from their work and self determined activities. Their discipline would be a self-discipline. Imposed discipline and a strict and rigid discipline can have no place in the pragmatic school.

A CRITICAL APPRAISAL OF PRAGMATISM

Pragmatism does not advocate any absolute standards. Education is to help man to create his new standards of life and living. But the fundamental philosophy of pragmatism has been severely criticised. In the absence of eternal values, there is very likelihood of a vacuum being created in social organism. It may lead to many vices like deceit, treachery and hypocrisy. With ever-changing values, we are not in a position to evaluate our conduct and that of our predecessors in terms of any set standards.

It is true that action is important and it may generate thinking. But it is equally true that all thinking does not proceed from action only. Truth can exist independently of anything. Truth is an end in itself and an instrumental truth may be shrouded in hypocrisy, selfishness and material mindedness. Practice cannot be identified with usefulness. Rusk stresses that, "If culture is to be saved, it must be by developing in pupils a love of knowledge for its own sake; the pragmatist is right in maintaining that practical activities must provide the incentive to learning, but the end must be the development of a disinterested activity,"

Further, by opposing the higher and spiritual values, it advocates extreme type of utilitarianism. Judging all activities in terms of human purposes and experiences, builds an inflated super-ego in man and leaves little scope for selfless humanitarianism. Anything may be justified on grounds of expediency. Truth may be tested, but not changed. Too much experimentalism is as bad as too much of faith and traditionalism. Pragmatism appears to be too radical and skeptical. It works towards denial of authority. Man has his limitations and to describe human purpose as the yard stick to perform actions. Cannot be accepted as the whole story of human existence.

In building aims of education, it leads us to a blind alley. The statement that the purpose of education is more education, leaves us vague because, beyond infinity only mathematical calculations are dealt with and not action. So far as methodology of teaching is concerned, pragmatism tries to build knowledge through projects and experiments. Hence, there are likely to be gaps in knowledge for which subject teaching becomes necessary. The curriculum may be given a vocational and social efficiency bias, but whole-sale condemnation of liberal studies and cultural subjects is not justified.

Rationalism and empiricism cannot replace irrationalism and intellectualism at all levels of human life. Accomplishment of a task cannot be judged by results alone.

Leaving aside the drawbacks of a purely pragmatic outlook, we can safely say that pragmatism has contributed much to the theory and practice of education. Its opposition to formalism and artificiality, its emphasis on practical results, its bias towards social efficiency, its questioning spirit and perpetual re-evaluation of traditions; all have greatly revolutionised education. It has accelerated the pace of democracy in educational institutions. Its humanistic and social approach in education ensures better citizens. To conceive education as a life-long process of reconstruction and re-institution of experience, puts education on a progressive pedestal.

CONCLUSION

To conclude, we can safely say that Pragmatism has contributed much to the theory and practice of education. Its opposition to formalism and artificiality, its emphasis on practical results, its bias towards social efficiency, its questioning spirit and perpetual re-evaluation of traditions, all have greatly revolutionised education. It has accelerated the pace of democracy in educational institutions. Its humanistic and social approach in education ensures better citizen. To conceive education as a life-long process of reconstruction and re-institution of experience, put education on a progressive pedestal.

10

Realism in Education

Realism is not a Philosophy of life like Idealism or Naturalism, but like Pragmatism it is an attitude of mind, a mode of thinking and an attempt to explain the nature of things. It is the doctrine that the objects of our senses exist independently of their being known or perceived by mind.

BASIC PRINCIPLES OF REALISM

Realism is an epistemological school. The basic principle of realism is the 'principle of independence'. If we put a question like this: Can a thing exist without being humanly known? Or, can a thing exist independent of our knowledge? The realist would say, 'Yes', whereas the answer of Epistemological Idealism will be in the negative. Now one who holds that an object known is independent of the knowing mind may still hold that independent object is spiritual in nature. Hence, he would be epistemologically a realist, but metaphysically an idealist. Plato was metaphysically an idealist but epistemologically a realist. Most of the modern Realists are either materialists or dualists or neutralists.

Realism, like idealism, admits of various types and degrees, because the object, may be held to be either wholly independent of and or distinct from the mind or to be partly so, and that to different extents. Therefore, the maximum of Realism is the presupposition that there is such a thing as knowledge; in other words, the perception and thought refer to some object, not the mere experience of perceiving and thinking. The maximum of Idealism, on the other side, would be the assurance that everything ever perceived or thought of existed, apart from apprehension and exactly in the form in which it is believed to exist. In other words, there is no such thing as error.

REALISM IN EDUCATION

Coming into the field of education Realism has acquired different meanings and even contradictory ones at different periods of history. Today Realism is a reaction against the book-centred academic, intellectual, liberal, literary or humanistic education. It favours child-centred, practical, specific, scientific and psychological education. Applied to education realism manifested itself in three different forms, namely: (a) Humanistic Realism, (b) Social Realism, and (c) Sense Realism.

Humanistic Realism

Although Realism is a reaction against humanistic studies today, yet it expressed itself through humanism during the Renaissance when it was believed that the ancient classics dealt with man's life more richly than the formal grammarian education of the middle ages. Thus, Humanistic Realism represented the survival of the idea of the Renaissance, but it did that in a different way. While, the classical humanists placed emphasis on form and style, the humanist realist opposed it in favour of content and ideas. This humanistic Realism was not only a rebirth of the ancient classical studies, but also a revolt against the prevalent traditional system of education. Medieval scholasticism was mere study of books and linguistic forms, while the purpose of the humanistic realist was to master his own environment through knowledge of the life of the ancient. It places substance before form, thought above words and practical efficiency in life above showy accomplishments. The Dutch international scholar *Erasmus*, the *Frenchman Rabelasis* and the English poet *Milton* were the most prominent representatives of humanistic realism.

We may review the ideas of *Milton* to have a clear understanding of Humanistic Realism, as *Milton's* 'Tractate on Education' remains one of the best expressions of Humanistic Realism. In the beginning *Milton* exposes the folly of the traditional curriculum and methods. Then he goes to analyse the work of the school and gives a scheme of education from 11 to 21 years. This course covers a variety of subjects such as Latin, geometry, 'moral training in the first stage; agriculture, architecture, natural philosophy, medicinal and mathematical science, poetry in the second stage; and ethics, economics, politics, History, theology, logic, public speaking in the third stage. It was a complete and general education which fits a man for all offices both private and public, of peace and war. Criticising this scheme of education, *Monroe* points out that the course was too heavy and meant for a College of Milton only.

The influence of Humanistic Realism was very little because it was not characterised by any external difference from the dominant formalism of those times, particularly in method, organisation and administration. Whatever influence it had, was through individual teachers only. Its spirit flourished more in the Universities, though they were artificial, formal and traditional. Yet, by its opposition of form and its placing emphasis on the realities of life, it directly led to sense realism that soon found a place in organised educational work.

Social Realism

The same force of revolt that gave birth to Humanistic Realism during Renaissance gave birth to Social Realism during the 17th and 18th centuries when the humanistic education turned into an extremely rigid formalism and ceased to be a progressive force. Social Realism was the natural reaction of practical men of the new world against a type of education that tended to perpetuate the pedantry of an earlier age, by devoting its energies to the production of the scholar and professional man to the neglect of the man of affairs. The exponents looked upon humanistic culture as insufficient for producing a man of the world. *Montaigue* was its chief representative. He would advise his scholar to spend his time at tennis, if education could not develop social qualities in him and made him only a book-worm. He takes a utilitarian view of education and interprets it as a preparation for the life of the man of the world. Social Realists were practical men and were against existing routine curriculum. They pleaded for direct contact with men and things particularly through travel. Consequently, it included a study of heraldry, genealogy, riding, fencing, and gymnastics, and a study of modern languages and the customs and institutions of neighbouring countries.

The idea of education through travelling was meant for aristocracy because travel involves expenditures. It is more a method of educational practice rather than a philosophy of education. Social Realism is not a completely distinct trend from other forms of Realism. It is, therefore, that *Montaigue* is confused as a humanist, a realist and a naturalist. He was against Humanistic Realism because he rejected book-learning and second hand knowledge. He was not a sense realist because things to him included thoughts as well, which Sense Realists neglect. He was not a Naturalist because the latter emphasised isolation while he emphasised society and contact with men. To *Rousseau* one's own experience mattered while to *Montaigue* the experience of others as well was significant. Social Realism has influenced modern Pragmatism for both are philosophies of life rather than of thought and both have narrow utilitarian end in view.

Sense Realism

In the 17th century through this very spirit of Renaissance, the individualistic attainment and religious, social and reformative influence gave way to the idea of reality comprehended through senses. Sense Realism contains the germs of modern education.

The aims of the sense realists were the following:

(a) to apply inductive method formulated by *Bacon* for his science in the field of education, with a view to organise and simplify the instructional process, and

(b) to replace the instruction in Latin, by instruction in vernacular and to substitute new scientific and social studies in language and literature.

The Sense Realists emphasised the training of the senses. They held that senses are the conveyers of knowledge, and learning takes place through the operation of the senses. This movement may be called the precursor of scientific tendency in education. The rapid growth in the knowledge of man regarding the world convinced the Sense Realists that Nature is the treasure-house of all knowledge and that this knowledge can be obtained through the training of senses. Their belief led to the formulation of a rudimentary science or philosophy of education and also a tendency to assign linguistic material a secondary place in the curriculum and attach greater importance to the material chosen from natural sciences and contemporary life. This attempt of their led to the formulation of Educational Psychology. Though the knowledge of child's mind was very meager in those days, yet the Sense Realists could assert convincingly that all studies should be adopted to suit the needs and interests of the child, and that "The child should acquire the idea rather than the form and should understand the object before the word, or the word through the object. This led to another change —that of the necessity of the use of vernacular which produced a practical and everlasting form.

The work of the Sense Realists corresponded to the spirit of the day. Distinguished with the futility of the classical learning in the cause of social betterment some people had started a movement, called the "Pansophic Movement" by turning to the new sciences and new methods for finding out a cure for social evils. The new ideals and new methods of the Sense Realists who tried to unify and systematise all knowledge and impart it in very simple inductive way had a great appeal. The use of vernacular in the teaching process made knowledge look comparatively simpler. By means of the new methods a man could master with in a very short time that amount of knowledge which put him to tremendous suffering and cost a considerable amount of time. The new writers placed emphasis on rationality rather than authority.

This attempt to simplify the instructional process led many thinkers in different lands to find out a way whereby education could be simple and easy to be imparted. The German historian *Karl Von Raumer* called this group of thinkers, 'Innovators'. Their chief pedagogical ideas were as follows:

(i) Education to proceed from simple to complex and from the concrete to the abstract.

(ii) Things before rules and words.

(iii) Students to be taught to analyse rather than to construct.

(iv) Each student to investigate for himself rather than to accept thing dogmatically.

(v) Only clearly comprehended things to be memorised.

(vi) Restraint and coercion to be replaced by creation of interest in studies.

(vi) Vernacular to be medium of instruction.

(viii) The order and course of nature to be discovered and a method based on this to be applied.

BASIC PRINCIPLES OF REALISM IN EDUCATION

Like Idealism and Naturalism, Realism also manifested in different forms in the field of education, but like Idealism and Naturalism it today has a broad meaning and it has also exercised a potent influence on education by emphasising the following basic principles:

(i) Since, we live in a world which is rapidly changing, it is necessary that we remain prepared to adjust ourselves to any psychological, intellectual and social changes that occur at any time.

(ii) A philosophy of education should be based on the realities of life and it can prove its worth by being practical.

(iii) No Ism' can solve problems of education. To be useful, education must be organised by harmonising values—past and present.

(iv) Things and objects exists independently. Human experience is limited. Truths of science are more reliable.

(v) The surest way of acquiring knowledge is the scientific way, but this does not mean that science has discovered all truths. There might be many truths which have not yet been discovered.

(vi) Curriculum should be many-sided and it should present to the children a rounded view of the universe.

(vii) Like Naturalism, Realism also lays emphasis on sense training, study of science, diversified curricula, catering education to varied interests, making methods of teaching interesting and basic theme on psychological principles.

(viii) Realism places more emphasis on curriculum and contents of studies than on behaviour training like Pragmatism. Education may be defined as behaviour training, but according to realism there is no possibilities of behaviour training without regard to the content of experience.

(ix) By emphasising the independence of objects realists outlook is more balanced than the pragmatic view which over estimates the worth of human experience.

CONCLUSION

Realism has exercised a very potent influence on modern education. The movement was not popular in the beginning but gradually it gained momentum and spread to different parts of the world. The increased interest in scientific studies, preference to the study of things before words, faith in the truths of science, enthusiasm for making curriculum broad-based, making methods of teaching interesting, sense training, direct experience—all these bear out influence and contribution of realistic trends of education. Realism places a great emphasis on curriculum and content of studies. As a philosophy it holds our attention while determining the contents of studies and as an educational trend and attitude it influences our thinking with regard to methods of instruction.

11

Existentialism in Education

Ever since the inception of reflective thought, the problem of being and Existence has loomed large in the minds of philosophers, saints and seers. In ancient Upanishadas we find direct reference to this question in the form of an inquiry into the quintessence or the element in man which survives death and destruction, that is, which is unaffected by becoming or change. The philosophers of East as well as West, of the ancient as well as modern times have all been seriously preoccupied by the problem of Existence. In short, no philosopher can avoid considering the ontological problems and thus all philosophies are at bottom existentialists. Then, how is the modern existentialist different and why do we not call other philosophies existentialism? The reason is that modern existentialism is concerned, unlike other philosophies, more with the problem of becoming than the problem of being; more with particulars than universals; more with existence than essence. As the father of modern existentialism, S. Kierkegaard puts it, the chief concern of an existentialist Christian is not the knowledge of rules and principles of Christanity but "how am I to become a Christian". The non-Christian or atheist existentialists substitute the word "Authentic Being" for the term Christian.

Thus the extentialists have emphasised "Action" and "Choice" instead of usual emphasis on knowledge and explanation, and replaced the question of what by how.

As a major school of philosophy, existentialism is a *'new comer'* and focuses on the person. Its origin as a philosophic outlook is not found until the nineteeth century. Although it may be correctly described as a modern twentieth century philosophy, yet any true account of Existentialism must begin with a reference to the work of Soren Kierkegaard (1813-1855). He was a Danish philosopher whose Journals form the intellectual basis for the modern development of Existentialism. His emphasis was on the individual and on human conduct.

BASIC POSTULATES OF EXISTENTIALISM

Unlike the traditional philosophies, existentialism does not attempt to offer final answers to the basic questions concerning reality, truth and value. The task of existential philosophy is to awaken man's interest in these questions, not to provide him with answers. The value of these questions lies in the fact that they represent an eternal quest to find meaning and purpose in the human condition. The existentialist views modern man as alienated from his world and his life as meaningless until he develops ultimate concern for these questions. Existentialists reject any system that offers wholesale explanation of man's relationships to his universe and the ultimate meaning of life. To the existentialist, the starting point for all understanding is the recognition of his individual existence in an indifferent world.

The basic postulates of an existentialist philosophy can be summarised thus:

Reality and Existence

According to the existentialist, the one reality man can be certain, is of his own existence. He is faced with the intellectual and physical reality of his own life. It is from this point that man becomes aware of the unique human condition that places upon him sole responsibility for what he is and what he will become. Each individual through the choice he makes, fashions his own world view of what he is. 'Man makes himself' and is responsible for the choices he makes.

Existence precedes essence. In other words the sheer brute fact that things exist is logically prior to any essence or definition we may read into them. Objects exist, and man interprets them; but before he ever regards them as the embodiments of certain characteristics, they simply are. The world is there; it is concrete and particular, and any essence that we abstract out of it is less real than the data from which it is abstracted.

Nature of Universe

By itself the universe is without meaning or purpose. The purposes we think we detect in the universe are nothing but a projection of our own desire for order. In reality we are 'cast' into an alien world, for which we were not specially created but within which we must sooner or later die.

Knowledge and Truth

For the existentialist, knowledge does not precede man's existence. 'Choice' is the key word in existential views about the nature of knowing. All knowing and truth arrived at by knowing, is individual and subjective. Man determines by conscious choice to accept or reject knowledge outside of his own experience. Self knowledge is the key to all knowledge. Man becomes the source of his own knowledge and truth by determining through his choices and experiences that which is real for him, and by accepting responsibility for his actions and beliefs based upon his choices.

Nature of Values

Since the essential reality of life for the individual is his outgoing engagement in making choices, the question of value is basic to the entire existential outlook. All of our choices actually represent an evaluation of various alternatives and a selection of one as superior to others. For the existentialist, man is ethically responsible for all his decisions. He has no higher authority to evaluate possible choices and no absolute code to follow.

Values determined for us by another, or assumed to exist above or beyond man's experience, are not real. Acceptance of them makes one less than a man since selfhood grows through making difficult choices and assuming full responsibility for them. The existentialist gives man freedom but requires responsibility. According to him each man has the responsibility for creating his own values and in doing so he is choosing freedom and responsibility.

The Human Predicament

Modern man's problem of existing in an indifferent world can be described by the word 'human predicament' or 'human condition'. Existentialism offers man no easy solutions and no escape from his responsibility for choosing his beliefs and actions. Life with this freedom and responsibility is often painful and never comfortable, but the efforts involved are precisely what life should be concerned with.

When man refuses to accept the reality of his existence and therefore, the human predicament, he ceases to participate in the world as a man and admits his failure as a human being. For the existentialist, then, man is not complete; he is in the process of 'becoming' and each man by his own life helps shape that process. The human predicament, thus, comes down to one basic choice: *"To affirm our existence in an indifferent world and struggle to become men or to reject it and with it all ultimate concern and contact with reality".*

Contingency of Human Life

Another significant concept of existentialism is the 'Contingency' of human life, the 'givenness' or 'thrownness'. (Dasien, being-in-itself of Sartre) of human life. Existentialists believe that Existence of a person means his period from birth to death. There was nothing before birth and would be nothing beyond death. In between we have been thrown into a social life and the characteristics of this social life are the contingent circumstances of our life. The contingency is often characterised by experiences of dread, horror, anguish, solitude, bewilderment, uncertainty and finally limited by death. It may be recalled that even *Buddha* recognised this contingency of human life as soon as he came out of his palce and thus human suffering was the occasion of his philosophising. As *Jean Wahl* puts it: "Man is in this world, a world limited by death and experienced in anguish; is aware of himself as essentially anxious; is burdened by his solitude within the horizon of his temporality." As such the whole gamut of metaphysics discussing about a transcendental being and purposes beyond death or an axiology discussing about transcendental values are mere imaginations of the mind designed to console an anguished soul and not the truth of existence.

Alexander Koyre, in an informal discussion with *Berdyaev, Gurvitch, Marcel, Jean Wahl* and others describes in a very simple way the contingency of human life : "We are there; I am there such as I am; and I neither know why nor how; the only thing I know, truly and inexorably, is that someday I am going to die. And that is what limits all my possibilities and my future. My future limited, finite and I knowing it—that is my situation in the world.

I know that my existence is precarious and short, and that I can lose it. This is the only thing that I have, and I can lose it at any moment; that is why there is the substratum of anxiety, fear and anguish." Therefore, the sources, process and content of philosophising must be the situation in which one is placed. We are all aware of our situation in life, limited by death, and existentialists rightly remark that man is the only being in the world who knows that some time he will die. That is why his existence is throughout permeated by dread, anxiety and fear. He cannot escape or transcend this situation. He has to be prepared to face dread, anguish, anxiety and fear resolutely and courageously. He must learn to live with anguish, dread and anxiety. He must learn to love death just as *Socrates*, *Lincoln*, *Kennedy*, *Gandhi* and a score of other greatmen for whom dying for a meaningful cause was of greater significance than living a purposeless life. There are a number of correlates in Indian philosophy for existential concepts for, e.g., anguish: Dukha, dread and horror: Bhaya, Bhiti (Vita), etc. But when existentialism advises us to live with these categories of contingency, Indian philosophy counsels us to transcend them. This is very clearly evident in the concept of a sthithaprajna in the *Gita*. One sloka runs like this—

दुःखेशु मनद्विग्नः सुखेंशु विगनस्पृह

वीतराग भयः क्रोध स्थितधिः मुनिरुच्छते ।।

(He who is not depressed by anguish, elated by joy, and at times of fear, anxiety, love, horror and anger maintains his equanimity and poise is a sage).

संभावितस्य चाकीर्तिर्मणादतिरिच्छते

(For a man enjoying popular esteem infamy is worse than death).

Gandhiji once had said that death in freedom is sweeter than life in bondage.

Another significant concept of existentialism is their view of man. In the age-long philosophical controversy of Free-will vs. determinism, existentialists prefer to view man as an infinitely free, responsible being. According to Sartre freedom is identical with existence. As such existentialism has even been described as a search for ways in which man's freedom to create may be widely established and understood. In *Marjorie Grene's* terms: "The revolutionary philosophy turns out to be philosophy of freedom— not just the philosophy of those who seek freedom but the philosophy of the very free act itself". According to existentialists, man is not only free but he is condemned to be free. He is only not free, not to be free. This is the tragedy of human life. This infinite freedom entails upon him a heavy sense of responsibility, and this situation of being burdened with a heavy responsibility is the cause of dread, anguish and anxiety. The peculiar quality of human reality is that it is without excuse. Man is always placed in a situation of 'धर्म संकट' ('Dharma Sankata'). A bold, honest, responsible and authentic existence would help man to face this situation.

EDUCATIONAL IMPLICATIONS OF EXISTENTIALISM

It is very difficult to discuss with a considerable degree of certainty and confidence about existentialistic education, as a good treatise on education by an existentialist is yet to appear. "The philosophy of existentialistsm has not displayed any particular interest in education." Therefore, the educational implications that have been discussed are those that are derived and deduced from their philosophy rather than those that are developed by existentialists. As *Kneller* feels: "Aside from casual references, such as those made by *Kierkegaard* and *Marcel* to their own schooling, existentialists, we repeat, do not carry their doctrine into practical theory or policy for school behaviour. We can only deduce curricular theory from philosophic doctrine helped here and there." But existentialist implications for education have been discussed below in a systematic way, of course supported by other sources.

Existentialism and Meaning of Education

In a broad sense education is that which helps an individual to realise the best that he is capable of. In doing so education must help the individual to realise the 'facticity' (contingency) of his existence, to face the categories of this facticity—dread, anguish, anxiety, and fear—resolutely and courageously and finally prepare him to meet death with pleasure. As such school life need not be a source of joy and happiness as for Rousseau, Froebel *Kindergarten* Pestalozzi and Montessori *'House of Happiness'* or a place of training for social adjustment as for Dewey, but need to be permeated by dread and anxiety. The former type of education is unrealistic according to the existentialist. "Education for happiness is a dangerous doctrine because there can be no happiness without pain and no ecstasy without suffering". Therefore, existentialists would welcome an education which throws open to children human suffering, misery, anguish and the dreadful responsibilities of adult life.

The world of education has hitherto been familiar with such concepts as education for complete living, for life, for happiness and for freedom. But existentialism speaks of a new kind of education—education for death. During and in between the two World Wars this concept of education was upper most in educational circles of United States, Germany, France and other European Countries where dying for one's own country constituted the supreme sacrifice. Students must develop a consistent scale of values, authenticate their existence by being commited to these values and so act as to be prepared to die for these values than to live without them. Brubacher presents a case for 'education for death' like this: "The attention given in our schools for education for death is 'grudgingly small' because death is regarded as a 'great misfortune'. This slighting of the study of death is anything but realistic, since history is replete with examples of self-sacrifice to the point of self-annihilation for the benefit of mankind." But much depends upon the teacher and his understanding of his role which is very delicate as he has to cultivate simultaneously both the values of life and values of death. He must resourcefully point to the need for death for the sake of continuity of group life. He must make the child feel that it has conquered death. This can happen only when the child can say that life is cheap in comparison to some great cause.

The message of existentialism for education is simple. It pleads for the affirmation of authentic freedom and individual uniqueness. It is against the 'conformity' in schools. The existentialist asserts that the individual does not necessarily "Realise" himself in the group at all but only exchanges his true self for the anonymous mask of the group. Instead of finding self-fulfilment, he actually loses himself.

In view of the five basic postulates outlined previously we may indicate the implications of existentialist outlook for education in the following manner.

Existentialism and Aims of Education

For the existentialist, education is the means for creating a general awareness of man's situation and as an instrument for helping him see both his problems and his unique possibilities. As Harper writes, "The end of education for an existentialist is making individuals aware of the meaning of homelessness, of being at home, and of the ways of returning." The aim of education which may find an approval of an existentialist may, thus, be put as follows:

- Promotion of the full, free development of the individual to deal with the situation in which he finds himself.

- To help develop within the individual the freedom to make choices, but freedom is not license. Rather, it is the freedom 'to commit oneself again and again to values and to persons.'

Existentialism and Curriculum

There is no specially prescribed curriculum by the existentialist. However, one may infer that such a curriculum would be characterised by three features: Open structure, changing content and challenging issues involving life in every aspect. The curriculum in the existentialist programme of education will have an open a rather than a closed structure. The content therein will undergo a change depending upon the problems faced by humanity at a particular stage of its socio-cultural existence. The issues which are important therein will be presented in a critical perspective.

For the existentialist, there is no such thing as 'disinterested knowledge'. He is concerned less with the gathering of evidence than with what the individual does for himself, with the evidence. Knowledge, properly conceived, brings freedom, since it deliverers man from ignorance and prejudice and enables him to see himself as he really is. The school must, therefore, completely revise its conceptions of knowledge. It must cease to regarded subject matter as an end itself or as an instrument to prepare the student for his future career, and consider it instead as a means for the cultivation of the self. "The whole emphasis of the curriculum, says George F. Kneller", "Must shift from the world of objects to the world of the person. Since the meaning of existence lies in man himself, the student should use his knowledge of external realities to come to terms more completely with his own nature."

The existentialists, therefore, attach great importance to the humanities, since history, literature; philosophy and art reveal in greater depth and immediacy than other subjects the nature of man and his conflict with the world. Over-specialisation and emphasis on vocationalisation should be avoided.

Existentialism and Teaching-Learning Strategy

According to the existentialist philosophy, since authentic existence involves the whole man, we should no longer regard learning primarily as mental discipline. On the contrary, the student should be urged to involve himself intellectually and emotionally in whatever he studies; he must appropriate to himself any exercise or problem or study he tackles.

The teacher should bring home vividly to the student that, whatever he does, he cannot escape the consequences of his actions: he must accept them as the issue of his own free choice, however thoughtless that choice may sometimes be. He should be taught to own his failures rather than attributing them to factors such as environment, family, temperament, or the influence of others.

The learner must be put in a situation by which he will recognise that frustration and conflict are not just undesirable states to be avoided at all costs; they stem from the inherent "Forsakenness" of the human condition, in which man's freedom has set him apart from the rest of the world. The school and the class room teaching-learning strategies should be so organised that the pupil will be acquainted with the "darker" side of life, with the pain, terror and seemingly inexplicable brutality of life, as well as with its beauty, ecstasy, and joy. The student must become personally concerned with the realisation of his own nature and with what Tillich calls the courage to be himself.

Existentialist believes that the teacher is not in his classroom to impart knowledge as the realist asserts, or as a consultant in problem situations as the pragmatist holds, or as a personality to be emulated as the idealist thinks. His function is to help each student personally in his journey towards self-realisation.

In an effective teaching-learning strategy, the teacher acts, himself as a free agent; his influence is not temporary but persists into adult life. He urges his students to challenge and criticise his own views and advises them not to be daunted by the fear of error, provided the approach they use is genuine. He exhorts them never to take the opinions of others, whether read or heard, for granted, and to scorn mere imitation and reproduction of ideas second hand. By virtue of the force of his own commitment to freedom and individuality, the teacher can generate a similar enthusiasm for these ideals among his students.

The teacher's task is not simply to stimulate latent originality. He must also encourage the student to commit himself to his work, to reflect on each item of knowledge until it is of importance to him personally. George F. Kneller observes that "This is an assertion not about the nature of truth but about the nature of learning. Knowledge is not more important than man, but less so, serving his foremost end, which is the search for authenticity." For the existentialist, the Socratic method is the ideal mode of education; since by it the student learns what he personally asserts to be true. Sartre has also advised the use of 'play' because in it the individual gives full rein to his creativity.

Existentialism and Discipline

Existentialism is a philosophy of personal freedom and individual responsibility. Such a concept of freedom with responsibility is applicable both to teacher and his pupils. In order to exercise an immediate and enduring effect on the pupil, a teacher must demonstrate his own independence by his word and deed. The discipline, for the existentialist, is largely internal and as such a trait of the individual.

In trying to handle a rebellious child, the existentialist recommends that the teacher should not strive to humiliate him or hold him up to the ridicule of the rest of the class. By all means, he may be punished by pointing out that certain behaviour will not be tolerated but he should not be talked down or scolded at a point of robbing him of his self-respect.

Existentialism and Evaluation

In the existentialist philosophy, proficiency or success in examination is not to be regarded as an end in itself. The student who can handle what little he learns is far more to be admired than the one who can merely produce a lot of information on demand. Thus, evaluation should be with reference to an individual rather than a group. It should be a criterion-referenced and not a norm-referenced testing which should be emphasised in any programme of education.

CRITICISM OF EXISTENTIALISM

In trying to understand the existentialist philosophy, there are certain obstacles identified by educators. The formulations of an existentialist cannot be studied objectively from without, but requires the student to identify himself with its doctrines from within. George F. Kneller rightly observes that the existentialist philosophers does not analyse issues from a safe distance but rather immerses himself in them both intellectually and emotionally.

There is also a general charge against existentialism that it has flourished best in conditions of social and economic collapse in

Germany after the First World War and in France after the second. The whole movement is characterised by '*anguished* introspection', 'resonant despair' and 'defiant affirmation,'

CONTRIBUTION OF EXISTENTEALISM TO EDUCATION

Existentialism developed as a reaction against the contemporary social, economic and political situation in which man has lost his self. This philosophy has widely influenced art and literature. In politics it has stood against war. Its followers are active pacifists. In the field of education the contribution of existentialism is as follows:

1. Total development*:* The existentialists have aimed at total development of personality through education. Education should aim at the whole man. It should aim at character formation and self-realisation.

2. Subjective knowledge: The present age of science has made too much of objective knowledge, so much so that the term subjective has come to mean unreal, non-sense, ignorant and irrelevant. The existentialists rightly point out that subjective knowledge is even more important than objective knowledge. They rightly hold that truth is subjectivity. It is a human value and values are not facts. Reduction of values to facts has led to widespread loss of faith in values. Therefore, along with the teaching of science and mathematics, the humanities, art and literature should also be given suitable place in curriculum at every stage of education. Most of the ills of the modern man are due to over-objective attitude. This requires a subjectivist correction in the light of existentialist ideas.

3. Importance of environment: The present industrial, economic, political and social environment is valueless. Therefore, it helps confusion and corruption, tensions and conflicts. The existentialists seek to provide an environment proper to self-development and self-consciousness. This environment in the school requires contribution from humanities, arts and literature. These will help in the development of individuality in the educand so that he may cease to become a cog in the social wheel. Rather he should develop to be a self-conscious and sensitive individual.

In spite of the above mentioned contribution of existentialism its disadvantages are obvious since, as a philosophy also it has never provided a balanced thought. Some of the existentialist theories, in spite of all their genius, verge upon pathological symptoms. Such is the philosophy of Kierkegaard, the father of modern existentialism. If truth is not objective, it is not merely subjective. Existentialist revolt against intellectualism has its merits but also its serious limitations. Existential methods may be useful in moral and religious education but it cannot work in the education of science and technology.

Therefore, the following limitations of existential philosophy of education may be noted:

1. Existential aim of education is as much one-sided as that of any other 'ism'.
2. Exclusive emphasis on humanities, art and literature is as much one-sided as emphasis upon science.
3. In their enthusiasm for self-realisation, the existentialists forget that a very important aim of education is earning a living. For that purpose the utilitarian aim of education has its advantages.
4. The existentialist method of teaching may be useful in moral and religious education but it will not work in the teaching of science and technology.
5. From a perusal of the advantages and limitations of existential approach in the field of education, it is clear that it serves as a corrective to contemporary gaps of education. However, it is far from being satisfactory as a complete philosophy of education.

CONCLUSION

To conclude, we can say that though the influence and popularity of existentialism continues to grow, acceptance of its emphasis upon the sober reality of death and the apparent futility of modern existence made it a difficult intellectual course to follow. For the present, pragmatic optimism and the assuring absolutes of idealism serve to maintain the primary position of these philosophies against the intellectual challenge of existentialism.

Part Three

EMINENT WESTEREN EDUCATORS

Jean Jacques Rousseau
John Dewey
Fredrich August Froebel
Maria Montessori

12

Jean Jacques Rousseau (1712-1778)

Rousseau was a revolutionary. "Without him", said Nepolean, there would have been no French Revolution." It may equally be admitted that without him there would have been no Social Revolution: at least it would not have come so soon. Rousseau was a revolutionary not only in politics, but he was also a revolutionary in education. A study of Rousseau's educational ideas is, therefore, very much significant for a student of education.

ROUSSEAU'S PHILOSOPHY

Rousseau's philosophy was a reaction against the contemporary social and political set-up which was saturated with formalism, despotism and hypocricy. Rousseau condemned the contemporary systems and denounced civilisation in most unequivocal terms. He held society responsible for all evils, religion for all superstitions, and social life for all snobbery and hypocrisy that pervaded all around. All governments he declared were despotic and tyrannical, and man was a victim of prejudices and conventions.

The key-notes to his philosophy are his concepts of 'State of Nature', 'Natural Man' and 'Natural Civilisation.' Rousseau has a profound faith in the original goodness of human nature.

"Everything", he believes, "Is good as it comes from the hands of Author of Nature, but everything degenerates in the hands of man." Thus, according to Rousseau, Nature is the only pure, clean and enabling influence. Human society is thoroughly corrupt. Therefore, man should be freed from the bondage of society; and he should be enabled to live in the "State of Nature." The only civilisation he should learn is natural civilisation. Human nature is essentially good, and it must be given fullest opportunities of free development. His native tendencies, his instincts and emotions and his inborn capacities must be permitted to be developed freely. The child must be enabled to grow in a free atmosphere.

ROUSSEAU'S EDUCATIONAL PHILOSOPHY

Emile is a novel in which the author has described the education of Emile, an imaginary child. The author described the methods of bringing the child in contact with Nature and removing the social evils. The child is left under the guidance of an ideal teacher away from the school and society. The teacher teaches the child in a natural environment. The book Emile consists of five parts respectively devoted to Infancy, Childhood, Adolescence, Youth and the Imaginary wife of Emile named Sofia.

Rousseau's philosophy of education is Naturalistic. He is against a system of conventional and formal education. For Rousseau, education does not mean merely imparting information or storing knowledge. It is not imposition from without, it is development of the child's natural powers and abilities from within.

Doctrine of Negative Education

The essence of Rousseau's philosophy of education is that, since human nature is essentially good, an attempt should be made through by education to preserve its natural goodness ; and it can be done by keeping the goodness of child's nature away from evil. This important thing is not to implant virtue but to preserve the soul from the vices which society puts in the child. It is Rousseau's concept of 'Negative Education'. The doctrine of negative education meant in srealm of physical education, a grant of freedom to the body and limbs, simple diet, no medicines and open-air life. In the realm of intellectual training it stood for no formal instruction and 'no reading'. Childhood, he said, is the sleep of reason. So far as moral training is concerned, Rousseau advocated the theory of 'Natural Consequences'.

The Theory of Natural Consequences

The theory of Natural Consequences means that a child should suffer the natural consequences for his mistake and follies. "If the child is slow in dressing for a walk, leave him at home; if he breaks a window, let him sit in the cold; if he disobeys and gets wet, let him have cold; if he over-eats, let him be sick. In fact, let him suffer the natural results of the contravention of the laws of nature."

This theory of Natural Consequences has been further discussed under the heading, Rousseau's concept of discipline.

Rousseau's Concept of Educational Aims

According to Rousseau the process of education should facilitate the development of the child's innate powers and capacities. It should not confine the child to the acquisition of knowledge only or prepare him for a particular vocation in life. It should prepare him for life itself. It should make him a man.

Besides this general aim of education, Rousseau, in his book 'Emile', has given specific aims for different stages of education. Emile is divided into five parts. The first four parts contain education for infancy, childhood, boyhood and manhood. In the fifth part, he gives a plan for the educational of women.

Education for Infancy (one to five years): For the period of infancy, Rousseau advocates physical education. He says that since "All wickedness comes from weakness, the child should be made strong so that he will always keep a restraint upon himself and will not be led into evil ways." He condemns all checks on freedom during this period. The child has a desire for physical activities. His spontaneous growth and training can be facilitated if he is placed under simple, free and healthy conditions. Rousseau regards habit as contrary to impulse. He therefore, insists that child development should not be arrested by any fixed patterns. The child should not be made to talk prematurely. Moreover, plain and simple language should be used with him. The education of Emile during infancy is to be purely negative and physical. All that the educator is to do, is to protect his instincts and impulses from vice and afford him opportunity for his natural activities.

Rousseau believes that education does not emanate from without infact, it springs from within. The first education should be the free and unrestricted expression of the natural activities of the child in his natural environment.

Education for Childhood (5 to 12 years): During the period of infancy, attention should be concentrated upon building up good health. No other training is to be given. When the infant grows into a child, he has different needs and he has also acquired some control of his limbs. Hence, during this period attention should be focused on training the senses and providing opportunities for the exercise of his limbs. No intellectual training during this period is to be given but moral training is to be given by example and through the theory of natural consequences.

Education during childhood should be exclusively directed towards the training of senses.

Education for Boyhood (12 to 15 years): This stage is the pre-adolescent period. So far Emile has been prepared for reviewing knowledge, his organs and powers have been perfected and exercised. He has gained surplus energy which is to be utilised by keeping him busy in instruction, labour and study. Hence, the aim of Education at this stage is to enable Emile to acquire useful knowledge which would satisfy his wants and stand the test of 'practical needs'.

During this period the child should be instructed in Natural Science. But the boy should discover science himself rather than learn it from others. Geography and astronomy should not be taught through maps, globes and other misleading representations. The spirit of inquiry should be stimulated in the child. He should be encouraged to observe the rising and setting sun and the moon during different seasons and draw the inferences himself therefrom. Let him understand the various problems of topography and neighbourhood and find out the solutions. To Rousseau, text books are of no importance for the boy. All valuable knowledge may be acquired most clearly and naturally through one's own experience.

Education for Manhood (15 to 20 years): It is during the period of manhood that Emile is to receive moral training. Hitherto his body has been developed and his senses have been trained. During manhood he needs training in human relationships. His sex instinct makes its appearance and it is necessary that he is given proper training in social and moral relationships. Rousseau advocates direct experience with regard to this training as well. For inculcating qualities of sympathy and social sensitiveness Rousseau says that Emile should be taken to infirmaries, hospitals, and prisons because there he can observe the example of human wretchedness at all stages. He is to observe concrete examples of miseries in all stages, but not so often as to make him hardened.

Care, however, is to be taken to ensure that the youth does not become cynical and hyper-critical. For this he should be given lessons in history. History is a study where one sees man simply as a spectator without feeling or passion. No formal instruction in moral education is to be given. Placed in the proper environment Emile would learn things through direct experience. But only contact with concrete things may not produce the desirable sentiments in the youth. Hence, his conduct should be directed on the reward and punishment level through the use of fables and stories; for by censuring the wrong doer under an unknown mark, we instruct without offending him. If he displays vanity, let him be exposed to flatterers, spendthrifts, and sharpers and allowed to suffer the natural consequences of his acts of omissions and commissions.

Female Education

In the fifth part of Emile, Rousseau has detailed out an education for Sophia who is to become the wife of Emile. By doing that, he expresses his views regarding the education of women.

To him, woman must not possess any individuality of her own. She should be regarded only as subordinate to the nature of man. He says, "The whole education of women ought to be relative to men. To please them, to be useful to them, to make themselves loved and honoured by them, to educate them when young..." The woman should undergo hardships at the hands of man, as the latter should suffer at the hands of nature. She should acquire physical charm by bodily exercise. Woman should be taught sewing, embroidery, lace work and designing so that they may decorate themselves to please men. The wives should be obedient and must be prepared to suffer injuries at the hands of their husbands without any complaint. They should be given religious training at an early age. "Every daughter should have the religion of her mother, and every wife that of her husband". Rousseau does not want that women should learn philosophy, art and science. She is only to learn the technique of pleasing man and to that end she should try to acquire a psychological insight into the nature of man.

Thus, we find Rousseau most radical, naturalistic and individualistic in the education of the boy, but hopelessly traditional throughout in the education of the girl.

Rousseau's Views on Curriculum

Although Rousseau has not set forth any principles underlaying the teaching of different subjects in the different stages of *Emile's* education, yet his discussion of the value of various studies is quite suggestive. Describing the details of education in the first stage, Rousseau, maintains that Emile will not be taught the usual subjects, for those do not fulfil the needs of childhood. Children are not capable of learning things which the adults can learn. Their ways of seeing, thinking and feeling are different from those of the adults. So, during the first period of the child's education, parents should pay little attention to positive instruction in the usual subjects, but should see that the child develops physically, has good health, his senses are properly exercised and he gets a chance of cultivating natural habits.

In the second stage, Emile's education is to be primarily negative. There will be no verbal lessons for him, no lessons in languages, history and geography. Emile is to learn by his own experiences. "No book should be used, for Reading is the curse of childhood." There is no place for moral instruction or positive education from five to twelve years, because these require the exercise of reasoning power on the part of the learner and this is not present in an active forms during this period. "Childhood is the sleep of reason." Positive education in this stage, consists in imparting physical education through a set of gymnastic exercises and exercises for the training of senses. Rousseau attaches great importance to sense training. He thinks that if the senses are not trained properly, independent reasoning and judgement are impossible.

With his bodily organs and senses trained. Emile is now prepared to receive knowledge in the third stage. Accordingly, he will be taught physical sciences, language, mathematics, manual work, a trade, social relations, music and drawing. The purpose of teaching drawing is to train his eyes and muscles, while that of teaching sciences will be to inculcate a heuristic attitude. Some manual work or trade will be taught to develop his powers of judgement, reasoning and cultivate in him habits of neatness, precision and work. Rousseau recommends carpentry and the making of scientific instruments. Social relations will be taught with a view to impressing on him the reciprocal duties of men, the need of co-operation in life and the economic dependence of man on man.

With the beginning of the adolescent period, begins the moral and religious education of Emile. Moral education consists in Emile's learning about his relations with his fellow men and such moral qualities as benevolence, kindness, service and sympathy. Moral education, says Rousseau, is to be preferably given through activities and occupations and not through lectures on ethics. Besides, moral education, history, religious instruction, aesthetics, physical culture, and sex instruction are to constitute the curriculum in the fourth stage. History will be utilised in the service of moral instruction. Rousseau recommends the study of biography for Emile. Aesthetics is included in the curriculum for the development of taste. Physical training is to be recommended for keeping Emile busy, diligent and hard work. It will keep at bay for a little longer the more dangerous passions. Sex instruction is to consist of direct moral exhortation on chastity and an explanation of the mysteries of creation in the world of plants, animals and men in a dispassionate manner.

Rousseau's Views on the Methods of Teaching

The methods of teaching as suggested implicitly by Rousseau, reflect his Naturalistic Philosophy. He lays stress on direct experience of things and on the principle of 'Learning by doing'. He says, "Teach by doing whenever you can, and only fall back on words when doing is out of the question." Rousseau is a great exponent of the theory of 'self-teaching'. He is deadly against didacticism. He says, "I like not explanations given in long discourses. Young people pay little attention to them and retain little from them. The things themselves! I shall never repeat often enough that we attach too much importance to words. With our chattering education, we make nothing but chatterers." The teacher is very often inclined to didacticism and moralising. The child can never feel interested in theoretical things. He wants activities. He hates all explanations and lectures from the teacher. He does not like abstract talks. He wants to manipulate concrete objects. Lecturing is the most unscientific and unpsychological method of teaching the young child. Rousseau has done a great service to education by making the school conscious of this wrong method. He advocates the adoption of the Heuristic Attitude which places the child in the position of a discoverer. Emile, for example, is to learn Science in a practical fashion by means of simple experiments performed with apparatus self-made and self-invented. The same principle is to be followed in teaching of Mathematics, History, Geography, Social Relations and Morality. While discussing the method of imparting moral instruction to Emile in the fourth stage. Rousseau remarks that the practice of virtue is to count far more than lectures on Ethics. "It is by doing good that one becomes good... occupy your pupil with all the good actions that are in his reach; let the interests of the poor always be his; let him assist them not only with purse, but with his personal attention; let him serve them, protect them, and consentrate to them his person and his time; let him be their advocate; he will never have nobler employment." Similarly, Emile will learn about social relations by his actual visits to shops and factories where people engage in industrial and mechanical arts, will be shown working together, but according to their talents and opportunities. Rousseau, like a modern educator, thinks less of teacher's exposition, much more of the learning experiences of the pupils.

Although Rousseau has not named any principles and methods as such, yet his scheme of education for Emile has furthered and stimulated thought in this direction with the result that we have now such methods as the Laboratory, Method, the Heuristic Method and such principles of teachings and learning as those of learning by doing and learning through sense experience.

Rousseau's Concept of Discipline

Rousseau's cry is "freedom" and "Absence of restraint" for Emile. It is only in an atmosphere of freedom that Emile can develop his innate powers spontaneously. Impositions are of no use. Punishments have no value as the child has no conception of right or wrong or of the 'why' of punishment awarded to him. The child's reasoning power is not so developed. He wants children to have their own way and suffer the unavoidable consequences or inevitable reactions of their conduct. He believes in discipline according to natural consequences. He says, "Allow the child to suffer the natural results of his own acts, "Without the intervention of human being to protect or to punish." The child is thus to suffer the consequences of his actions and he will set himself right. If he breaks a window-pane, let him sit in the cold wind that gushes in as a result of his folly. If he climbs a tree, let him fall and learn not to attempt it". Rousseau goes to this extent if the child puts his hand into fire, let him burns his hand and learn by the natural consequences of his fault not to do it again. Thus, according to Rousseau, "Children should never receive punishment as such, it should come as a natural consequence of their fault." Rousseau advises the teacher not to intervene in matters of moral guidance as a means of disciplining the child. He contends that the child's nature is essentially good, and any intervention is, therefore, harmful.

School Organisation

The title given above may be a little misleading because Rousseau objected to the system of school education. He contended that the child is born innocent and pure, that he is only defiled and distorted by the defective environment of the school. In fact, the only suitable environment of every kind is defective and impure. It is better to separate the child from his parents, to take him away from school, and leave him by himself in a natural environment. The educator's only task is to look after the child, because in natural surroundings the child will himself look after the development of his natural abilities. Even if schools are created, they can be utilised by stressing the natural surrounding instead of insisting on creating a social atmosphere. In the predominantly natural surroundings the child will be able to develop naturally.

ROUSSEAU'S CONTRIBUTION

Rousseau's contribution to the theory as well as practice of education is indescribable. There is hardly any side of education which his philosophy did not affect. He challenged traditionalism in education on all fronts. He questioned the traditional aims of education, the traditional curriculum, the traditional methods of teaching and traditional concept of discipline.

Rousseau rendered a great service to the educand, by psychologising education. He emphasised that the education of the child must be based on the study of his nature and organised in conformity with it. He rightly stressed that traditional aims, rigorous discipline, and telling method can never produce good educational results. Full and free development of the child's inner powers alone should be the aim of education.

Rousseau stressed the fact of individual differences between the child and child, as also between one stage of development and another in the case of same child. This concept exercised a marked influence on the determination of the curriculum and methods of teaching at different stages.

Movement for learning by direct experiences of things and heuristic teaching have been the contribution of Rousseau. It is he, who awakened the educator to the need of introducing physical activities and sense training in the education of the children.

Rousseau emphasised the goodness of the child's nature and as such advocated complete freedom for him. This attitude virtually laid the foundation of all later and modern movements for self-education. He gave a death blow to authoritarianism in education.

Thus, one of the most important contributions of Rousseau is his assertion that the child is a positive factor in education. The function of education is to ensure his proper development at each stage of his growth. Rousseau's ideas inspired the thinking of Pestalozzi, Herbart, Forebel, and many other educational thinkers of the 19th Century, who expanded them further and adopted them for class-room practices.

It may be summed up in the words of Ross. "Rousseau was decidedly contrary in his attitude towards established institutions... Certainly he has irritated many people, but, like Socrates, he has been a gadfly stinging his contemporaries and his successors into thought. He was the fore-runner of so many, who have followed in the trails he blazed through the forest, until now they have become the broad-highway of common travel." Certain it is that the educational ferment he started has not died down even yet.

13

John Dewey
(1859-1952)

John Dewey, greatest of the pragmatists and generally recognised as the most outstanding philosopher his century has produced, made significant contributions to virtually every field of philosophy as well as to such other areas of inquiry as education and psychology. Active for 70 years as a scholar, he was a prolific writer publishing approximately fifty books band more than eight hundred articles. Many of these have been translated into various foreign languages. New volumes are still coming out with more Dewey material, mainly correspondence, and books and articles on him are appearing at a rapidly increasing rate.

While Rousseau stressed the original nature of the child and Froebel idealised his spiritual nature, the social aspect of education was left to Dewey who stressed that education is a process of living in society. John Dewey, the American philosopher, psychologist and great teacher, challenged the old static cold-storage ideal of knowledge; he brought education more in accord with the activities of the present day life; brought fusion of psychological and sociological aspects of education.

DEWEY'S GENERAL PHILOSOPHIY

Dewey is a Pragmatist, holding that all thought is subordinate to action. Philosophy is only a means to guide the individual to live his practical life successfully. No opinion, belief, hypothesis or principle is worth anything unless it works—that is, serves some practical purpose. No philosophy is true in its own right, unless it helps man in solving the practical problems of his life. Truth is thus nothing eternal, absolute or unchangeable; it is purely purposive, changeable, relative and practical.

Dewey emphasises the importance of science and of scientific methods as central in determining approach to human affairs of all kinds. In the scientific method, he found principles and procedures that gave him the concepts of experience. According to him, knowledge and thinking are closely associated with action. People ordinarily believe that knowledge arises apart from action and regard it as an independent existence. Dewey does not agree with this point of view. He believes that knowledge can never arise from action. It is only as a result of action that knowledge is acquired. For Dewey the only reality is one's experience of objects, physical and social surroundings around him. It is through experience that true knowledge increases and the modification on one's behaviour takes place. Such modification determines and modifies his subsequent experience.

Dewey believes that "All knowledge has come as a result of activities of individuals in their struggle for existence. The struggle for food, shelter and clothing resulted in certain activities which ultimately formed certain tendencies as instincts, impulses and interests which are inherited by each individual and transmitted from generation to generation." These inherited tendencies are not as fixed and definite in human individuals as they are in the animals. These tendencies are general urges which prompt the individual to respond to the various stimuli present in the environment. It is through the play of these tendencies or general urges that human intelligence has developed to its present level. Therefore, Dewey thinks that the natural play of these tendencies should be considered as the starting point of the educational process of the child.

Dewey was convinced of the organic relationship between the individual and the society. He wants the individual to commune not with nature alone but with his fellow-beings and to understand and appreciate their achievements. The environment of the individual is both natural and human. He should value the one as much as the other. The self, he believes, cannot grow in solitude. Nor can it grow in the mere contact with nature. For the growth of man, it is essential that he should live with the rest of mankind. This is a natural condition. The make-up of individual includes reflections of multitude of man ; his thoughts are their thoughts. Just as the knowledge of the physical world has led man to control the physical world to some extent, similarly the understanding of social inter-relationship brings about maximum human development.

DEWEY'S PHILOSOPHY OF EDUCATION

Dewey defines education as the "Development of all those capacities in the individual which will enable him to control his environment and fulfill his possibilities." It is a process that begins with the very birth of the child, and goes on throughout the whole life. It is a process which has two sides one psychological and the other sociological. Of these two, the psychological is the basis.

The Psychological Factor in Education

Dewey regards the child as the core of the whole educational process. He says, "Education must begin with a psychological insight into the child's capacities, interests and habits. We must know what they mean. They must be translated into terms of their social equivalents—into terms of what they are capable of in the way of social service." Dewey looks at the child's capacities and interests in a social context, thinking that it is in the social context alone that they can be developed. Dewey speaks of four instincts or fundamental interests of the child, viz., (i) the interest in conversation, (ii) the interest in inquiry or finding out things, (iii) the interest in construction, (iv) the interest in artistic expression.

Dewey thinks that the child's interest in conversation is the greatest of all educational resources. But all these four interests may be accepted as the basis of the curriculum of the school, because these represent the great racial activities, such as communicating each other's thoughts procuring food, obtaining shelter, and making clothing. Dewey believes that if education is conducted on these lines, the child will develop into a healthy personality and will acquire such traits as will help him in reconstructing new experiences.

The Social Factor in Education

Dewey cannot conceive of an individual apart from the society. To him, both the individual and the society exist at the same time.

It is only by living in a society that the individual becomes human and acquires the necessary modes of responses and conduct which make him an individual. If the individual is dependent upon society, the society, too, is an organic unity of individuals. The activities of the individual centre round social inter-course, relations and interactions. Whereas, Dewey starts with psychological basis—child's instincts and innate powers, the sociological side to him is equally important, perhaps more. The knowledge of the social conditions is essential for the proper appraisal and assessment of the child's powers. "All education proceeds by the participation of the individual in the social consciousness of the race." The social consciousness continually shapes and modifies the individual's powers and personality. Dewey maintains that the child is to live in and for the society to which he belongs, hence the stimulation of the child's powers, through the social medium, constitutes true education. The social medium is educative because it affects every fibre of one's character and mind, forms habits of language and enlarges vocabulary, cultivates social manners and conduces to good taste and aesthetic appreciation. At birth, the child's capabilities are undeveloped. They are developed as he begins to take increasingly greater interest in home and other social activities. In the beginning, the activities of the child are self-centred. Therefore, he must be helped to realise the ends and purposes of society. For this, it is necessary to organise the school for co-operative activities. Thus, Dewey has emphasised the need of recognising the school programme for promoting community work. This idea of socialisation is Dewey's educational contribution of the highest importance.

Dewey's Concept of the Aims of Education

Dewey does not believe in an 'ultimate aim of education'. In his 'Democracy and Education' writing on education he says, "It has all the time an immediate end, and so far as activity is educative, it reaches that end—the direct transformation of the quality of experience. Infancy, youth, adult life—all stand on the same educative level in the sense that what is really learned at any and every stage of experience constitutes the value of that experience..." Thus, Dewey finds the aim of education in the process itself. The aim of education is not to reach any pre-fixed final goal. In fact, the aim is the immediate end that attracts and engages the learner's attention. Education is to re-make experience. Hence, it always tends to move further towards new activities and reorganisation of experience. As Dewey says, "The process of education is a continuous process of adjustment, having as its aim at every stage an added capacity of growth. "The individual has always to re-adjust himself to the environment. So long as such process of re-adjustment is continued, education goes on. Since, this re-adjustment never stops, and the individual is always in the process of learning things, education never stops in life. Evidently, no such final goal or end of education can be conceived at which education can be considered to have been completed. Furthermore, the education is not to be determined by the teacher. It is the child himself who has to determine or choose his own aim.

Dewey emphasises that education is life itself, and not preparation for life. A remote aim of education can not be appealing to the child. It is only an immediate aim that can be interesting to him. The whole process of education becomes discouraging to the child, if he is required to put in efforts for an aim which is not immediate, pertaining to his felt need. The child lives in the present. The future is meaningless to him. Hence, it is absurd to expect him to do things for some future preparation. As the child lives in the present, the educative process will be naturally based on the present needs and interests of the child.

Functions of Education

Discussing the functions of education, Dewey holds that education is a necessity of life. It is needed for living a socially desirable life. It is that power which bridges the gulf between the innate nature of the immature child and the social standards and demands made upon him. It gives him social consciousness through the school as a special environment. The school as a special environment has been deliberately planned with a view to realising some social purpose. The ordinary environment of the child is too complex to be assimilated properly or to influence the mental and moral disposition of the child. The school will simplify this environment by eliminating its unworthy features and "Will co-ordinate the diverse influences of the various social environments into which the child enters—family, street, workshop, religious associations etc." The school as a special environment will cultivate, within the young, the attitudes and dispositions which are necessary for a continuous and progressive life in society.

Not only does education perform the social function through the school as a special environment, it directs, guides and controls the inborn propensities of the child. These propensities have to be directed in socially desirable channels or sublimated. The undesirable expressions of these innate propensities have to be controlled. But this control or restraint, according to Dewey, should not be alien to the child's nature; it should not amount to repression.

Education helps the child in the process of growth by enabling him to form habits and sentiments wherewith the child can control his environment and his native impulses. This growth is not a accretion or storage of ideas from without, it is unfolding of the innate powers from within. Thus, education is, as Dewey says, growth and all one with growing. This is so because the child is an ever-growing and changing personality.

Besides these functions, education constantly re-organises or reconstructs the human experience. It preserves that much of the experience which is valuable and re-weaves it in the light of present needs and demands. This function of re-weaving and re-vitalising the social fabric or heritage is performed through special agencies like the school. The child who is an ever-growing individual, too, takes part in this function of re-construction. The growing child selects and reorganises his cultural heritage according to his own needs in a changing and new world. It is for this reason that his creativity needs to be encouraged.

Dewey's Conception of an Ideal School

Dewey regards school as an institution, essential to social life. To him school is an absolute social necessity. The school is not a place where some knowledge is imparted and an attempt is made to develop certain habits in children. For Dewey, the school is a place where the child learns by his own experiences. At the school the child will make many experiments in life, in order to learn how his life is directly dependent on the continued growth of the society. As a social institution, the school will try to develop a social consciousness in the child. So that he may be able to derive the maximum benefit from what the society has to offer him. The school should try to develop in the child powers which he can use for furthering the ends of the society as a whole.

The school is to be a representative of the society outside it. As already mentioned in a different context. According to Dewey, "The school is to be a reflection of the larger society outside its walls, in which life can be learnt by living. But it is to be a purified, simplified and better balanced society".

Dewey's ideal school will not cut the child off from the home. It will gradually grow out of the home life. It will preserve, continue and rebuild the activities with which the child is familiar in the home. It should reflect the ideal home and its conditions, should re-touch them if needed, in order to give them more perfect form and scientific garb. Dewey would like his school to be a genuine community like the family where the pupils are engaged in common pursuits and educative experiences. "The school, in fact, should be an enlarged family, in which discipline the child receives more or less accidentally at home is continued in a more perfect form with better equipment and more scientific guidance."

Dewey's school will be a place where moral education is provided not in the form of separate lessons, but through its social and conjoint activities. He thinks that "the best and deepest moral training is precisely that which one gets through having to enter into proper relations with other in a unity of work and thought."

The school should try to make the society conscious of its own needs, by giving the people a clearer conception of the needs and problems of the modern life. As such, the school is to provide ideals in the light of which these needs will be determined. But these ideals will not be divorced from the life of the community; they will arise out of it.

The Place of the Teacher

What is the place of the teacher in the ideal school? Dewey has answered this question in his own way. Unlike Rousseau, Dewey gives an important place to him. He is a social servant whose duty is to maintain a proper social order and to see that the children grow in a social atmosphere. The teacher is not to impose his personality or his ideology on the child. His business is to select the influences which should enrich the child's experience and to help him in properly reacting and responding to such influences. Even in the matters of discipline, he is to simply guide the child on the basis of his richer experience and riper wisdom.

Dewey's Conception of the Curriculum

We may infer from the above account that Dewey has no sympathy with the traditional curriculum. Dewey does not like the division of knowledge into isolated branches. He says that "We violate the child's nature and render difficult the best ethical results, by introducing the child too abruptly to a number of special studies, of reading, writing, geography etc." To Dewey, it is the child's own activities, around which the school subjects should be organised, and not around science, literature, history or geography. It is with the 'activities' that the child has participated in the home that the school should begin its work, and not with the teaching of reading, writing and arithmetic Dewey says, "The beginning is made with child's expressive activities in dealing with the fundamental social material—housing (carpentry); clothing (sewing); food (cooking); these direct modes of expression... bring out the factors of social communication—speech, writing, reading, drawing, modeling etc." Thus, the curriculum in the primary school should be organised according to the fourfold interests of the child—in conversation, inquiry, construction and artistic expression.

According to Dewey, the curriculum should consist of "Educative experiences and problems". The aim is to enrich the experiences already gained by him. The problems should be so organised as to inspire the pupil to add to the existing knowledge and ideas. It should be noted that Dewey uses the word 'educative experiences' in a special sense. According to Dewey, only those experiences are educative which pay due regard to the natural inclinations of the child in the context of the social, political, physical and economic conditions of the community. According to him, "An educative experience is creative and leads to further experience. It has the power of modifying the experiences and the modification thus effected, affects the subsequent experiences." An educative experience subordinates books teachers and apparatus to the natural inclinations of the pupil and takes into consideration the social, economic, political, physical and occupational conditions of the community.

Besides laying down the general principles of the choice of subject, in the school, Dewey has advised us as to how to organise the curriculum. He suggests that it develops critical discrimination and the ability to reason. But this will be possible, Dewey says, if different subjects are taken from the materials of day to day life, the subject-matter of each subject links the present with the past and they are taught in such a away that their usefulness in the immediate present is emphasised. Moreover, different subjects should be naturally correlated and, therefore, they should not be presented as distinct studies, but as types of the process by which society keeps itself going.

Dewey's Conception of the Methods of Teaching

Dewey's views on method of teaching are in line with his pragmatic philosophy. He emphasises that direct experience is the basis of all method. To him, knowledge should arise from concrete and meaningful situations. Hence, spontaneous activities of the children should provide the natural condition for the growth of knowledge. This means that learning should be the result of doing. Nothing should be learnt directly for its own sake. According to Dewey, the method of teaching should be based on the principles of learning by doing, activity, purpose and connection with the life of the child. It is to integrate the various subjects, his activities and experiences. Kilpatrick, one of the most famous of Dewey's followers, is of the opinion that Dewey had in mind the following rules when he conceived of the project technique, which was later on developed into Project Method by the former.

1. The pupils must propose what they actually wish to do.

2. They should be allowed to do only those things which build up certain attitudes.

3. All learning should be done only, if it is necessary for what the pupils have actually proposed.

4. What the pupils are allowed to do, should be guided so as to enrich the subsequent stream of experience.

Thus, the Project Method of teaching is different from the method employed in traditional schools. It utilises the child's interests for teaching the various subjects. In the Project Method the child's interests and purposes are the important things, and the various subjects are regarded merely as means for satisfying those interests and purposes.

Dewey's Conception of Discipline

Dewey believes that discipline should be social through and through. The natural impulses of the child ought to be directed and disciplined through the co-operative or conjoint activities of the school. "Out of doing things that are to produce results, and out of doing in a social and co-operative way, there is born a discipline of its own kind and type." It is such a discipline that will lead to character training, not the discipline that is the result of force, imposition or authoritative instruction. Dewey believed that the child's activities—intellectual, social, moral and physical, are disciplinary in their effects if they are carried out in co-operation with others and are directed towards the realisation of certain purposes. Discipline is inherent in the relation of members of the school society in pursuit of common ends.

The teacher's duty is to provide the right type of physical environment that will enrich the child's experience and will direct his activities in a co-operative manner. The individual will thus develop social attitudes, social interests and social habits. Even his will be socialised. Thus, according to Dewey, the main purpose of school discipline is the cultivation in the pupils of social attitudes, habits and ideals of conduct through the conjoint activities of the school, which has been organised as a community.

DEWEY'S CONCEPTION OF DEMOCRACY IN EDUCATION

According to Dewey, democracy means "Equality of opportunity for every one; it means freeing intelligence for independent effectiveness, the emancipation of the mind as an individual organism to do its own work." It does not simply mean freedom of action. The freedom of action must be preceded by freedom of thought.

Dewey wants that education should reflect democratic principles on all sides. Teachers, in a democratic system of education, will have some regular say in matters of school organisation, selection of text books and others. The school authorities, managers and supervisors are not expected to dictate to them in determination of educational methods. Dewey deprecates the minute and close supervision which is exercised on the teacher at present. This will mean restriction of his intelligence and imprisonment of his spirit. It is contended by some critics that teachers, on account of their incompetence and efficiency, should not be given such powers. Dewey characterises such an injunction as undemocratic.

Dewey disapproves of a system of education which subjects the mind of the child to outside and ready-made material. A democratic system will aim at the development of moral, self-directing individuality. It will encourage his emotional as well as intellectual freedom by providing outlets for his growing intelligence. It will not train children for docility or obedience, but they will be trained to think, to act and to develop qualities of initiative, independence and resourcefulness—qualities of an intelligent citizen in a democracy.

Dewey advocates the employment of methods that give much scope to the child's participation in the process of learning and those which emphasise the child's view point. The curriculum will undergo change and will stress the subjects that are vocational in character. It is these subjects that will conduce to individual efficiency so necessary for good citizenship in a democracy. Discipline in a democratic system of education will be free and through self-government in the school.

DEWEY'S CRITICISM

Although Dewey's views on educational principles were enthusiastically received, they were also subjected to criticism on the following grounds:

1. Difficulties of not accepting truth to be permanent: Pragmatist philosophy does not treat truth as permanent and objective. Instead as Dewey explains, all truth is relative to time and space. No philosophy is always true or correct. It has its utility only in a particular set of circumstances. And utility is the final criterion of truth. In actual practice, of course, Dewey's philosophy is fairly useful, but when his own principle are applied to his own theories, the latter also become relative to time and space and thus have only a limited utility. Hence, the principles of pragmatism itself becomes only relatively true because it does not accept truth as something permanent.

2. Materialistic bias: Pragmatism was born out of reaction to idealism, and consequently it manifests a distinctly materialistic bias, in contradiction of the spiritual bias of idealist philosophy. At the same time, Dewey wants to realise democratic ideals of freedom, equality and fraternity through education. But it is difficult to understand how this can be done unless he accepts an idealistic basis for his system of education. If worldy success is the only criterion of truth, few if any people will concern themselves with moral superiority, since the latter has no obvious relationship with material success.

3. Absence of any aim of education: The achievement of democratic ideals through education seems to be implicit in Dewey's educational philosophy, because he rarely ascribes particular aim to education in explicit terms. For him, education is life itself, and it is not possible to determine any objective for it. Most scholars disagree with this opinion because they believe that education can progress only when it has some definite aim and objective. There is always some definite purpose in sending the educand to school. And even though school resembles society in many ways, it has a distinct existence within the larger framework of society. Hence, the aims of education must be defined.

4. Excessive emphasis upon individual differences: Modern educational psychology accepts that the curriculum of education must take into account the individual differences of children and that children must be educated according to their individual and unique interests and inclinations both in respect of curriculum and also of the method of teaching. While in theory this is quite acceptable, any attempts to apply it in practice lead to immediate complications. It is almost, if not completely impossible to provide a separate educational plan for every individual child in a school. It is for this reason that all schools now a day's provide a uniform pattern of education imparted in the same manner. Besides, the teacher may have to educate the educand in a subject in which the latter is not at all interested. Thus, it is not possible to eliminate many complex and difficult subjects from the curriculum only because the student is not interested in them.

5. Limitations of learning through doing: There is no doubt that the child should learn by actually doing things, as Dewey suggested yet the theory has its limitations. Many facts known to an individual are acquired from another person. It is almost impossible for one individual to experience every fact known to him. Thus, the educand should try also to benefit from the experience of his teacher, educator and colleagues. The educator must also supplement the educand's efforts at self-education with guidance and communication of his own experience.

DEWEY'S IMPACT ON MODERN EDUCATION

Many of Dewey's ideas have had great impact on modern education. Some important facts in this connection are:

1. Impact on the aims of education: Nowadays, one of the important aims of education is teaching of democratic values. Dewey insisted on developing social qualities in the child. In modern schools these aims of education have been accepted as valid.

2. Impact on educational methods: The greatest impact of Dewey's ideas is seen in the method of education in more recent times. Dewey suggested that education should be based on the child's own experience, and also that the method of teaching should vary according to the interests and inclinations of each individual child. These ideas influenced modern teaching techniques and led to active teaching in schools. One such school is the Activity School. The project method is also a result of Dewey's ideas. Even in the other schools, attention is paid to the principles of child psychology which guide the educator in creating an atmosphere suitable for developing social consciousness in the educand.

3. Impact on curriculum: The impact of Dewey's ideas on the subject of curriculum led to the introduction of manual skill subjects into modern curriculum. Social importance is now being attached to various kinds of games, objects, the use of certain tools and implements, etc. In selecting the subjects to be taught, attention is now paid to the individual interests and abilities of the child.

4. Impact on discipline: As a result of Dewey's theorising on the subject of discipline, now the educand is entrusted with much of the work done in the school. In this manner the educand is trained in self-control and democratic citizenship. Apart from this, once the educand has to face responsibility, he is compelled to think scientifically and reason out things for himself.

5. Universal education: Dewey's thinking and ideal also led to faith in universal and compulsory education. Education aims at the development of personality. Hence every individual must be given the opportunity to develop his personality through education. The current stress on the scientific and social tendency owes much to Dewey's influence. He pointed out that education was a social necessity, in that it was not merely a preparation for life, but life itself. It aimed at the development of both the individual as well as society. This leads to the comprehensive development of the individual.

DEWEY'S CONTRIBUTION

Dewey was a great educationist and a great philosopher. He is more for change than for permanence, more for practice than for theory, more for experimental enquiry than for speculation, more for contemplation. One could remark that Dewey underestimated the action than for significance of ideas. Ideas are more powerful and lasting than actions, the influence of which is limited to a particular time and place.

But whatever the limitations of his philosophy or the way of trying to do without philosophy, we cannot but be grateful to Dewey for his service to education. He emphasised the importance of including activity in education. In fact, he wished activity to be made the medium of all teaching and learning. His contribution to the 'activity movement' in education can never be exaggerated. He stressed learning by doing.

Dewey emphasised the necessity of relating education with the practical life of the child, for educating him successfully. He thus stressed the psychological point of view in education. At the same time, he did not fail to emphasise the social sanctions that govern education. He rightly stressed that education is intended to be a means of preserving, transmitting and advancing the culture of the community, and realising its standards and ideals. For the fusion of these two stand points in education, we owe the credit to Dewey.

By denying the existence of any eternal and absolute values, and characterising all values as man–made, Dewey emphasised the need for developing the creative powers of the children. The credit of emphasising the development of the creative powers of the educand, goes to Dewey.

One of the gifts of Dewey is the Project Method. In the Project Method the child's interests and purposes are the important things, and the various subjects are regarded merely as means for satisfying these interests and purposes.

Dewey has rightly stressed the need for devising education in such a manner that it may train the pupils in co-operative activities and democratic living in their community. Training for citizenship forms an integral part of education, and training for citizenship essentially involves training for a vocation.

CONCLUSION

To sum up, we can say that Dewey challenged the old static cold-storage ideal of knowledge; he brought education more into accord with the activities of the present day life. Rusk remarks, "The general principle underlying the developments in his philosophy and his applications of these in education appears to be that both philosophy and education should reflect the main currents of contemporary thought and incorporate the techniques that have so signally contributed to modern, industrial and social progress." In the words of Russell, Dewey has an outlook which is in harmony with the age of industrialism and collective enterprise.

14

Fredrick August Froebel (1782-1852)

By reason of irregular training, Froebel neither adopted nor developed a consistent philosophic attitude. As he himself explains in a letter to Kraus, he continued 'without ceasing to systematise, symbolise, idealise, realise and recognise identities, and analogies amongst all facts and phenomena, all problems, expressions, and formulae; and in this way, life with all varied phenomena and activities become, more and more free from contradictions, more harmonious, simple and clear, and more recognisable as a part of the life universal.

Froebel follows Rousseau when he wants to take shelter in 'nature' but with a different motive. While, Rousseau considers nature as a great teacher, Froebel wants that man should become intimate with it, not so much with reference to the outer forms of her phenomena as with reference to the spirit of God that lives in her and rules over her.

FROEBEL'S GENERAL PHILOSOPHY

Froebel's philosophy is a philosophy of Absolute Idealism. He assigns high place to Spiritual Education and the inherent worth of the individual. The key-point in his philosophy is that there is a fundamental unity of existence of nature and man in the absolute which is Self-conscious Spirit. He believes that the purpose of all existence is to reveal God.

The two great ideals that he preached are "Unity in Diversity", and "His Theory of Development."

Unity in Diversity

Froebel views the whole universe as a unity emanating from the Absolute or God. He remarks, "In all things there lives and reigns an eternal law. This all-controlling law is necessarily based on all pervading, energetic, living, self-conscious and hence eternal unity. This unity is God. All things have come from the Divine Unity (God), they have their origin in the Divine Unity. The Divine affluence that lives in each thing is the essence of each thing." Within this all-inclusive unity, Froebel includes every existing thing viz. man, animal, plant, inanimate object and human society. Each one of these is an individual and also a unity. All of them are bound into one great cosmic unity, which may be called God or a Spiritual Being. He says that "In everything there works and stirs one life, because to all, one God has given life. Every creature, every object is matter informed by spirit... God is the pre-supposition, the condition of their existence. Without God they would not exist. God is the one ground of all things. God is the all comprehending, the all sustaining. God is the essential nature, the meaning of the world".

From this follows his principle that there is unity in man, nature and God. "Nature and man," seem to him "Mutually explaining each other through all their numberless various stages of development." Man should become conscious of the Absolute Unity of the universe. He should also know the diversity of things and appearances which are perpetually unfolding themselves within that unity. The varied phenomena in man's life, work, thought, and position, he believes, can be summed up in the unity of man's existence. Therefore, the purpose of education, according to him is to expand the life of the individual until it should comprehend this existence.

Theory of Development

His theory of development is very clear and consistent. Froebel says that 'there is an Absolute goal towards which all things are growing'. This Absolute is present but only implicitly in every existing thing. Development or growth of anything consists in making this Absolute explicit by a gradual unfolding process. "The absolute goal", he says, "is realised through the presentation of symbols which represent the various aspects of the Absolute. Without such symbols the conception of the Absolute is not possible". Those symbols, he calls 'gifts', a reference to which would be made later

His doctrine of development is that everything develops according to a universal or creative force. May be animal, vegetable or mineral, they have a drive to develop along those lines suited to their characteristics. "By development" he does not mean, "an increase in bulk or quantity (though it may include this), but an increase in complexity or structure, an improvement in power, skill and variety in the performance of natural function". To him, "A thing appears fully developed when its internal organisation is perfect in every detail and when it can perform all its natural actions or functions perfectly".

Applying the theory of development to mind, he says, that mind is developed when it has the power, skill and variety in dealing with knowledge and putting knowledge to all its natural uses. To Froebel mental growth is organic. In order to make a plant grow, we induce it to become active in its own natural way. We may seek shortening the duration of time needed for its growth, but we have to stimulate the plant's own activity. The activity of a thing's own self is self-activity. Knowing, feeling and willing are the three major activities of the mind. Exercises directed towards mental development must be in complete accord with the process of knowing, feeling and willing, and at the same time proportionately balanced according to their strength. We find the result better, if the activity is that of the whole mind.

To Froebel, the soul itself is an activity to be active is inherent in our nature. With our birth, we bring certain tendencies which always prompt us to action. Thus, mind is a purposive activity. Froebel believes that mind is a unity, just as life is also a unity. Mind has no independent faculties. All its powers and forces are organically related like branches and leaves of a tree. For sound mental growth of the child, Froebel suggests that there should be no gulf between home and school. The influences of the two should be organically connected. Otherwise, the purpose of education is sure to be defeated.

Froebel contends that the unity between the various stages of mental growth—Infancy, Childhood, Youth, Manhood—should not be lost sight of, otherwise education would be of no avail. There should be a connection between the various activities of the mind and the various aspects of life. Froebel calls this relation between the two "inter-connectedness." The realisation of this inter-connectedness should constitute one great aim of education.

FROEBEL'S PHILOSOPHY OF EDUCATION

Froebel's philosophy of education is the direct outcome of his general philosophy.

Let us now discuss his Educational Philosophy:

His Concept and Aims of Education

Education, he says, is a development by which the individual realises that he is one unit of the all-encompassing unity. It is a development by which his life broadens, until it has related itself to nature, until it enters sympathetically into all activities of society; until it participates in the achievements of the race and aspiration of humanity. "Education, he advocates, is but the realisation of the evolutionary process in its highest stage, which the individual should attain. Such development takes place "In accordance with eternal, self-governed and self-developing laws. Thus, he believes that development proceeds through the divine self. The aim of education should be that the child should develop according to his natural and systematic course of development. Education has failed, if it has neglected or prevented the development of certain aspects of the child's nature or if it has caused 'the distortion of originally good human powers and tendencies by arbitrary interference. If the child's nature has somehow been marred, it should be redirected into the original course of development. If the child displays activities contrary to the true principle of growth, they must be recognised and corrected in order to keep the development progressing along the right lines. Thus, according to Froebel education should be a 'Controlled-Development.'

Instruction, he commends, should lead the child's spontaneous activities and native interests to some tangible expression of the knowledge. "Education seeks neither to eliminate nature, nor to leave it severely alone." It helps nature and guides it to attain higher ends.

Stages of Development in Education

Like Rousseau, Froebel, recognises in education, the stages of development and desires that each one of the stages—infancy, childhood, boyhood and youth—should be fully exploited to prepare the pupil for the succeeding stages. While in infancy, he emphasises the sensory development, in childhood his emphasis is on play. While childhood is characterised by making the internal external, in boyhood the process is reversed. Education in boyhood has to be determined by environment and not by endowment as in childhood. Feeling now gives way to thought and play to instruction. It is now to be curriculum-centred and not child-centred. The characteristic activity of childhood is play, but that of boyhood should be work. The child takes interest in the process, the boy takes interest in the product. The range of the pupil's environment in boyhood is considerably widened. This provides him with new patterns of activities in the shape of vocational occupations to be imitated and learnt through training. Of course, this work is not those of adults. Learning of some vocation should still be dominated by the spirit of play and not work. The only difference between the two stages is that in childhood the pupil intended domestic between activities, in boyhood he imitates neighbourhood occupations. His activities, now, are Projects—practical problems, demanding co-operative effort and giving intellectual and moral training.

The Curriculum

All-round development being his aim, of education, Froebel wants that the curriculum at the boyhood stage should consist of four main divisions:

(a) Religion: Religion he says should be the basis of all education. No other knowledge is possible without it.

(b) Natural Science: Nature, he has often repeated, is the manifestation of God. Its study will mean the contemplation of outer facts, while religion requires inner contemplation. Therefore, both are necessary to have a complete man. Insight into nature reveals the laws that govern human life. This creates a sense of the reign of law. "From every object of nature and life there is a way to God." In this study of Natural Science, he also emphasises the importance of Mathematics. In his opinion this subjects is a connecting link between the mind of man and the natural world. "Mind and Mathematics", he says, "are inseparable as the soul and religion".

(c) Languages: Languages help in establishing the inner living connection among the diversities of thing and thus complete the work of education.

(d) Expressional Work: Froebel believes that there is need for the expression of the soul in outward forms. This expression may take the form of singing, drawing, painting and modeling. The school does not aim at aim at "Making each pupil an artist in some one or all of the arts but to secure to each human being full and all-sided development".

Importance of Play: Play of childhood is of paramount importance. It is nature's device for directing the growth of the child according to the social pattern. Childhood is a period of play and not of work. "Play", says, Froebel "is the highest phase of child-development of human development at this period; for it is self-active representation of the inner impulse. Play is the purest, most spiritual activity of man at this stage... It gives, therefore, joy, freedom, contentment, inner and outer rest, peace with the world. It holds the source of all that is good."

Play, if it is to have any educative value, should not be motivated by any ulterior purpose. However it need to be organised and controlled by suitable materials in order to harmonies the feelings and the activities of the children while engaged in activities. "Without rational conscious guidance", Froebel says, "Childish activity degenerates into aimless play instead of preparing for those tasks of life for which it is destined".

Value of Hand-Work: According to Froebel all constructive work should be the beginning and the end of the educational process. Rousseau recognises industrial training on social and economic grounds. Pestalozzi introduced manual activities for developing sense perception. Frobel emphasises the manual and industrial training because, it gives expression to some of the most dominant urges of the childs. All constructive work, he believes manifests outwardly what the child feels inwardly. Such manifestation of ideas is the basis of the higher power of expressing the intellectual, moral and spiritual life in action.

Nature Study: Similarly, he commends the introduction of the Nature-study in the school curriculum. By prescribing this study he is the least concerned with the facts about nature. He desires that the child should "Have moral improvement religious-uplift and spiritual-insight" by coming into contact with nature. Nature-study affords the child opportunities for varies activity. It suggests material for reading, 'language work' constructive work and number work. He does not want nature to be analysed and dissected. He wants to study nature as life the plant as development, the animal as acting, and the organ as functioning.

FROEBEL'S THEORY AND PRACTICE OF KINDERGARTEN

Froebel, in his conversation with the under-training at Burg-dorf, learnt that the pre-school age of the children was entirely neglected. His conception of harmonious development led him to attach great importance to early years and his work.

"The Education of the man", chiefly deals with the education of children. It became obvious to him that all school education was yet without a proper initial foundation and he realised that until the education of nursery years was reformed nothing solid and substantial could be achieved. It was at Burg-dorf that he bagan to think over the training of children and prepared for them a gradual course of exercises, modeled on the games in which the children were interested.

Chief Charactestics of Kindergarten

The Chief Characteristic of Frobel's Kindergarten are discussed below:

1. Self-activity.
2. Creativeness.
3. Social participation.

1. Self activity: By self activity, Frobel means that the child should not be forced to indulge in any activity which is suggested by parents or teachers, but in those whereby he can satisfy his own impulses and fulfill his desires. Education, he believes is a process of individual growth which is directed by inner forces in the child. This growth differs from that of a plant, as the child has perception and reason. He can be made conscious of the working of God within him. Froebel believes that the divine spirit reveals itself in the activities of the child, if their activities are spontaneous.

The teacher should provide appropriate experiences for such purpose. But while directing the process he must follow nature; never thwart it for he is but nature's assistant. "Education" says, Froebel should not be prescriptive categorical or interfering. It should provide for free self-activity and self determination on the part of man—the being created for freedom in the image of God.

Self-activity arises out of one's own interests and is sustained by one's own power. It alone can lead to the evolution of mind and can secure the aim of education it is therefore essential that all processors of educational instruction must originate with the interests of the child. The child must be stimulated to achieve certain ends through spontaneous activities if they are properly directed and influenced by the teacher. Fuller harmony between the inner and outer, between the thought and the external world cannot be created, if the child is not aided by the teacher.

Self-activity manifests in the child a desire to enter into life around it 'the desire to help, to find out, to discover and to participate in the affair of daily life. Froebel believes that there is no conflict between theory and practice and no discrepancy between ideas professed and the actions performed.

2. Creativeness: With self-activities is connected Froebel's principle of 'creativeness'. Through creativeness, new forms and combinations are made and expression is given to new images and ideas. He says, "plastic material representation in life and through doing, united with thought and speech, is by far more developing and cultivating than the merely verbal representation of ideas". "Man", he says, "is by nature an active and dynamic being". He is not a receptive and passive observer of events. He must create something. Thus, according to Froebel, the result of education consists in what the child gives out from within himself. It does not consist in what the child learns from outside. Each child has a tendency to make new forms and combinations which suggest the new ideas and images arising in him. The child produces something which may appeal to the adult as absurd and meaningless. But the divine principle is active in the child as well as the adult. So whatever he produces follows from some ideas connected with his creative urge. Thus, Froebel concludes that the best development of self-activity is essentially creative. He devotes special attention to this attribute of creativeness in the child.

3. Social Participation: Whereas Rousseau advocates isolated and un-social education for 'Emile', Froebel lays great emphasis on the social participation. He believes that increasing self-realisation or individualisation through self-activity comes through a process of socialisation. The social instant being a primary instinct of man, the individual can be truly educated only in the company of other human beings. Man's life is bound up with participation in institutional life. The home, the school, the church, the vocation, the state—all are the medium for individual activity and a means of social control. "The school", says Froebel, "is an association for the child, wherein he discovers in a, simplified and idealised form the relations of society". It is a means of social progress and individual development. Similarly in the society a child receives the development and also prepares for the future life. Through imitation of co-operative activities in play, he obtains not only physical but also intellectual and moral training. His growth, therefore, should be in harmony with the unity and purpose of humanity to which he belongs.

A NEW METHOD OF TEACHING

According to Froebel the child expresses his feelings and ideals through singing, gestures and constructing objects. He, accordingly, believe that everything to be taught to the child must be expressed to him through singing, gestures and construction. This is a unique device which Froebel most remarkably invented. He recommends that history should be taught through dramatisation or through songs. Froebel aims at stimulating the child's imagination and thought by placing concrete things before him.

However, the teacher should be very careful in the selection of songs, games and pictures, because the child feels very much amused by them and tries to express himself while he is in their association. Froebel does not regard songs, gestures and construction as isolated means to educate the child. He thinks of them as three co-ordinate forms of expression in the child. He saw an organic relation between them. The whole process becomes one organic whole. For example, when the story is told or read, it is first expressed in song, then it is dramatised in movements and gestures and finally it is illustrated by constructive work from blocks, paper, clay or other material. In this way ideas are given, "Thought stimulated, the imagination verified, the hands and eyes trained, the muscles co-ordinated and the moral nature strengthened." In the Kindergarten all efforts are put into concrete objective forms. The higher motives and, sentiments' are aroused.

Gifts and Occupations

Gifts and occupations are the other means which Froebel used in the Kindergarten system. The gifts suggest to the child some forms of activity. They are arranged in an order to be determined by the principle of development. Occupations are the activities suggested by the gifts. The very order and arrangement of the gifts lead the child from the activities and thoughts of one stage to those of another.

The First Gift: The first gift consists of a box of six woollen balls of different colours. The child is to roll them about in play. Rolling is the occupation. These woollen balls are meant to give to the child an idea of colour particular stuff, form, motion and direction.

The Second Gift: In the second gift there are a cube, a sphere and a cylinder of hard wood. In occupation with these things the child marks the difference between the movements of the different articles. He sees that the cube is stable and the sphere is unstable. He also notices that the cylinder is stable in certain positions and unstable in others. Thus, the cylinder is noticed as possessing the quality of both the cube and the sphere. It is a concrete example of harmony of two opposite things in one.

The Third Gift: In the third gift there is a large wooden cube divided into eight equal parts. These cubes are meant to make the children understand the relation of part with the whole. From these cubes the child may make a number of objects such as chairs, tables, benches, and stairs etc.

The Other Gifts: Among the other gifts are included sticks and rings. While playing with these gifts the child gets the ideas of lines, surface points and their inter-connections. The child has to engage himself in making a number of constructions with papers, sand, clay, wood and other materials.

The Role of the Teacher

In the Kindergarten one should not think that the teacher is to remain entirely passive. As a matter of fact, his responsibility is not lessened in any way. While the children are offered gifts, the teacher has to suggest the occupation connected with them. He has to demonstrate certain activities to them.

Froebel's socialistic and liberalising tendencies were not liked by governmental authorities during his days and the Kindergarten system of education was banned.

THE ESTABLISHMENT OF KINDERGARTEN

Froebel developed the later part of his life to founding the Kindergarten on which his fame mainly rests.

The name 'Kindergarten' came to Froebel one spring day in 1840 as with some friends he was proceeding from Keilhau to Blankenburg when from a hill he saw the valley of the Rinne, a tributary of the Saale, stretching out before him like a great garden and exclaimed, "I have found it. Kindergarten shall the name be". It was not till 1843 that institution of the Kindergarten, as we now know it, was founded, the date usually given is 1840.

'Froebel considered' childhood as the most important stage of the total development of man and humanity'. In his Reminiscences he gives his reason thus: "The earliest age is the most important one for education, because the beginning decides the manner of progress and the end. If national order is to be recognised in later years as a benefit, childhood must first be accustomed to law and order, and therein find means of freedom". For this stage of childhood Froebel elaborated his gifts, the first being the ball, the second the sphere, the cube and the cylinder.

Gifts and Occupations

In his gift Froebel personifies playthings and assumes that children will be able to appreciate the symbolism involved. He also believed that the quasi-philosophic conceptions which underlie the games will impress themselves on the child's mind and determine his attitude to life. He was obsessed with his philosophical formulae that his psychological insight cannot save him from such absurdities as assuming that the child when dealing with the second gift, that is, during the second half of the first year of his life, has some dim perception of the nature and destiny of man. In his account of the same play, he affirms: man himself "in play, even as a child, by play should perceive within and without how from unity proceed manifoldness, plurality, and totality, and how plurality and manifoldness finally are found again in and resolve themselves into unity and should find this out in life." In reviewing the first plays he observes: "In and by means of the ball (as an object resting in itself, easily movable, especially elastic, bright, and warm) the child perceives his life, his power, his activity, and that of his senses, at the first stage of his consciousness, in their unity and thus exercises them... The ball is therefore to the child a representative or a means of perception of a single effect caused by a single power. The sphere is to the child the representative of every isolated simple unity; the child gets a hint in the sphere of the manifoldness as still abiding in unity. The cube is to the child the representative of each continually developing manifold body. The child has an intimation in it of the unity which lies at the foundations of all manifoldness, and from which the latter proceeds. In sphere and cube, considered in comparison with each other, is presented in outward view to the child the resemblance between opposites which is so important for his whole future life, and which he perceives everywhere around himself, and multifariously within himself".

By his methodological arrangement of the gifts and occupations Froebel founded a new type of educational institution. Although his system too readily lent itself to formalism by later generations of teachers who had not the spirit of the master, it ameliorated the lot of countless children. His theory is also open to criticism, on the ground of its excessive symbolism.

CRITICISM OF FROEBEL'S EDUCATIONAL THEORY AND PRACTICE

The following have been the chief points of criticism raised by some educators against Froebel's educational theory and practice.

1. Many critics hold that Forebel's law of evolution does not explain definitely how to proceed in the development of child's life.

2. Froebel's emphasis upon play in education cannot be acceptable because it detracts the child from serious learning.

3. Froebel's insistence upon play, constructive work, and many other subjects has under-rated the importance of true knowledge and leads to disrespect of learning.

4. Some criticise kindergarten methods because of over emphasis on form and mathematical knowledge. He represents the gifts. He sings a song connected with them and thereby tries to help the child to form appropriates ideas. The songs and pictures used by Froebel are crude and rough.

FROEBEL'S CONTRIBUTION

No educational theory has been followed more faithfully in actual practice than that of Froebel. Therefore, modern education will ever remain indebted to him. Almost all modern tendencies in education can be traced back to what Froebel stood for a century ago. We may not agree with many educational procedures outlined by Froebel, but it was he who first drew the attention of the society towards the education of very young children. The formalism of the Kindergarten system may be subject to much criticisms. But its methodical arrangement of plays and occupations invited the active interest of many who lack the spirit of the master to give 'play' a place into school.

We admit that the songs and pictures used by Froebel are crude and rough, but he never meant that they should not be improved upon. He gave direction to the teacher to modify songs and pictures suiting the needs of the time. The underlying principles of Froebel's philosophy may not be intelligible at times, but his doctrines are of immense practical use. Just as Jesuists and Comenius introduced a systematic methodology of instruction, similarly, Froebel gave a methodology of play to be applied in educational procedure.

The educational ideologies of Froebel were deeply coloured by the philosophy and scientific principles of his time. The essence of his contribution to education may be put in the words 'self-activity' and 'creativeness'. The meaning of these words is being understood more and more as time passes on. Froebel stood for the recognition of the child's individuality in the school. Now the school is being regarded as a place where the teacher should try to discover the individuality of the child and devise means to develop the same activities, such as, play, songs, and making objects, etc., have been given an importance in the learning process of the child. Needless to say that all these tendencies in modern education may be traced back to Froebel's fundamental doctrines.

Froebel's permanent contributions to education may be summarised in the following:

1. Inner self-activity directs the development of the child.

2. The natural course of evolution of the child's activities should be the main guide in the education of the child.

3. Early education should be organised around play.

4. The child's physical, mental and moral powers should be developed and harmonised through constructive activity.

5. Spontaneity and social control may be harmonised through creative activity.

6. The curriculum should be based on activities and interests of children.

7. The education of women should be regarded as essential for the development of the human race.

8. Education can ensure the future evolution of mankind.

9. Knowledge should not be considered as an end in itself. It should be evaluated in terms of the activities of the individual.

CONCLUSION

In conclusion, we may say that it was Froebel who said that education is a natural process, that the child is an organic whole in itself, is an integral part of the society and that the whole universe is an organism of which all smaller organisms are members. His faith in man's relationship with nature, his advanced scientific thought, his belief that human life should be in harmony with the universal spirit are his greatest contributions. He was the first modern educator who stood for spiritual evolution. Education to him is the process by which the race and the individual evolve to higher and higher levels. His emphasis on 'Play', 'Self-activity' and 'Creativeness' have gone a long way in changing the concepts and practice of educational theory.

To conclude this Dewey says, "Froebel's recognition of the significance of the native capacities of children, his loving attention to them, and his influence in inducing others to study them, represent perhaps the most effective single force in modern educational theory in effecting widespread acknowledgement of the idea of growth."

15

Maria Montessori (1870-1952)

Madame Maria Montessori (1870-1952) was an Italian lady-doctor who later became a world famous educationist. She entered the field of education through her interest in mentally deficient children. She studied those children very intensively and reached the conclusion that mental deficiency was due to dullness of senses and that if their senses could be properly trained, those children could acquire some knowledge. And she actually succeeded when she tried the experiment. This led her to employ that very method on educating normal children and she achieved far better results. Taus, her approach to education is scientific and rational as against that of Froebel's meta-physical. She is the originator of the 'Montessori Method'.

CONCEPT AND AIMS OF EDUCATION

According to Madam Montessori, "Education is the active help given to the normal expansion of the life of the child." She said that every child is different from others, phyically as well as mentally. Each has peculiar powers and endowments. So the child's individuality must not be crushed or suppressed through collective teaching. Each child should be paid individual attention and allowed to progress at his own pace. Education should enable each child to adjust himself to his immediate environment. She wanted that each child should develop from within and not from without. Education should guide the process of unfolding the hidden powers of the child in a way that he becomes what he is destined to become.

Educational Principles Underlying Her Philosophy

Below are given the principles underlying her philosophy:

1. Development from within: Like Froebel, she believed that education of a child is from within. "If any educational act is to be efficacious, it will be only that which tends to help towards the complete unfolding of the child's individuality. The child has a body which grows and a soul which develops." She is of the opinion that education must help in the complete unfolding of the child's individuality.

Suitable environment should be provided so that the child may grow and develop the potentialities that he has within him.

2. The doctrine of freedom or liberty: This doctrine is the outcome of the concept of education as development. Her belief is that there should be no hindrance or interference in the way of child's growth and development. She believes that the freedom is the birth-right of every individual and she advocates the spontaneous development of the child through full liberty. She does not believe in putting' restraints as she thinks that these may 'mar or stifle the innate powers of the child' She says, "The school must permit the free, natural, manifestations of the child if he is to be studied in a scientific manner."

3. No material rewards and punishments: According to her, they are incentives unnatural or forced effort and the development that comes with their help will also be unnatural. She writes, "The jockey offers a piece of sugar to his horse that he may respond to the signs given by the reins, and yet neither of these runs so superbly as the free horse of the plains."

4. Principles of individual development: In the words of John Admas, Dr. Montessori "Has rung the knell of class teaching." She believes that every child is peculiar to himself and he progresses at his own speed and rate and collective methods of teaching crush his, individuality, she treats each child as a separate individual and recommends that he should be helped and guided in a manner that helps him in his proper growth and development.

The teacher is concerned with his mental as well as his physiological development.

5. Principle of self-education or auto-education: Montessori has shifted the emphasis from teaching to learning. She believes that self-education or auto-education is the only true education. She advocates that the child should remain undisturbed by adult interference. She has devised the didactic apparatus which attracts the attention of the children, keeps them busy spontaneously, leads them to learn the powers of movements, reading, writing and arithmetic, etc.

6. Principle of sense training: Montessori asserts that our senses are the gateways of knowledge and therefore on their training and development depends the acquisition of knowledge throughout life. She pointed out that the senses are very active between the ages of one and seven and that a lot of learning takes place during this period. She advocates that the sensory training is the key to intellectual development.

7. Principle of motor efficiency or muscular training: She has also attached importance to muscular training as a part of the early education of children. She believed that muscular training facilitates other activities like writing, drawing, speaking etc. She takes, muscular activity as purely physiological in character. She stresses that running and walking etc. all depend on muscular training.

8. The teacher as the directress: She replaces the word 'teacher' by the word "directress" As she thinks that the function of the teacher is to direct and not to teach. Her motto should be. "I must diminish to let you grow."

9. No place for fairy tales: She would like to banish fairy stories from the curriculum of young children since these tend to confuse children and to hinder them in the process of adjusting themselves to the real world. The principles advocated by Dr. Montessori have Revolutionised our traditional notions about education. She has shown a real insight and feeling. She is a thinker of the first rate. The present educators must work towards completion of the ways and principles she has advocated.

Functions of a Teacher

"The Educator" says Montessori, must be as one inspired by a deep "worship of life". She thinks that a teacher should care for the child like a gardener who cares for the plant so that the natural growth of the child is properly guided and aided in the process of unfolding itself.

Knowledge of each child: The teacher should have an intimate knowledge of the mind and character of each individual. He should keep the physiological records of each child's development—his weight, height and other measurements.

The directress and not the teacher: Dr. Montessori has replaced the word 'teacher' by the word 'directress' and she thinks that the primary duty of the person in authority is to direct and not to teach. She insists that the directress should have an extensive knowledge of psychology and laboratory technique.

Doctor-cum-scientist-cum-missionary: In the words of Montessori, the Directress should be partly doctor, partly scientist and completely religious. Like a doctor she should avoid scolding or suppressing the patient in order to avoid worst situations. Like a scientist she should wait patiently for the results and should conduct experiments with her material. Like a religious lady she should be there to serve the child.

Faith in the personality of the child: She should allow the child to grow according to his/her own inner law. Her business is to provide with suitable environments. She should provide children provide for opportunities to think for themselves.

Moral qualities: "Virtues and not words are the main qualifications of the Directress." She must acquire moral alertness, patience, love and humanity. She must banish anger which is a great sin and which prevents from understanding the child. The soul of the child, which is pure and very sensitive, requires her most delicate care. Her motto should be "I must diminish to let you grow".

PRACTICAL WORKING OF MONTESSORI METHOD

Froebel called his school "Kindergarten" or "The Children's Garden." Montessori called it "The Children's House." It is the place where children are taught in homely atmosphere, which is very congenial to the development of pupil's individuality.

"The children house" is a many-roomed school with a nicely' laid-out garden. It has separate rooms for study, lunch, manual work, games amusement and rest etc. All these rooms are properly equipped and furnished. These are looked after by the children themselves, who not only clean and dust them but also lay the tables and set the chairs. The Montessori school has no fixed time-table because class is only a unit of organisation and not a unit of teaching. There are no punishments and rewards. The child sense of achievement is the only reward and self-development is the greatest pleasure. Each child is free to choose his own activities, interest and inclinations.

TYPES OF EXERCISES

For children below the age of Sixty-three types of exercises are given in a Montessori School.

Exercises for Practical Life

In Children's House, pupils are given exercises for practical life. They are taught how to wash their bands and clothes, how to sweep the rooms, dust the furniture, set the tables, clean their nails, brush their teeth, polish, their shoes and comb their hair. Exercises are also given to train children in movements, necessary for dressing and undressing themselves. It is, in fact, a training in liberty, for freedom. According to Montessori, it does not consist in having others at one's command to perform the ordinary services, but in being able to do these oneself and in being independent of others.

Montessori has also devised certain formal gymnastic exercises, which develop coordinated movements in the child. For these exercises, she has also devised special apparatus. Muscular education and training is given through walking, holding objects and hand work. Rhythmic exercises are also provided. These exercises only make children healthy but also give them training for practical life.

Exercises for Sense Training

Montessori attached more importance to sensory training than learning, thinking or reasoning. She, therefore, devised apparatus for providing exercises in sense training. The Didactic Apparatus sharpens the pupils' senses, and accelerates learning. The varied material includes blocks, cylinders, paper, cabinets, coins, tables, pencils and wools of different colours, boxes, balls, cubes, rods, and water of different temperature. This material is meant to give perception of size, form, weight, touch, hearing and colour etc. The sense of touch is developed by presenting water at different temperatures to the child. Sand-papers of graded roughness are also used for this purpose. Perception of size is developed through handling a series of wooden cylinders of varying heights and diameters. Series of blocks and rods of graded diameters are also used for this purpose. Sense of hearing is developed through boxes, containing pebbles and other sound producing material. Sense of weight is cultivated through blocks and tables of wood of varying weights. Colour sense is trained through samples of wood of different colours arranged and graded according to the depth of colour. As we have already stated under the 'Principle of Self-education', 'the procures of learning through the Didactic Apparatus, conforms to the three psychological! steps of association, recognition and recall'.

Didactic Exercise for Teaching 3'R's

After sensor training, children arc cut in reading, writing and arithmetic. In her system writing starts before reading. For this purpose, she depends upon the psychological principle of "Transfer of Training". In her own words, "Preparatory movement could be converted and reduced to a mechanism by means of repeated exercises, not in the work itself, but in that "which prepares for it."

Teaching of Writing: The procedure of teaching of writing consists of following steps:

(a) Recognition of the forms of letters: For this purpose, letters of the alphabet are cut in sand-paper and pasted on cardboard. The children are asked to pass their finger over these letters. In this way they gradually learn to manipulate a pencil. The same exercise is 'practised with closed eyes'.

(b) Learning of Phonetic Sounds: While the pupils are tracing out letters teacher tells them their sounds, which they are asked to 'reproduce'. This prepares them for reading.

(c) Control of Pen: Then the pupils are asked to place the metal frame on a piece of paper and draw a line round it with a coloured chalk. The same thing is repeated by placing the metal inset. In this way two intervening figures are produced on the paper. The intervening figure is then filled up with another piece of chalk, while making upward and downward strokes the pupils are not allowed to move their pencils or pieces of chalk, outside the outline. Thus they learn the necessary control of pen.

Teaching of Reading: About reading, Montessori says, "Reading is the interpretation of an idea, from the written signs and not merely barking a print. Until the child receives transmission of ideas from written words, he does not read." Her material for reading consists of slips of paper or cards on which words and phrases are written in bold scripts. The child is given a card, containing the name of a familiar object. He tries to utter the sounds and then repeat them faster. When the child is able to pronounce the word correctly, he is asked to place the card under the object, whose name is written on it. Similarly sentences, describing actions on expressing commands are written on paper or card-board. The child selects a card, reads it mentally and does the action contained in it.

Teaching of Arithmetic: After sufficient writing and readings, Montessori wished that children should be introduced to the four fundamental rules of arithmetic. But there is no originality in the methods of teaching arithmetic as advocated by her. It is the same old procedure of teaching by means of coloured beads, numerical rods, wooden–spindles and-paper numbers, simple boxes, printed shells and such other attractive material as could be made available. Thus addition, subtraction, multiplication and division were taught. The device, generally used, was the Long Stair, consisting of a set of ten rods varying in length, from one to ten decimeters. Each rod was divided into a number of parts, painted red and blue respectively.

Besides these exercises, care of plants and animals is also taught for developing the sense of responsibility. Lessons are also given in patience, faith and mercy. Building, with blocks, sticks and manual training are also recommended.

Place of the Teacher

Montessori recommends "Consciously controlled and systematically directed Education for young children." This control and direction is to be provided by the teacher, who should be an expert guide and excellent organiser. The teacher in Montessori system is called a "directress", who should be well-versed in child psychology. Montessori says, "The broader the teacher's scientific culture and practice in experimental psychology, the sooner will come for her the marvel of unfolding life and her interest in it. The teacher must allow full freedom to the child and not to interfere with his activity. She is simply to observe and intervene only when absolutely necessary. She is to act as a stage director in this self-educative process. Virtues and not words are the main qualifications of the teacher. She should be partly a scientist, partly a doctor and completely religious."

Discipline in Children's House

Discipline comes by an indirect route, by developing activity in spontaneous work. Every individual is expected to learn how to control himself by his own efforts and through calm, silent activity which is directed towards no external aim but is meant to keep alive that inner flame on which our life depends. Montessori writes, "In truth, the 'good' an; those who move forward towards the goodness which has been built up by their own efforts." Such discipline can never be attained by way of commands, by sermons, by any of the disciplinary methods universally known.

Directress of the 'Children's House'. She moves about slowly and silently. She supervises in such a way as anyone who needs her is aware of her presence at once: Whilst those who do not need her do not notice her existence.

Merits of Montessori Method

Madam Montessori profound love and affection, keen sensitiveness, artistic imagination and exceptional sympathy, for children have given a new touch to the theory and principles of education. In fact, she has ushered in a new era in child education and especially of small children at the nursery stage. The chief merits of the Montessori method are:

1. Reverence for small children: To Madam Montessori "the child was God." Her school was the temple and duty of the temple was the essence of childhood. She further writes, "Today there stands forth one urgent need-the reform of methods in education and instruction, and he who struggles towards this end is struggling for the regeneration of man." The method as suggested by Montessori gives an important place to the child.

2. Scientific bases of the method: The method is based upon scientific grounds. Madam Montessori was a scientist and she applied scientific principles based on experience and not upon prejudices.

3. Individual teaching: Individualism is the key-note of the Montessori method. Her method is a reaction against collective teaching.

4. Freedom for children: She ranks among the forefront educators who want to give education in a atmosphere of complete freedom. In her method discipline is that of self-control and self-directed activity.

5. Sense training: The Montessori method aims at educating the children through the sense training. It is based upon the maxims 'proceed from concrete to abstract', from 'general to abstract.'

6. Unique method of reading and writing: Spepcial importance to the learnmg of writing as seen provided in the methods. She takes into consideration the muscular movements in the process of writing. Properly graded and correlated exercise for reading and writing are provided.

7. Learning through living: She has provided practical exercise in her school which enable children to learngood habits of and order. The students learn the lesson of dignity of labour and self-help by attending to their needs themselves. Many practical lessons are provided.

8. Social-value of the method: Though her method inalvidualistic 'in nature, yet it is full of social values. The social value of serving–at the table and lunching together and cleaning plates etc. is beyond doubt. The students perform many other activities cooperatively.

LIMITATIONS OF THE MONTESSORI METHOD

1. Mechanical and artiqcial nature of didactic apparatus: Too much Importance has been given to the didactic apparatus. The cities argue that the apparatus handcuffs both the teacher and the pupil. The pupil is expected to do different types of exercises with the help of the apparatus and the teacher also has' to teach through the didactic apparatus with the result that the free expression of the children is limited and so the work of the teacher. The apparatus is unreal and unnatural.

2. More emphasis on biological aspects and less on psychological: The teacher in this system takes special care in keeping records of the height, skull and limbs of each individual child. She hardly observes temperament and other emotional, traits.

3. Belief in transfer of training: The idea of sense training in the Montessori method is based on the old theory of 'formal training 'of the senses.' She feels that by training particular faculties through particular senses it will be possible to get advantage of that training in other. life situations through transfer of training to the desired field. Modern psychology disapproves of this idea.

4. Neglect of the training of imagination: There is no place for fairy tales in the Montessori system. Fairy tales used in a proper way form art of the literary training of children and help in the development of imagination.

5. Lack of suitable teacher: The successful working of the Montessori system depends upon teachers who possess extensive knowledge of child psychology and acquisition of laboratory-procedure. It is not possible to find such teachers. in sufficient numbers.

6. Little scope for projects and correlation: The present tendency is to teach all subjects together "in the form of projects. Learning by doing is the key-note of the present methods of teaching. In the Montessori method the childern have to depend upon the mechanical apparatus".

7. Vea expensive: It requires a lot of money to set up a school on the lines as suggested by Dr. Montessori. It is very doubtful if we could spare huge sums on such schools.

HER CONTRIBUTION TO THE FIELD OF EDUCATION

Dr. Maria Montessori's work has considerably influenced modern educational theory and practice especially in case of children at nursery school stage. Her gospel of love, respect and sympathy for the child has been accepted all over the world. Her system of child education has become so popular that the word "Montessori" becomes synonymous with "child". All values of her system have been absorbed and put into practice by the modern nursery schools. Her main contribution is as follows:

1. Scientific concept of education: Dr. Montessori started life as a doctor and, so such, formulated her method of teaching young children in the light of her experience and experiment. She gave us observation, experimentation and other scientific methods in education. She never insisted on material and method as the last words in the field of child education. She rather gave a scientific approach to education by breaking away from old, traditions.

2. Psychological approach to education: Like Froebel, she has also given emphasis on sense-training, which is based on psychological principles. By introducing exercises for practical life, she has enabled children to meet everyday situations themselves. She has advocated Auto-education in an atmosphere of freedom and in the spirit of play. She has also emphasised child's development from within through his own efforts. All these principles have made *learning* more important than teaching which is universally accepted today.

3. Emphasis on individual teaching: As against collective and class-reading, Montessori stresses individual treatment of each child. Because of individual differences in physical and mental make-up, each pupil should be observed, studied and handled in a different manner. Thus, like the modern educators, she made child as the "Unit of teaching" in place of class.

4. Love and respect for small children: Montessori often said that child education was the most important problem of humanity. It is, therefore, that it should receive the best attention of the Government and the public. In her own words, "The child's soul which is pure and very sensitive requires our most delicate care". For her, "Child was God, her school was the temple and deity of the temple was the essence of childhood." The profound love for children that she had, compelled her to travel from one corner of the world to another to start institutions for them, based on her system. She also stayed in India from 1939 to 1951 and conducted a number of training courses for teachers in her system of child education. It is under her influence that a large number of nursery schools for children have sprung up in our country also, on Montessori lines.

5. Learning through exercises: The most conspicuous contribution of Montessori is Didactic Apparatus, which she devised for imparting sense-training, muscular co-ordination and instruction in 3 R's. It was really a new experiment to teach writing before reading.

6. Special Role of the teacher: In her system of education there are not *teachers* because they do not teach. They are simply directors because they direct and guide the movements of children. They only provide the proper environment and material at the right moment and then observe auto-development of children. Thus, in Montessori system the child is more active than the teacher. He learns by participating fully in the reading-learning processes. "Thus, the teacher has to play a different role altogether. Instead of facility of speech, she has to acquire the power of silence; instead of teaching, she has to observe; and instead of the proud dignity of one who claims to be infallible, she assumes the vesture of humanity."

She has greatly contributed to the field of education. She has been called as the liberator of the child's soul. In her times collective interest and verbal teaching stood as a bar against individual instruction. At such a time her system came to take care of the individual child. "The most characteristic feature of the method itself is its individualism... such individualising of instruction shares with the most recent developments in other fields of educational activity." Her method is completely a result of the experiments that she has conducted on children these experiments were completely based on experimental psychology. "The technique of our lessons is governed by experimental psychology. And this trend, without doubt, is in contrast to that of the past which was governed by speculative psychology." Another significant contribution that she has made is that of her concept of a 'teacher'. The teacher of a Montenssori school is not a teacher in the ordinary sense of the term but, an observer or a 'directress'. "The old time teacher, who wore herself out in maintaining discipline of immobility and wasting her breath in loud and continual discourse, had disappeared and the didactic material which contains in itself the control of errors is substituted." Her system will develop in the child a zeal to attend school and also an interest to learn. Thus, in a Montessori school, we may find the child working at a 'self-imposed' task for several days. Her system took far more complete charge of the child than did the ordinary school. So there will be a better scope to train the children in decent social habits.

CONCLUSION

In spite of the above-mentioned limitations, the outess method has come to stay in all progressive countries. The word "Montessori" is freely associated with schools, meant for young children. In the opinion of Rusk, "The permanent elements of method are more likely to the practical activities and exercises, subsidiary to tbe didactic apparatus. But the most significant feature of the system is the individualization of instruction. Although this is characteristic of most recent advances in educational practice, Sir John Adams considered himself justified attributing to Montessori, the credit of sounding the knell of class teaching".

Part Four

EMINENT INDIAN EDUCATORS

Mahatma Gandhi
Rabindranath Tagore
Swami Dayananda Saraswati
Swami Vivekananda
Aurobindo Ghose

16

Mahatma Gandhi (1869-1948)

Gandhiji, the father of Indian Nation, the apostle of Truth and violence, stirred three hundred million people to revolt, shook the foundations of the mightiest imperial power with his unique weapon of Spiritual Force and wrested independence from its unwilling-iron hand.

Of his many gifts to the nation, the experiment of new education is one of the greatest. New education aims to create a new type of Individual in our society. The whole effort of education is to remake individuals, to shape human-beings in such a way that they can contribute to the well-being of society. It seeks to prepare citizens for a new society by teaching young people to live together as a community on the basis of co-operation, love and truth.

GANDHIJI'S PHILOSOPHY

Gandiji's view on the nature of Reality is monistic, as can be seen from his writings "I believe", he says, "in the absoluted oneness of God and therefore also of humanity. What though, we have many bodies? We have one soul. The rays of the sun are many through refraction. But they have the same source." He again says, "I believe in education, I believe in the essential unity of man and for that matter of all that lives." Gandhiji further says in unequivocal terms. "I subscribe to the belief or the philosophy that all Iife in its essence is one, and that men are working consciously or unconsciously towards the realisation of that identity. This belief requires a living faith in living God who is the ultimate arbiter of fate." For Gandhiji, God is the reality behind the universe which is always in a state of flux. 'God alone is real, the world is an illusion. He alone persists in the midst of change. That God does not need any proof. It is an indefinable, mysterious power that pervades everything. "God is Life, Truth, Light. He is Love. He is supreme Good."

In Gandhiji's view, there is no other God than Truth?

Truth

What is truth? This is a difficult question, but Gandhiji's sloves it for himself by saying that it is what the voice within tells us. Gandhiji would say, Truth is God rather than God is Truth; because the atheists in their passion far discovering truth do not hesitate to deny the very existence of God. The definition "Truth is God", give Gandhiji the greatest satisfaction. Though Gandhiji believes that Truth is God, but unlike ancient seers his concept of truth is not theology ridden, rather it is a secular concept. Truth is eternal and absolute, but man can realise only a part of it. Man should adhere to truth firmly and should be ready even to die for that. But he should not impose his truth on any one else. It should not be presented in a bitter form, but at the same time it should not degenerate into hypocrisy. It should be practiced in all walks of life.

Non-Violence

If Truth is God, how to realise it? Gandhiji says that the only means for the realisation of Truth is *Ahimsa*. Truth is God, is the ultimate goal of human life and *Ahimsa* is the means to this end. "Ahimsa and Truth", says Gandhiji, "are so intertwined that it is practically impossible to disentangle and separate them. They are like two sides of a coin, or rather a smooth unstamped metallic disc. Who can say, which is the obverse, and which is the reverse? Nevertheless, *Ahimsa* is the means; Truth is the end. Means to be means must always be within our reach and so Ahimsa is our supreme duty."

Non-violence is not, for Gandhiji, a negative attitude. It is positive and dynamic. As Dr. Radhakrishnan puts it, "It is not non-resistance or submission to evil. It is resistance to it through love. *Satyagraha* is the belief in the power of the spirit, the power of truth, the power of love by which we can overcome evil through self-suffering and self-sacrifice."

Summum Bonum of Life

Gandhiji firmly believes that the ultimate aim of man's life is the realisation of God. Man is a part and parcel of the social structure through which alone he can realise this summum bonum or the highest goal of his life. Society or humanity is composed of human beings who are bound together by the bond of a universal brotherhood, Man and Society can realise God who is Truth, only through *Ahimsa*, which implies love for all human beings he should practice the ideal of service unto all. In such a society there is no domination of the strong over the weak and no exploitation in any form. The whole social structure is based upon moral principles of justice and non-violence.

GANDHIJI'S SOCIO-POLOTICAL PHILOSOPHY

Gandhiji's socio-political philosophy consists in the evolution and establishment of an ideal society which is a stateless democracy in which social life has become so perfect that it is self-regulated and self-disciplined. "In such a state everyone is his own ruler. He rules himself in such a manner that he is never a hindrance to his neighbour. In the ideal state, therefore, there is no political power, because there is no state." Such an ideal democracy will be a federation of Satyagrahi villages communities. In such a society every individual will be a believer in non-violence and will live a life of love, renunciation and social service. In such a non-violent society individual freedom will be reconciled with social restraint through truth and non-violence.

GANDIJI'S EDUCATIONAL PHILOSOPHY

With the object of realising his ideal of spiritual Society as a stepping-stone to the realisation of God or Truth, Gandhi evolved an educational system as, a dynamic side of his philosophy. There is a unity running through his concrete schemes and plans, making them a complete system of philosophy.

Gandhiji's Educational Philosophy and Basic Education

There is a tendency even among great educationists, to identify Gandhiji's Educational Philosophy with Basic Education or Wardha

Scheme of Education. The Wardha Scheme of Education is, no doubt, an integral part of Gandhiji's educational philosophy, but it is a scheme or a programme of education not synonymous with Gandhiji's philosophy of education, which aims at bringing about a revolution in the hearts and minds of man all over the world. His thoughts on education well-cohere, into a complete educational philosophy, which is the coping-stone of his general philosophy. The Wardha Scheme is primarily concerned with the education of children between seven and 14 years of age and that too, in India of British rule.

Gandhian Concept of Education

"By education", says Gandhiji "I mean an all-round drawing out of the best in child and man body, mind and spirit. Literacy is not the end of education nor even the beginning. It is one of the means whereby man and woman can be educated. Literacy in itself is no education." The literary training in a school lays more emphasis on the tools and subject rather than on the personality of the educand which, according to Gandhiji, is the main concern of education. What does Gandhiji mean by drawing out the best?' This best is nothing else but the inner voice of Truth. Education which draws out the best or Truth consists in the development of the mind and body with a corresponding awakening of the soul. It is the function of education, therefore, to bring about a harmonious development of all the four aspects of the human personality, viz., body, mind and spirit, "True Education", says Gandhiji, "is that which draws out and stimulates the spiritual, intellectual and physical faculties of the children."

Aims of Education

Gandhiji's aims of education are implied in the meaning of education, and they are correlative to his ideal of life. He has given two sets of aims viz., the immediate and the ultimate. Among the immediate aims, we may mention the 'bread and butter' aim, the 'cultural aim, the harmonious development of all powers, the moral or character development aim and the aim of 'liberating' the educand. The ultimate Aim of Gandhiji is related to the ultimate goal of life—the aim of self-realisation, the knowledge of Truth and God.

The Bread and Butter Aim: Gandhiji advocated bread and butter aim among other aims of education. It was in this context that he arrived at his theory of self-supporting education. He remarks: "This education ought to be for them a kind of insurance against unemployment." Elaborating the same idea, he further says, "The child at the age of 14, that is, after finishing a seven year course, should be discharged as an earning unit. Even now the poor people's children automatically lend a helping hand to their parents—the feeling at the back of their minds being: what shall my parents eat and what shall they give me to eat, if I do not also work with them? That is an education itself. Even so the state takes charge of the child at seven and returns it to the family as an earning unit. You impart education and simultaneously cut at the root of unemployment." It may be remembered, however, that Gandhiji never wants the child to be a mere bread-earner and to earn while he learns.

The Cultural Aim: As against the bread and butter aim. Of education, there is the cultural aim, according to which knowledge is worth having apart from any material use that it has for its possessor. Knowledge of this kind is the goal of liberal education. The advocates of the cultural aim of education tend to think that, because a person had been engaged in intellectual work, his mind is thereby, trained to behave better ever afterwards in all new situations. It should, however be borne in mind that knowledge is not the same thing as culture. "A man's culture is not be judged, says Dr. S. Radhakrishnan, by the amount of tabulated information which he has at his command, but by the, quality of mind he brings to bear on the facts of life."

Being practical to the core, Gandhiji would not enter into an academic discussion of culture. His conception of culture is typically Gandhian, and he would not care what others talk of it. In his talk to the girls of Kasturba Balikashram, New Delhi, April 22, 1946, he said : "I attach far more importance to the cultural aspect of education than to the literary. Culture is the foundation, the primary thing which the girls ought to get from here. It should show itself in the smallest. detail of your conduct and personal behaviour, how you sit, how you walk, how you dress, etc., so that anybody might be able to see at a glance that you are the products of this institution. Inner culture must be reflected in your speech, the way in which you treat visitors and guests, and behave towards one another and your teachers and elders." Thus, to Gandhiji cultural aim is an important aim of education. But in his view, culture is not the product of intellectual work, but the quality of the soul, permeating all aspects of human behaviour.

The Complete Development or Perfection of Nature Aim: The complete development or perfection of nature is another aim that Gandhiji advocates. According to this view, our various innate and acquired powers should be so trained as to bring about a harmonious development of all those powers. This aim accords well with Gandhiji's concept of education an all-round drawing out the best in the child and man—body, mind and spirit. The complete development implies, therefore, the education of 3Hs—hand, heart and head rather than the education of 3Rs. The development of the mind and body must go hand in hand, with a corresponding awakening of the soul in order to save it (education) from being reduced to a mere lopsided affair. It is only a complete development that can give us a whole man.

In the light of this aim, we can easily see how the present education is a lopsided affair. It consists mainly in the training of the mind. The training of the soul as well as the heart is necessary because, it can lead to refinement of emotions and impulses; it can awaken our deepest feelings of love, sympathy and fellowship qualities that constitute Ahimsa.

The Moral Aim: The moral aim is also emphasised by Gandhiji in the sense of character formation or character development. Gandhiji attaches so much importance to character training that he was prepared to relegate to it a subordinate position or even sacrifice literary training, if the choice were to be made between the two. To the question, 'What is your goal in education when India obtains 'freedom?' he promptly replied: "Character building. I would try to develop courage, strength, virtue, the ability to forget oneself in working towards great aims. This is more important than literacy. Academic learning is only a means to this great end." "The end of all knowledge", he further says, "should be the building up of character." Character development, for Gandhiji, implies the cultivation of such moral virtues as courage, strength of conviction, purity of personal life, righteousness, self-restraint and service of mankind. This character is to be built up in terms of non-violence and universal love. Gandhiji believes that such moral virtues, properly cultivated, will enable the individual to realise Truth.

Liberating the Educand Aim: Another subordinate aim of education, according to Gandhiji, is that it should liberate the individual learner. Education should lead to political, economic, intellectual and spiritual freedom. To Gandhiji, 'spiritual freedom is more important than other freedoms.' Spiritual freedom alone can initiate an individual into the higher life of the spirit.

Self-realisation Aim: The highest aim of education, according to Gandhiji, is realisation of God or self-realisation. All other aims are subordinate to this supreme aim of life and education. We have considered different aims of education as put forth by Gandhiji. With all these aims as the bases of educational activities, Gandhiji regards self-realisation as the *Summum-Bonum* of life and education. This is the ultimate goal after which human beings ought to strive. In his Autobiography, he clearly says: "Long before I undertook the education of the youngsters of the Tolstoy Farm, I had realised that the training of the spirit was a thing by itself. To develop the spirit is to build character to enable one to work towards knowledge of God and self-realisation. And I held that this was essential part of the training of the young, and that all training without the culture of the spirit was of no use, and might be even harmful." Gandhiji believes, "that those who defer preparation for this invaluable experience until the fourth stage of life, i.e., Sannyasa, attain no self-realisation, but old age. Amounting to a second and pitiable childhood, living as a burden on this earth." He regards the life of a brahmachari and that of a sannyasi as spiritually similar." In his letter to his son, Mani Lai, he writes; "You have realised my ideal of education if you learn real virtues and saturate your life with them. Armed with these virtues, you will earn your living in any part of the world and will be on your way to the knowledge of God and self realisation." Gandhiji's ultimate aim of education, viz., self realisation includes and embraces all his immediate and subordinate aims.

Are Gandhiji Aims, Individual or Social: We have dwelt at length on the immediate and ultimate aims of education as formulated by Gandhiji. It would, therefore, be in the fitness of things for us to consider whether his educational aim is social or individual or both. Gandhiji does not hesitate to state that "the individual is the one supreme consideration", and "I look upon an increase of the power of the state with the greatest fear, because, although while apparently doing good by minimising exploitation, it does the greatest harm to mankind by destroying individuality which lies at the foot of all progress." Gandhiji has no doubt in his mind that individuality should be preserved and developed, if we are to achieve any progress, either material or spiritual. At the same time, Gandhiji believes in the good of the state whose service and interests should be the aim of its individual citizens. Service, he thinks, is an essential part of education.

Gandhiji thus, strikes a balance between the ideals of social service and individual development. He says, "I value individual freedom, but you must not forget that man is essentially a social being. He has risen to his present status by learning to adjust his individualism to the requirements of social progress. Unrestricted individualism is the law of the beast of the jungle. We have learnt to strike a balance between individual freedom and social restraint. Willing submission to social control and restraint for the sake of the well-being of the whole society enriches both the individual and the society of which the former is a member". "Individual development and Social progress are, thus, interdependent. "The individual can reach his highest development in and through a spiritual society. Acharya Kripalani, commenting on Gandhiji's synthetic view point, says that the inter-relation can only be ignored at the peril of the individual and the society. Any over-emphasis on the one will be at the expense of the other. Such over-emphasis destroys the balance which a true and lasting civilisation needs. Sometimes the individual with his anarchic tendencies produces confusion in society. At other times, society so crushes the individual that his initiative and personality are lost and he becomes a mere automation. "Humanity has been oscillating between the thesis of the individual and the anti-thesis of the society". But Gandhiji succeeded in achieving the proper synthesis between individual and society in his philosophy of life and education. The ideal of self-realisation, the highest aim of education, combines both the development of individuality and social progress.

The Method and Procedures

How can such objectives be realised? Only a suitable method and a suitable curriculum can help in realising these objectives. The system of education as it prevails is too, literary and academic to fulfil these aims. It cannot train the whole man. Gandhiji believes that in order to train the whole man education should be craft-centred. A system of education in which a craft as the centre can lead to the highest development of the mind and the soul. The craft chosen should be manual and productive. It is to be taught scientifically and not mechanically. it is to be a starting point of other subjects as well; "A meeting point of both physical and social environment represented by such subjects as general science, social sciences and creative and expressional arts." When teaching the craft and through craft other subjects, stress should be laid on the principles of co-operative activity, planning, accuracy, initiative and individual responsibility in learning. Gandhiji attaches a spiritual significance to the craft-centered method. The notion of education through handicraft arose from the contemplation of Truth and Love permeating life's activities. True education should be easily accessible to all and should be of use to every villager in his daily life.

Craft-centred education lays emphasis on such important principles of teaching as provision of useful experiences and activity as well as correlation of subjects. All this helps to develop an all-round personality in which knowledge, action and feeling are evenly balanced. The craft-centred education will fulfil other objectives as well, such as 'the bread and butter aim.' There are influences in the craft-centred education which are favourable to virtuous dispositions even to a richness and fulness of culture. Its effect on character in general is very wholesome, irrespective of the fact whether the craft is a going to be one's vocation for life or just an antidote to that lethergy, listlessness and weakness of all which is not consistent with and which is very, often generated by too much intellectual work, pure and simple. The craft is again in consonance with Gandhiji's ideal of non-violence. It will save people from exploitation, selfishness and usurpation—all expression of violence. The craft centered education will bring a new age from which class and communal hatred is eliminated and exploitation is eschewed, The craft will not only stimulate the creative urge of every individual, but also will develop co-operativeness and team work.

The craft chosen, as the medium should make education self-supporting. The child, after completing his course of education should be able to earn a living for himself; and education imparted in the Basic School should be self-supporting to an extent that the craft product of the children should meet the expenses of teacher's salaries. This is in accordance with Gandhiji's emphasis on 'bread and butter aim' and his realistic approach to the problem of education.

The Craft in the school should be the craft of the locality as far as possible. Only then, some positive relationship between education and life could be satisfied. It is thus, a method which not only stresses the importance of student's activity, experimentation, discovery and discussion rather than passive reception and absorption of information, but one which establishes an intimate relationship of the school with life and reality.

The Curriculum and Concept of Education

The curriculum and content of education, besides the method, is another means of realising the objectives. Gandhiji suggests the following studies in the Basic Scheme in order to develop the whole man—his intellectual, physical and spiritual powers.

These subjects are to be taught through the craft as the centre of correlation:

(a) A Basic craft in accordance with the local conditions.

(b) Mother-tongue.

(c) Arithmetic.

(d) Social Studies.

(e) General Science including nature study, botany, zoology, physiology, hygiene, chemistry and physical culture.

(f) Art Work.

(g) Music.

(h) Domestic Science for girls.

Gandhiji's Concept of Discipline

Gandhiji thinks that the highest form of discipline comes through self-control and not by being free to follow stray impulses. "It is rather by denying himself such freedom that he becomes master in his own house, achieving the higher freedom to follow light that is in him unhampered by the chains of his lower nature." Gandhiji believes that real freedom comes through self-discipline, discipline that arises spontaneously from the inner springs of life rather than that which is imposed from without. Thus, he gave us the concept of "Voluntary Discipline" which is a synthesis of freedom and external control. Such self-discipline arises from a life of restraint, fearlessness, usefulness and self-sacrifice—discipline through a practice of non-violent conduct. Gandhiji's craft-centred education encourages conjoint and co-operative activities. And out of these, emerges a sort of social control or social discipline. That Gandhiji had in his mind the concept of social discipline is evident also from his emphasis on the ideals of citizenship through education.

Gandhiji's Views on Higher Education

No doubt, Gandhiji is not in favour of so-called higher education which consists of mere intellectual training unrelated to the real needs of the society and the individual, he is not against higher education if it is improved. He says, "I would revolutionize college education and relate it to national necessities." He adds, "Thus for claim I am not enemy of higher education ... under my scheme there will be more and better research institutes . . . There will be truly original work instead of mere imitation. "As regards universities Gandhiji says that "State Universities should be purely examining bodies, self-supporting, through the fees charged for examination." They should guide the whole field of education and should prepare and approve courses of studies in various departments of education. But he wants university charters to be given liberally to any body of persons of proved worth and integrity. It is his opinion that "it is not for a democratic state to find money for founding universities. If the people want them, they will supply the funds. Universities so founded will adorn the country which' they represent": "All education in a country has to be demonstrably in promotion of the progress of the country in which it is given." Education should be based on realities. "To be based on realities is to be based on national, i.e., State requirements." Gandhiji considers it 'criminal' to pay for a training which benefits neither the nation nor the individual and held that the "university becomes self-supporting when it is utilised by the state."

"The state must pay for it," he says, "Whenever it has definite use of it". But this does not mean that there will not be many institutions which are conducted by voluntary contributions. Higher Education, being selective, whether in industries, or fine arts, can and must normally be left to private enterprise. but it does not absolve the state from running such seminaries as may be required for supplying state needs.

It is his firm conviction that the vast amount of so-called education in arts, given in our college, is sheer waste and has resulted in unemployment among educated classes. "The aim of university education," according to Gandhiji, "should be to turn out true servants of the people, who would live and die for the country's freedom."

EVALUATION OF GANDHIJI'S EDUCATIONAL PHILOSOPHY

Gandhiji's Philosophy of Education is sound psychologically, sociologically and biologically. Gandhiji saw that the child can make intellectual progress only through activity which is purposive and productive. Working on a craft will involve planning, experimenting and reflection. It will accustom the child to look closely to attend to details to measure correctly, thus developing his observation. Manual work not only encourages intellectual development by associating muscular action with cerebral effort. "It also develops the child's imagination, for he must visualise in advance what he expects to make. It develops his reflection and encourages the co-ordination of the process by putting to work all the senses and organs. As children are to learn by doing, they will be able to satisfy many of their urges and achieve a balance, as it were, between the intellectual and practical phases of experience. Both body and mind will be educated in co-ordination. The child will thus, acquire not the superficial literacy, but the real literacy of the whole personality. The Basic Scheme which reflects Gandhiji's philosophy of education gives ample opportunities for self-expression. Ordinary education cannot foster the creative urge for self-expression but the Basic Education, as outlined in the scheme, provides "An effective outlet for the creative urges innate in every human heart." The scheme satisfies some of the fundamental psychological needs of children the need for affection and self respect, the need for creativeness and activity and the need to develop a sense of security. Gandhiji expected the teacher to understand the child and love him, to make him happy and thus satisfy his needs for affection. Manual work, will satisfy his need for creativeness and will develop self-reliance and self-confidence leading to self-respect and security.

Pedagogically too, Gandhiji's educational theory is sound. The craft-centred education will give greater concreteness and reality to the knowledge acquired by children. The principle of correlation will relate knowledge of life with other forms of knowledge. The very concept of 'education' and 'aims of education' show Gandhiji's breadth and depth of insight at the same time. According to Gandhiji, education is not mere literacy it is an all-round development of the whole man.

Sociologically considered, Gandhiji's philosophy of education is as sound as considered psychologically. Education should fit a man for playing a useful role in the non-violent social order. He will cultivate the character appropriate to a social being. He will learn the art of discipline, self-government, breadth of vision, tolerance and good neighbourliness'. And as, this social order is to be democratic, every member of society has a right to free education. The introduction of the craft will bridge the gulf between manual and intellectual labour. It will remove the cleavage that exists in Indian society between the leisured and the labouring classes. It will cultivate a true sense of the dignity of labour and of human solidarity. This will make for better social unification. Mahatma Gandhi regards his plan as "the spearhead of a silent social revolution fraught with the most far-reaching consequences." In the words of Gandhiji, "It (the plan) will provide a healthy and moral basis of relationship between the city and the village and thus go a long way towards eradicating some of the worst evils of the present social insecurity and poisoned relationship between the masses." Gandhiji wants the ideals of useful citizenship to be encouraged through education. He regards the school as a co-operative community where students can learn lessons of love, truth, justice, co-operative endeavour, equality and brotherhood of man and social service. With these ideals in view, students will grow into citizens who will form a society known as the Sarvodya Samaj in which the aim is to attain a new humanism based on non-acquisitiveness, non-violence and truth.

Gandhiji's philosophy of education is biologically sound, in the sense that it lays emphasis on man's capacity "To go beyond the process of modifying the relations of his organism to fit the environment for promoting his best interests as well as, those of the society in which he lives." That man should be able to fit himself in a successful existence under the conditions of a complex and changing civilisation is what the biological aim in education demands the demand of adjustment. And that was the implication of Gandhiji's belief that education should aim at developing the individuality of the whole man.

Dr. M.S. Patel has beautifully summed up Gandhiji's philosophy of education from the three angles that we have referred to above. Assuming that manual work or crafts is the core of his educational philosophy, it, "from the psychological point of view, balances the intellectual and practical elements of experience and may be made an instrument of educating the body and mind co-ordination. From the sociological point of view, it will conduce to a true sense of dignity of labour and of human solidarity, which would be an ethical and moral gain of incalculable significance." It will develop in the children the qualities of co-operation, brotherhood and service, which would make for a peaceful life in society, minimising all possible causes of friction.

PHILOSOPHIC TENDENCIES IN GANDHIAN EDUCATIONAL PHILOSOPHY

An interesting thing about Gandhiji's philosophy of education is that it combines the essentials of the three philosophical tendencies such as naturalism, idealism and pragmatism. Of course, his philosophy is fundamentally idealistic and naturalism and pragmatism are merely contributory to it.

This philosophy is naturalistic in as much as it considers the nature of the child, how he learns and what his essential needs are. Like a biological naturalist, Gandhiji stresses the child's nature and its full development through education. This is borne out in such statements as "Children take in much more and with less labour through their ears than through their eyes" or that "Children should be educated in an atmosphere of freedom—freedom from superimposed restriction and interferences. Gandhiji, like the naturalists, believes in the essential goodness of child nature, emphasises activity or learning by doing and shows aversion to artificiality and pedantry; He, like them, attempts to liberate education from the four walls of the school-room and wishes it to be given in a wider sphere of the natural surroundings of the child.

Gandhiji is an idealist to the core. He has stressed the dignity of man; and the significance of the spiritual values in life like an idealistic thinker. Other important aspects of idealism are the ultimate aim of self-realisation, the ideal of service unto humanity, preservation of moral values the emphasis on religious education in the true 'sense of the word, and development of a harmonious personality, Like Froebel, Gandhiji believes' that education should awaken the latent potentialities of the educand to fuller development., "Both of them discern the divine plan, a symbolism which means that behind all activities there exist spiritual meanings and values."

While being a naturalist and an idealist, Gandhiji is also a Pragmatist. He believes that the absolute to be realised through sustained experimentation. His autobiography entitled as "*My Experiments with Truth*," shows that Gandhiji is a pragmatist; Education should equip the child 'with knowledge and skills necessary to deal effectively with the situations of real life. Again, there is a lot of similarity between the craft-centred activities and the learning activities as described by the pragmatists in the Project Method. 'Gandhiji has tried to relate knowledge to the life of the people; the basic craft, like a project, is to be a socialised activity which makes for all type of social relationships, social participation, division of labour and willing responsibility to the community. Like the pragmatists Gandhiji has emphasised the significance of correlation' of the various subjects and social function of education or the school. In the words of Dr. Patel, "Gandhiji's philosophy ... of education is naturalistic in its setting, idealistic in its aim and pragmatic in its method and programme of work....... All these tendencies are not separate in his philosophy. They, fuse into unity, giving rise to a theory of education which would suit the needs of the day and satisfy the loftiest aspiration of "the human soul."

CONCLUSION

If we want to evolve a sound system of Indian Education we will have to first determine our national goals in the light of aims of education as suggested by Gandhiji. As regards the methods of teaching and the contents of education we will have to make our educational theory and practice, life-centred as suggested by Gandhiji. As suggested by Gandhiji our educational theory and practice must fulfil our, three basic needs—food, shelter and clothing; it must be based upon three basic urges of the child—love, freedom, and creativity, and it must inculcate three basic values-Truth, Beauty and Goodness among our students.

As regards Higher Education, it should be as suggested by Gandhiji, highly planned, professional and creative.

To sum up we can say that Gandhiji's system of education develops on all round vigorous personality, physically and mentally alert, keenly aware of its environments and fired with the desire to improve it. If such persons could be multiplied by the million and Gandhiji feels they can be, the face, of India rather the "Whole world can be changed, Gandhiji planned this system of education" as a spearhead of a silent social revolution fraught with most far-reaching consequences. And all this would be accomplished without the horror of a bloody classwar, because the schools will be co-operative communities where students will learn lessons of love, truth, justice, co-operative endeavour, equality and brotherhood of man and social service. With these ideals in view, students will grow into citizens who will form a society known as the 'Sarvodaya Samaj' in which the aim is to attain a new humanism based on non-acquisitiveness, non-violence and truth.

17

Rabindranath Tagore (1861-1941)

Tagore is primarily a poet; but his poetry is imbued with philosophy. The poet seeks beauty, the philosopher truth. Both the paths lead to the same Supreme Reality. Tagore's poetic rapture is 'soaked in his question for the Beyond'. In his presidential address to the Indian Philosophical Congress Tagore said, "In India, philosophy ever sought alliance with poetry because its mission was to occupy the people's life and not merely the learned reclusion of scholarship. Instead of being logically intellectually Tagore's philosophy is, a sight of the soul rather than a reasoned account of metaphysics; an atmosphere rather than a system of philosophy'.

TAGORE'S GENERAL PHILOSOPHY

On the basis of Gitanjali, it is sometimes said that Tagore represents the teachings of Hinduism. But, neither the Hindu 'Karma' nor the Hindu doctrine of 'transmigration of soul' can be found in Tagore, although the idea of incarnation is met with in some of his poems. When asked whether his father had belief in transmigration of soul, he gave vent to his mind thus, "My father never believed in that fairy tale".

From the inheritance point of views he is a Brahrmo-Samajist. His grand-father was the right hand man of Raja Ram Mohan Rai. His father kept the same torch burning. So after his father, Tagore was a member of the Adi-Brahmo-Samaj and thus he took his cue from Upanishads which formed the back-bone of his philosophy.

On deep study, we find that Tagore is out and out a Vedantist. He believes in One Supreme Being, the Braham. He believes that the various manifestations of nature all represent him and the Braham pervades through all these forms. Among this empirical diversity there, is, thus an innate unity. This results, therefore, in there being a Spiritual Bond between man and man. Like a Vedantist he believes in "Aham-Brahmosmi" or 'I am the Brahma'. Thus, according to Tagore, the true salvation comes when an individual feels the truth contained in the words, "Aham-Brahmosmi". The Vedantistic philosophy also led him to have an implicit faith in the Brotherhood of Man and Fatherhood of God and in the need for universal religion.

Like Rousseau, Tagore is an "Individualist" and "Naturalist". He believes in the right and freedom of the individual to shape his life in his own way. But in the individual's development he ultimately wants the unity of mankind. He says that every individual is different from another and everyone is unique, in every one of us the Creator manifests himself in a unique manner and every individual tries to realise the creator in his own way. In the creator and through him, we find unity not only among human beings but also between man and nature.

Tagore, a great lover of nature gives a very important place to Nature. This, he says, is the manifestation of the creator (Braham). Through its various forms, colours, and the rhythms the Braham reveals himself through many ways. He reveals himself more clearly through nature than through man. Tagore, therefore, wishes human beings to have a close communication with nature and with its purifying and vitalising influences. Just as a man realises his relationship with human beings, he should realise his relationship with nature.

'Experience of the Spiritual World, religion as the right centre of life's activities and the unity of thought and truth are the key-note of Tagore's philosophy. There should be a spiritual relationship between man and man. This knits human beings into communities. Tagore's individualism, therefore, is compatible with the growth of social units. He encourages the individual to reorganise the social groups on the basis of the individual's spiritual worth. By this, he does not mean parochialism intellectual, social, political and spiritual. The essential unity of the universe is evident to him. True, that he advocates internationalism, but not from the economic or political point of view. He realises and stresses the spiritual bondage of the universe. Having an explicit faith in the fundamental unity of mankind, he preached human brotherhood.

Tagore, like most of the ancient sages and seers, believes 'that man should Iive for the Ultimate Truth. He wants man to "Have access to the life that goes beyond death and rises above all circumstances". His advice is "Let us find our God, let us live for the ultimate truth which emancipates us from the bondage of the dust and gives us the wealth, not of things but of inner light, not of power but of love."

TAGORE'S EDUCATIONAL PHILOSOPHY

Tagore's educational philosophy conforms to his general philosophy. He approaches education as he approaches life as a poet, from a comprehensive standpoint. "Education", he says, "Is a permanent part of the adventure of life ... it is not like a painful hospital treatment for curing them (students) of the congenial malady of their ignorance, but is a function of the health, the natural expression of their mind's vitality". To him, the object of education is the freedom of mind through the path of freedom, though he has its risk and responsibility too. In his words "The best function of education is to enable us to realise that to live as a man is great requiring profound philosophy for its expression, and heroism in its conduct." "Most people", he says, "Have forgotten that children are living-beings. They are more living than grown-up people, who have built their shells of habit around them, while the children are always pliable". Therefore, he wants that children should not have mere schools for their lessons, but a world whose guiding spirit is personal love. "Love and action" he believes, "are the only media through which perfect knowledge can be obtained".

Tagore's educational philosophy is based on three cardinal principles namely, (a) Freedom, (b) Creative Self-expression, (c) Active Communion with Nature and Man. For Tagore, "Education has its only meaning and object in freedom; freedom from ignorance about the laws of universe, and freedom from passion and prejudice in our communication with the human world." The genesis of the ideal of freedom lies in his own experience as a child and his experience of the prevailing system of education. About his early education he remarked, we had to sit like dead specimens of some museum, whilst lessons were pelted at us from without like hail-storms on flowers. He spoke of the existing school as being an "Education factory, lifeless, colourless, dissociated from the context of the universe within the bare white walls scaring like eye balls of the dead". Our education has taken us away from nature and its vitalising and life-giving influences. It is dissociated from social contexts. An education divorced from the streams of life and confined within the four walls of the class-room becomes artificial and loses its value. The first and the foremost work, in his opinion, is to bring the child's mind in contact with nature. Let the child imbibe and learn freely and spontaneously from the book of nature. Let him be happy and free. Education should be natural in content and quality. Through contact with nature the child will be introduced to the great world of reality spontaneously and joyfully.

Tagore does not want education to be shut off from the daily life of the people. However, the utilitarian aim of education is not ignored by him. According to him, educational institutions, in order to obtain their fullness of truth must have close association with economic life. The highest mission of education is to help us realise the inner principle of the unity of all knowledge and all the activities of our social and spiritual being. Society in its early stage was held together by its economic co-operation, when all its members felt in-unison a natural interest their right to live." It was this idea of economic co-operation that formed the basis of Shanti Niketan which was not only to be the centre of intellectual life of India, but the centre of her economic life also. "It co-operates with the villages around it, cultivates land, breeds cattle, spins cloth, and presses oil from oil seeds. It is producing all the necessaries, devising the best means, using the best materials, and calling science to its aid. Its very existence tends to depend upon the success of its industrial activity carried out on the co-operative principles, which unites the teachers, students and villagers of the neighbourhood in a living and active bond of necessity.

Tagore's Views on Aims of Education

While considering the educational aims of Tagore, we should bear in mind that he was not an educationist in the strictly academic sense, and he never wrote any thesis on education, like Rousseau's Emile, or Spencer's Education. Nevertheless, in his countless writings, we find some direct and indirect utterances about the aims of education. Those are presented them here in a systematic form.

Physical Aims: Tagore was conscious of the importance of the education of the body. He attached so much importance to the healthy physical development of children that he strongly advocated their free, spontaneous movements and play in joyous, natural surroundings, even at the expense of studies, if necessary. "Even if they learnt nothing" he says, "They would have had ample time for play. Climbing trees, diving into ponds, plucking and tearing flowers, perpetrating thousand and one mischiefs on Mother Nature, they would have obtained the nourishment of the body, the happiness of the mind, and the satisfaction of the natural impulses of childhood."

Intellectual Aims: Tagore deplored the fact that the existing system of education encouraged slavery to books. Our mercenary education, inspired by narrow utilitarian motives of passing examinations and entering a job as quickly as possible and imparted through the medium of a difficult and alien language, led us to cram rules, definitions, facts, and ideas since early childhood without giving us either the time or the incentive to pause and think and assimilate what we had learnt. Thus, our intellect had never been exercised in a real sense, nor had our mind received any genuine intellectual food and nourishment. The natural consequence had been the starvation and stunting of our intellect on a nation-wide scale. We, thus, never succeeded in attaining the stature of intellectual maturity either as an individual or as a nation.

The power of acquiring ideas through independent efforts, of critically examining them, and thoroughly assimilating them, was therefore, considered by Tagore the most important aim of intellectual education. He writes, "Power of thinking and power of imagination are undoubtedly two very essential faculties for adult life. So, if one is to grow into real manhood, these two factors cannot be eliminated from Iife." Again, he writes, "Ever since childhood, instead of putting all the burden on the memory, the power of thinking and the power of imagination should also be given opportunities for free exercise".

"This ability of acquiring", writes Dr. H.B. Mukherjee, "and assimilating ideas independently from books was considered by Tagore as only just a fraction of the intellectual equipment of an individual. He was far from advocating bookishness of any description; he indeed, condemned it whenever the occasion arose. On the contrary, he always stressed the importance of the ability to learn directly from Nature and life. This is, in fact, a fundamental basis of his philosophy of Education in Nature." There is education,

Tagore says, "in the mere effort of knowing a living person directly instead of through books. It not only gives some knowledge but develops the faculty of knowing to such an extent as is impossible in class lectures." Again, "Our intellect, emotions, or imagination, if divorced from reality, become feeble and distorted."

While developing the ability to learn directly from real life situations, a true intellectual education, in Tagore's opinion, must also aim at making the students familiar with and adjusted to the facts and conditions of real life and habitual environments. He asserted that unrealistic education was responsible for producing in our countrymen intellectual dishonesty, moral hypocrisy, and ignorance about their mother land. Hence, he argued that the first and fore most problem deserving our attention at the present moment is the problem of creating harmony between our education and our life.

Moral and Spiritual Aims: Tagore, as a moral teacher, has put forward a number of moral and spiritual values. One of these is the value of discipline, which is certainly a most fundamental element in the moral education of an individual. By the word, "discipline", Tagore does not mean either external order or blind obedience. Explaining its meaning in Siksa Samasya, he said, "Real discipline means protection of raw, natural impulses from unhealthy excitement and growth in undesirable directions. To remain in this state of natural discipline, is happy for young children. It helps their full development."

"Inner discipline," writes Dr. H.B. Mukherjee, "of the self is at once the spirit and the fruit of all Tapasya and Sadhna. All worthy activities great or small succeed because of this spirit of austere devotion to the cause or the task. "Nothing great and Noble", he (Tagore) declared, "can be achieved except through severe suffering and sacrifice." Time and again, he exhorted his countrymen, and specially the young people, to imbibe fully this spirit of Tapasya, of austere devotion, and to apply it to every sphere of national endeavour. He pointed out that Japan could rise to great heights in a very short time because of the power of her-people to devote themselves intensely to any work of importance. The West also attained ascendancy in the modern world through the same spiritual and moral force.

Another ideal of great value recommended by Tagore is the ideal of peace and tranquility. "The essential spirit of the forest," he says, "Is the santarasam, the spirit of peace and tranquility, which is the consummation of all emotions; just as white is the consummation of all other colours. Attainment of this spirit of peace and tranquility in one's character is an ultimate end of the process of self-discipline. This, in its turn, produces, the spirit of humility which is a tremendous spiritual, force and can be attained only by the strong."

In conformity with the ideal of self-discipline, Tagore advocates, a simple way of life achieved through the reduction of all unnecessary material equipment. "We should demonstrate the ideal", he said, "of reducing the unnecessary in life in every respect in our school..." Easy accessibility, simplicity, and naturalness—these comprise true civilisation. The complexity of ponderous accountrements is sheer barbarity; in fact, it is a rubbish-heap of sweating incompetence. That the dignity of man does not suffer through the want of some lifeless materials, but, on the contrary, it frequently becomes brighter with a natural glow this truth will have to be learnt in schools since childhood, not through futile precept but through living examples. Getting rid of the luxury of materials, the child will acquire greater familiarity with the use of his hand and feet, the floor and the earth.

"Tagore laid stress," writes Dr. Mukherjee, "On another fundamental ideal which aims more at inner development than an outward expression. It is the attainment of an inner freedom, an inner power and enlightenment. This ideal of inner freedom may be expressed as the liberation of the self from all kinds of slavery. It aims at, emancipation of the, intellect from the domination of bookish knowledge." "The character of good education," according to Tagore, "is that it does not over power man; it emancipates him.

Tagore's Views on Curriculum

Curriculum is the means to achieve the aims of education. Hence, Tagore's approach to curriculum was as wide and comprehensive as his aims of education. The main aim of education, according to him, was the development of complete manhood for the realisation of a full life. Naturally enough, the curriculum envisaged by him partook of that idea of fullness and referred to all aspects of human life, physical, intellectual, moral and spiritual from one point of view; individual, social, utilitarian, non-utilitarian, etc., from another.

This is the reason that Tagore advocated a fullness of experience for children so that they might acquire knowledge from multiple sources through the sub-conscious process. His chief complaint against the existing curriculum in the Indian schools of his time was that it concentrated exclusively on the mind, and was hopeless circumscribed by the narrow mercenary and utilitarian aims. Everybody was desirous, he said, somehow to get through an examination and secure a job. There was, thus, no incentive to any serious course of study of a comprehensive nature. The students had the bare minimum in view; but the bare minimum, he pointed out never suffices for a healthy growth. Introducing a biological analogy in Siksar Herpher, Tagore significantly observed that, though a human being is only three cubits and a half in height, none can live and grow happily within a space only just as high. An ample space is necessary for free and healthy development. And this is as true in the intellectual sense as in the physical. Such ample space can be provided only through a full and wide curriculum that would ensure a fullness of experience to the growing children. "It was my desire," Tagore pointed out, "That I would establish in the Santi Niketan Ashram a field for the pursuit of culture not merely the cultivation of knowledge within the narrow limits determined by the text-books prescribed in your schools but also all kinds of arts and crafts, dance, music and play, as well as all knowledge and skill necessary for rendering service to the villages."

Tagore's conception of the curriculum as fullness of experience shows that he viewed curriculum "Not in terms of certain subjects to be learnt but in terms of certain activities to be undertaken." As Nunn has written, "The school must be thought of primarily not as a place where certain knowledge is learnt, but as a place where the young are disciplined in certain forms of activity." We find, accordingly, writes Dr. Mukherjee, "That at the Santi Niketan school, and later on at Visva Bharati, not only did the teaching of the various familiar academic subjects like History, Science, Nature Study, Geography, Literature, etc., include a variety of relevant practical activities like drama, excursion, gardening, regional study, laboratory work, drawing, original composition, collection of museum and herbarium, etc., but a multitude of so-called 'extra-curricular' activities like games, social service, student self-government, etc., formed a regular feature of the normal working of the institution in order to bring into play all the essential faculties of the children. From this point of view, the curriculum introduced in Tagore's Institutions has been "Activity. Curriculum" in a large measure.

Tagore's View on Method

The most significant point in Tagore's philosophy of method was that the process of education should be full of life. He deprecated the mechanical and life-less system of education. His main grievance against the schools of his time was that they were not centre of learning, but educational factories, turning out the same kind of stuff through their mechanical system of education. He developed an abhorrence to this system in his childhood when he was sent to a school. Since, that very time, he longed to save children from that ordeal. In this respect, his views were like those of the Naturalists, who stood against dead formation and sought to breathe into education the fresh air of light and life, placing it on the natural interests and impulses of the child.

Another point, which Tagore stressed was that education should be imparted on realistic lines. Just as the curriculum envisaged by him was to reflect the customs, traditions, social ideals, conditions and problems of everyday life of the pupil, so also the method was to be based on real life situations, concrete facts of Nature, and social life. Thus, facts of Nature are to be studied through actual Natural phenomena and through the wild life in Nature, and facts of history, geography, and other social sciences are to be studied first hand from direct sources as far as possible.

Tagore's realistic approach was psychological. Expressing his views about it, he said, "Learning can become sound only when it proceeds from the near to the distant from the familiar to the unfamiliar. If our learning continue to be based mainly on what does not exist all around and what is not present before us, then such knowledge must be feeble. If we can fully and properly grasp what is familiar, only then can we apperceive what is unseen and unfamiliar."

Realistic approach to the learning process, as conceived by Tagore, 'presumed the idea that knowledge should be acquired through independent efforts and thinking'. Tagore said, "In contact with the real objects that are present before the pupils their power of observation and reasoning will develop." Again, "There is education in the very effort to give up books and study men who are living and present. It not only leads to knowledge, but it develops the power of knowing to an extent which is never possible through class teaching." In his letter to Tanayendra Nath Ghose, dated the 10th of March, 1929, Tagore made a plea for a realistic education which is based on the study of life and society, and is independent of books. He wrote, "The students must be led to think. A variety of questioning and answering has to be conducted on what they have studied in books. Indeed, we should think that their education has been real if they venture to criticise the matter contained in the text books. Different problems of everyday life should be presented before them and discussion should be conducted on their solution. Note down many such problems in your note-book. Moreover, they visit Sriniketan, but they view it from outside and do not know what its essential problems are they should be made aware of them and asked to offer solutions. What is the economic foundation of the village; what does the co-operative principle mean; why is it necessary for our country; what drawbacks are there in the nature, habit, and custom of the rural population that they are dying through want of food and water and through diseases and addictions? We should see that they ponder over and discuss these problems—remember, this education is much greater than class teaching."

Another important principle in Tagore's educational method was the activity principle. This principle as conceived by Tagore has a much deeper meaning than that by which it is familiar to us. It is based on the philosophy of Tagore that body and mind are inseparable. He asserted that physical activity not only invigorates the body but also energises the mind. This is the reason that he advocated compulsory training in some craft for the students of his school. He also affirmed that such instances are found where skill in a physical activity has released the suppressed energies of the mind. "It is my firm conviction," he said, "that there is a close relation between physical and mental education, physical and mental movement. The rhythm of our life is disturbed if a proper harmony is not established between the two." It is on this ground that he regarded the mobile-school as the ideal school. "Teaching while walking," he stated, "is the best method of teaching". It is so not only because walking facilitates learning many things through direct observation, but because it keeps our awakened mental faculties; constantly alert and receptive through contact with ever-varying scenes and objects and the rhythmic marching together of the inner and the outer... Such dynamic learning is entirely fruitful for living human being. The static education within the classroom, on the other hand, causes a divorce between the body and the mind, without initiative. In his document 'Movement in Education', he explains this idea very clearly. "To compel the mind to use only one portion of the body in the learning process" he states, "is not natural". In the process of taking in and of digesting our food, a whole symphony of life is being performed in which heart, eyes, tongue, and ears are playing their part. The same process should occur when you are taking your lessons or trying to swallow useful information. Life should be entire, a co-ordination of all the different faculties and functions. According to this principle, the children of Shanti Niketan recite or think aloud, while walking. They carry their note-books with them to sketch or record "all the picturesque details of the life around them."

Even in class teaching, Tagore applied the activity principle to such an extent that many would feel surprised. He wrote, "I would allow all our boys and girls during class to jump up, even to climb into a tree, to run off and chase after a cat or dog, or to pick some fruit off a branch ... I tried to keep in mind the need of the child to use the whole of its body in acquiring a vocabulary and in mastering a whole sentence. Most of our teachers used to get disgusted when they heard the children of my class laughing and shouting and clapping their hands." A boy would say to me, 'May I go for a run?' 'Yes, of course,' I would say, because I knew that by this means some tedium would be broken and that, when again he felt lively, it would be much easier for him to receive and to digest. It is while children feel dull, from the passivity of their minds and through being asked to be inert receptacles, without any activity of body that they cease altogether to assimilate the non-living lesson." It is from the view point of the physical activity theory that Tagore emphasised the importance of dancing and dramatic arts. He said to Elmhirst, "In the developing of your own school I advise you to make the practice of drama and of the histrionic arts compulsory for all children. We must make dramatic performance a regular subject of education. Children need the opportunity to give expression of their sentiments through perfect and graceful movements of the body. Never allow this capacity to use the whole body as a medium of expression, to die out."

MAIN FEATURES OF TAGORE'S EDUCATIONAL PHILOSOPHY

Tagore's educational philosophy is based on naturalism, humanism and internationalism all saturated with spiritualism.

Tagore's Naturalism

Tagore finds a fundamental unity between man and nature. Therefore, he wants that 'the child's education must be organised in natural surroundings'. He believes that education given in natural surroundings develops intimacy with the world. Because of this intimacy the child develops of his own accord the power of communication with it. He says, "Children with the freshness of their senses come directly to the intimacy of this world. This is the first gift they have. They must accept it naked and simple and must never again lose their power of immediate communication with it." Tagore does not want that the natural senses of children should be debased in an urban atmosphere.

Like a true Naturalist, Tagore was very much influenced by Robinson Crusoe. He writes, "I still believe that it is the best book for boys that have ever been written. There was a longing in me when young to run away from my own self and be one with everything in Nature."

Tagore puts more faith in an individual than in any institution. He does not want that the child should be crushed into the heavy traditional methods of instruction. The individual child is more important to him than the books, method and the teacher. The chief teachers upon whom Tagore places his main reliance are the open spaces around the grooves, the tree, dawn, evening and moonlight, the wind and rainfall. Such teachers, he believes, nourish the child nature spontaneously. Nature inspires the human beings differently at different stages of human development. For the young child, Nature will become an unconscious symbol of super-personal growth and evolution, something that need not be questioned and which provides an ever-ready background for its dreams and its play. For the adolescent, Nature will become an object of either scientific or lyrical curiosity. The adult will see in her the soil on which his country and, his people grow, the cultural and economic background of human existence. Nature to him, is the focus where the interests and aspirations of human beings meet. It is, therefore, essential not only to know Nature, but to live Nature. Man attains thereby the greater and deeper freedom. He will find fulfilment in the struggle from the dim dream lands of childhood towards the light of maturity.

School, according to Tagore, should be a place where the sunrise and sunset and the silent glory of stars are not daily ignored; where nature's festivities of flowers and fruits have their joyous recognition from men. It should be such a place where the young and the old, the teacher and the students sit at the same table to partake of their daily food and the food of their eternal life. Tagore says that we have come to this world to accept it, not merely to know it. The highest education is that which does not merely give information, but makes our life in harmony with all existence.

Tagore wants an equilibrium of the 'Natural' and 'Civilised' forces in man. The art of education, according to him, should consist in training the child to inhibit all those impulses that are anti-social. "For our perfection, we have to be vitally savage and mentally civilised; we should have the gift to be natural with nature and human with human society." That is, why, he suggests that besides communion with nature, there should be communion of man with man. This would enable children to learn social behaviour and co-operation in educational activities.

Education, in the academic sense of mere acquisition of knowledge or information never appealed to the versatile genius of the poet. Education to be real, must be of the whole man, of his emotions and senses as much as of his intellect. A large part of man, believes Tagore, can never find its expression in the mere language of words. It must have many other languages—lines and colors, sounds and movements for the satisfaction of his aesthetic urge. The poet regards the language of sounds and movements to be the best means of self-expression side-by-side with this provision for creative self-expression, he stresses various forms of hard work. He says, "However great a scholar may be, if he has not educated his body, he has to live a life of dependence on others in many ways he is an incomplete man. There is a close and inseparable connection between the faculties of mind and body. Each gains strength by co-operating with the other. If the education of the body does not proceed along with the education of the mind, the latter cannot gather strength." "Hard work, music and arts", he says, "are the spontaneous overflow of our deeper nature and spiritual significance" .

Tagore Humanism

To Tagore, 'man is the measure of everything'. Throughout his life, he has been striving to make the people of the world conscious of this Supreme Truth. His conception of the universe is purely human. All values and virtues are to be realised through man. When our universe is in harmony with Man, the eternal, we know it as truth; we feel it as beauty. This world is a human world the scientific view of it is also that of the scientific man." Tagore thinks of a Universal Mind of Humanity. This Universal Mind transcends separate individual minds. Tagore regards God also as human. He says, "God is the Eternal Person manifested in all persons". He observes that "He is there where the tiller is tilling the hard ground and where the path maker is breaking stones." To Tagore, civilisation should be evaluated in terms of what value it attaches to man and not in terms of how many scientific inventions it has produced. He says, "The decay and fall of a civilisation is due to the causes which produce callousness of heart and lead to the cheapening of man's worth." It is this love for man that stimulated Tagore to turn to the education of children and he founded a school at Bolpur. Because of his humanism, he was a great lover of children and advises the teacher to be like children and not to think himself as their superior, but should regard himself as one of their elder brothers. While addressing a group of pupil-teachers, he advised them to cultivate the eternal spirit of child, if they desired to take up the task of training the children of Man. Tagore shuns all violence and force in the process of education.

Tagore's Internationalism

Tagore's Internationalism knows no bound. He is an ardent prophet of world unity. All through his strenuous life, he has worked for a closer contact between the East and the West. He wants that the East should give its best to the West and in turn it should assimilate the best that the West has to offer. He felt grateful to both the East and the West and believed that the problem of the world could be solved only, if a judicious synthesis was attained between the contributions of the two for the benefit of man. He wanted to achieve this synthesis in his Visva Bharti which was accessible to all persons in the world irrespective of caste, colour, creed and sex.

Tagore's Universal Humanitarianism is the corner stone of collaboration between East and West, says Lesny. He is the apostle of enlightened humanity and a strong champion of world unity.

Tagore's Idealism and Spiritualism

Tagore's educational philosophy is saturated with Spiritualism. He wants to achieve the essential unity of the universe through God. For Tagore the object of education is to give man the unity of truth. The sense of unity of truth may be given by emphasising the inter relationship between intellectual, physical and spiritual life. Tagore believes in a spiritual world which is the innermost truth of this world. The experience of the spiritual world must be gained by children by living in it and not by theological instructions. Tagore wants to make 'the purpose of education nothing short of the highest purpose of man, the fullest growth and freedom of soul'. He says, "It is India's mission to realise the truth of the human soul through its union with the world-spirit. Tagore fight against the dominance of materialistic outlook of Iife and he was an Idealist to the core. But he believes that education should be related to the life-currents of the people for which it is meant". He says, "Our centre of culture should not only be centre of the intellectual life of India, but the centre of her economic life also." Here, Tagore shows a pragmatic approach to education.

TAGORE'S VISVA BHARATI

We have referred to Tagore's Visva Bharati at Shanti Niketan. So, it is in the fitness of things to discuss here briefly the philosophy underlying this International University which was formally inaugurated on December 22, 1921, by the great scholar. Dr. Brajendranath.

A University, Tagore believes, should not be a mechanical organisation for collecting and distributing knowledge. It should be a medium of enabling people to offer their wealth of mind to others. The conception of his Visva Bharati, is in accordance with his notion of Greater India where humanity will strive to reach a reconciliation of different races with different religions and civilisations. Tagore believes that this Greater India or New India will not belong to this race or that, this religion or that religion, but to humanity. Tagore's Visva Bharati is a symbol of his passionate faith in the Brotherhood of Nations. In 1934 while responding to Professor Gilbert Murray's invitation to help in bridging the gulf between various nations through international co-operation of thinkers in all countries, Tagore wrote, 'Willingly therefore, harness myself in my advanced age to the arduous responsibility of creating in our educational colony at Shanti Niketan a spirit of genuine international collaboration based on a definite pursuit of knowledge, a pursuit carried on in an atmosphere of friendly community life, harmonised with Nature and offering freedom of individual self expression," This is the ideal on which Tagore has based his Visva Bharati.

Purpose of Visva Bharati

Tagore had three main purposes in establishing the Visva Bharati. He has described them as follows:

1. To teach different cultures of the East, especially those that originated in India or found shelter within her shores.

2. To establish 'The Institute of Rural Reconstruction' in order to lay the foundation of a happy, and contented human life in the villages, and lastly.

3. To seek to establish a living relationship between the East and the West, to promote inter-cultural, and inter-racial amity and understanding, and fulfill the highest mission of the present age 'the unification of mankind'.

Objectives of the Visva Bharati

The Memorandum of the Association of Visva Bharati lays down the objectives of Visva Bharati in the following words:

1. "To study the mind of man in its realisation of different aspects of truth from diverse points of view.

2. To bring into more intimate relation with one another, through patient study and research the different cultures of the East on the basis of their underlying unity.

3. To approach the West from the standpoint of such a unity of the life and thought of Asia.

4. To seek to realise in common fellowship of study the meeting of the East and West, and thus ultimately to strengthen the fundamental conditions of world peace through the establishment of free communication of ideas between the two hemispheres.

5. And with such ideals in view to provide at Shanti Niketan aforesaid centre of culture where research in the study of religion, literature, history, science and art of Hindu, Buddhist, Jain, Islamic, Sikh, Christian and other civilisations may be pursued along with the culture of the West, with that simplicity in externals which is necessary for true spiritual realisation, in amity, good fellowships and co-operation between the thinkers and scholars of both Eastern and Western countries; free from all antagonism of race, nationality, creed or caste, and in the name of One Supreme Being Who is Shantam, Shivam, Advaitam."

Departments of the Visva Bharati

The Visva Bharati has now been recognised as a full-fledged Central University by the Government of India by a special Act passed by the Indian Parliament. The following are the various constituent departments of the Visva Bharati:

1. Vidya Bhawan (School of Research)
2. Siksha Bhawan (College)
3. Patha Bhawan (School)

4. Kala Bhawan (School of Music and Dancing)
5. Sri Niketan (Institute for Rural Reconstruction)
6. Shilpa Bhawan (School of Industries)
7. Vinaya Bhawan (Teacher's Training College)
8. China Bhawan (School of Sino-Indian Studies)
9. Hindi Bhawan
10. Islamic Research Section.

Atmosphere in Visva Bharati

Many of the classes at Visva Bharati are held in the open air. The development of individuality in all its aspects, is the aim of this unique institution. Every student is free for giving expression to his tastes and aptitudes. The curriculum is so broad as to provide far the various aptitudes of the students. The social side of the students is not ignored. The institution tries to keep itself in touch with the poor, unhappy and downtrodden masses of the neighbourhood. Thus, Tagore has tried to make the Visva Bharati a centre of Indian Renaissance. He has made it a venue for International Understanding. He also made it a place from where solid work may be done for social and economic reform of the nation. Above, all he made it a place, where from India many give the message of humanity to the whole world. Tagore is physically no more now, but his personality still pervades the Visva Bharati.

CONCLUSION

In the words of Calcutta University Syndicate "Through him (Tagore) India has given her message to mankind and his unique achievements in the fields of literature, philosophy, education and art, has won imperishable fame for himself and has raised the status of India in the estimation of the world."

Tagore had a benevolent function to perform. His was the ideal that human personality should be developed in an atmosphere of freedom and fellowship, through impulses of life lived in nature and in close touch with varied creative activities of the human mind. There (Shanti Niketan) prevails the atmosphere of Nature's own beauty with her varied gifts of colour and dance, flowers and fruits with the joy of her mornings and the peace of her starry nights. The place of Visva Bharati in the educational system of India is great. While it is preserving and furthering the cultural heritage of India, it is combining it with the best from the West in art, science and literature. The ideal of developing the human personality in an atmosphere of freedom and fellowship through impulses of a life lived in nature and in close touch with varied creative activities of human mind have found a true expression in Visva Bharati.

Tagore loved humanity and the purest form of humanity—the child. To him he gave respect, love, freedom, sympathy and scope for initiative.

18

Swami Dayananda Saraswati (1824-1883)

Swami Dayananda Saraswati was a great social and religious reformer of modern India. He was the champion of Arya Samaj movement and its founder. He revived the ancient Vedic Wisdom of India and worked for the upliftment of ignorant masses of his motherland. Truly, he was the saviour of Hinduism and maker of Modern India.

SWAMI DAYANANDA'S GENERAL PHILOSOPHY

A thorough protagonist of the Vedic culture and religion, Swami Dayananda Saraswati was shocked to see the appalling condition of his countrymen who leaving his own ancient faith were gradually embracing Christianity and were under the sway of Western Culture. Being Pro-Vedic and holding that the life in the Vedic ages had reached its highest level in culture and illumination, and himself being an ardent scholar and a seeker after the ultimate truth, he devoted his whole life in reviving the Vedic studies and discipline in India. He founded the Arya Samaj, because social reform formed an important part of his religion. He laid emphasis on the Vedic knowledge as a means of attaining emancipation, the highest end of life. He tried to revive the Vedic Culture through educational centres. He also laid down the Vedic Scheme of Education.

Swami Dayanandaa fought against the superstitions, the Pauranic Hinduism and the Dharma Shastras which were largely responsible for leading the masses towards darkness, idol-worship and disunity. To him, the Vedas are the source of all knowledge and character. Character or righteous living as taught by the Vedas and Smritis is the highest virtue. This is the end-all and be-all of human existence. Let a man, therefore, always take the path of righteousness.

Dayananda's Humanism

Dayanada's philosophy of knowledge has been elaborated in the second, third, fourth and ninth chapters of '*Satyartha Parkash*'. Explaining the aim of the author in writing the book Dayananda said, "Though the human should possess the capacity for ascertaining truth, yet through self-interest, obstinacy, wrong-heartedness, ignorance and the like, it is lead to renounce truth and incline towards untruth". I have freed myself from these influence while writing this book. It is not my object to hurt any one's susceptibilities or to injure anyone. On the other hand, my aim is to further the advancement and advance the well-being of mankind, to help (all) men in the ascertainment furthering of what is right and to handle them to accept truth and reject falsehood. In my opinion there is no other way of elevating the human race. Dayananda tries to fulfill this humanistic ideal both positively and negatively. While on the one hand he says, "Of course, any suggestion, made by persons actuated with the spirit of furnishing the welfare of humanity, on being found good, will be most acceptable." On the other hand he ruthlessly criticises those who supported untruth and rejected whatever is thought to be harmful for human welfare. Taking sides due to prejudices, according to Dayananda, was not only foolish and wrong but below the diginity of man. This emphasis on human dignity exhibits the humanism of Dayananada.

His Concept of Religion

Swami Dayananda regards religion as the true conduct of life. The central doctrine of religion, according to him, is the worship of God by means of prayer, meditation and the daily Havana. There is no place for idol-worship or pilgrimages and even for a priestly class. His religion is the religion of a common man. He believes in the equality and brotherhood of man and believes that it is the obligation of all human beings, to work for the welfare of all human beings. In brief, the essence of his religious doctrine is that a religious and God-loving man is not only to make his own life noble and beautiful; he is also to devote himself to helping other people to live virtuous and happy lives.

His Views About God

Swami Dayananda believes in the oneness of God. According to him God is one and the various names such as Agni, Vayu, Surya, etc., are the different names of the same God-head. God is pure Universal Spirit. God has no form. Dayananda does not believe in the finite and human form of God. According to him, the assumption that the infinite, all-pervading and eternal Lord can take on a human form, is the height of illogical thinking. He holds that God permeates the whole Universe. He is personification of Sat-Cit- Amanda. He creates, sustains, and dissolves the Universe.

His Ideas About Transmigration of Soul

Swami Dayananda believes in the transmigration of soul. He holds that the soul is immortal and eternal. Death of the body does not mean the end of the soul. Due to ignorance the soul is in bondage in this world. This ignorance is the cause of sin. Salvation lies in the emancipation of the soul from pain and suffering.

Characteristics of Knowledge

Explaining Vidya or right knowledge in the tradition of *Vedas*, Dayananda has written, "This fourfold incorrect knowledge is called Avidya or Ignorance. The reverse of it viz., to look upon what is temporal what is eternal as eternal, what is pure as pure, what is impure as impure, pain as pain, pleasure as pleasure, what is soulless as soulless, what is soul-possessing as soul-possessing, is called *Vidya* or knowledge." Distinguishing between knowledge and ignorance Dayananda writes, "That by which the true nature of things is known is called knowledge whilst that by which the true nature of things is not revealed, and instead, a false conception of things is formed, is called Ignorance."

Thus, in pointing out the aims of knowledge, Dayananda has maintained a pragmatic and practical outlook. Though in the Vedic Tradition he considers salvation to be the aim of knowledge but this salvation is not an extra terrestrial goal. It includes the realisation of human perfection as an individual as well as a collectivity here on this earth. It is hence that Dayananda has laid so much emphasis on right knowledge and right conduct. In the second chapter of his famous book 'Satyartha Prakash' he has written, "Fathers, mothers and tutors should always give their children and students good counsel and they should also advise them to imbibe their virtue but avoid their vices."

SWAMI DAYANANDA'S EDUCATIONAL PHILOSOPHY

Swami Dayananda attached great importance to educational institutions and felt a necessity of their establishment. It would serve as permanent means of enlightenment for the public and in the work of reform and regeneration. He established about seven schools at various places in U.P. His educational thoughts and principle as contained in 'Satyartha Parkash', are in accordance with the Vedic Philosophy interpreted in the light of contemporary socio-political and religious conditions of India. In order to understand his educational assumptions we refer to certain basic points.

Education as a Life-long Continuous Process

Swami Dayananda believes that education is a life-long continuous process. Though formal education of a child begins after his 'Upnayana Ceremony,' education informally begins from the time of conception. As mind is the product of food, Dayananda recommends Sattvik food to the parents: such a food, besides producing health, strength, energy and intellect, also produces mental tranquility and good temper.

Therefore, a pregnant mother must be particular about this fact. The parents must have a selective environment for themselves and must remain in close commune paving the way for the advent of a blissful life. During the whole period of pregnancy the mother has to be on her guard against all sorts of distractions and evil effects. According to Swamiji, "No other person can equal a mother in her love for her children, and in her anxiety for their welfare. Swamiji has given details how education has to be imparted in accordance with each period of the child's physical and mental growth. Summing up, we can say that the character of the mother influences the character of the child in the womb. Therefore, the upbringing of the child begins not at its birth but at the conception.

Education for all

Swami Dayananda considers it a sacred duty of the parents to look after education of their children. To give their children the highest education possible, to instruct them in the ways of truth, to make them refined in character and manners, in short, to devote all their wealth, body and mind for this objective. To accomplish this objective is the paramount duty, the highest virtue, and the glory of the parents.

Apart from this duty of the parents, "Both state and society should make it compulsory upon all to send their children (both male arid female) to school after the fifth or the eighth year. It should be made a penal-offence to keep a child at home after that age."

To have the society in perfect order, Swamiji asks the teachers not to neglect the education of classes other than Brahmans, viz. Princes and other Kashatriyas and intelligent Shudras "Because, if Brahmans only were to acquire knowledge there could be no advance in knowledge, religion and government, nor increase in wealth, or, Brahmans, whose sole duty is to acquire knowledge and disseminate it, depend for their living on Kashatriyas, etc., to whom they are law givers. Brahmanas would be relieved of all restraint and fear from Kashatriyas, who, being uneducated, would be quite incapable of judging the soundness or unsoundness of their teachings. They would thus gradually use their powers for their own selfish ends, drift into hypocrisy and do whatever they like, and their example will be followed by other classes. But when Kashatriyas and other classes are also well-educated, Brahmans study still harder to keep ahead of other classes, and walk in the path of righteousness. They could never then falsely teach and lead selfish, hypocritical lives. It follows, therefore, that it is in their own interest, as well as that of community at large, to try their best to teach the Veda and other true Sciences and Philosophies to Kshatriya, etc. It is Kashatriyas, and other classes, that are the real cause of advance in knowledge, religion, and government, and of increase in wealth, etc. They never live on alms, they, therefore, can have no reason to be partial in religious or scientific matters. When all the classes are well educated and cultured, no one can set up any false, fraudulent, and irreligious practices.

All this goes to prove that it is the Brahmans and sanyasins, who keeps Kashatriyas, and others in proper order, and vice versa. Therefore, all persons of all classes should be given good, sound education and be well instructed in the principles of true religion.

Functions of Education

The function of education is to provide this Vidya. Prior to defining right knowledge or Vidya Dayananda pointed out the following characteristics of Avidlya or ignorance. These have to be removed through education:

1. "The false notion that the transient world and worldly things (such as bodies) are eternal or in other words that the world of effects, that we see and feel, has always been existing and will continue to exist for ever, and that by virtue of the power of yoga the physical bodies of godly men become imperishable is the first kind of Avidya (ignorance).

2. To regard impure things, such as lustfulness and untruthfulness, as pure is the second kind of Avidya (Ignorance).

3. To believe that excessive sexual indulgence is a source of happiness, whilst it really causes pain and suffering, constitutes the third variety of Avidya (ignorance).

4. To consider dead material things as possessed of soul is the fourth kind of Avidya (Ignorance).

Aims and Objectives of Education

Education aims at removing the above mentioned fourfold ignorance or incorrect knowledge. Besides this, negative aspect of the aim of education, it has a positive aspect in the provision of right knowledge. Elucidating this right knowledge in the tradition of Vedas, Dayananda wrote, "This fourfold incorrect knowledge is called Avidya or ignorance. The reverse of it, viz., to look upon what is temporal as temporal, what is eternal as eternal, what is pure as pure, what is impure as impure, pain as pain, pleasure as pleasure, what is soul less as soul less, what is soul-possessing as soul-possessing called Vidya or knowledge." Distinguishing between knowledge and ignorance Dayananda wrote, "That by which the true nature of things is known as called knowledge whilst that by which the true nature of things is not revealed and, instead, a false conception of thing is formed, is called Ignorance.

Thus, while pointing out the aims of Education; Dayananda maintained a pragmatic and practical outlook. In the Vedic tradition he considered salvation to be the aim of education but this salvation is not an extra-terrestrial goal. It includes the realisation of human perfection as an individual as well as a collectivity here on this earth. It is hence that Dayananda laid so much emphasis on right knowledge and right conduct. In the second chapter of his famous work *Satyartha Prakash* he wrote, "Fathers, mothers and tutors should always give their children and students good counsel and they should also advice them to imbibe their virtues but avoid their vices."

Child Education

Dayananda devoted the second chapter of his work 'Satyartha Prakash' it to the upbringing of the children. In this context he elaborated his educational theory about child's education, and showed sufficient insight in the education and psychological principles. He held that no one can achieve knowledge without the guidance of three great teachers—the father, the mother and the preceptor. Child's education starts in the family. Emphasising the importance of family in education, Dayananda wrote, "Blessed is the family, most fortunate is the child whose parents are godly and learned." Education of the child pre-supposes education of the parents. The mother educates the child through her immense love. The parents should present good examples before the children. the children tend to copy the parents. As soon as the child is able to understand, the mother should instruct him in refined manners. The initial teaching of language is carried on in the family through the parents. The mother should see that the child uses his tongue properly. Besides proper speech the child should also develop proper conduct. He should again be trained in manners while addressing his superiors and inferiors. And finally what is most important is that", "Parents should endeavour to inculcate in the minds of their children an intense desire for the love of knowledge, elevating company, and control of the senses."

Education in the School

The child's education, according to Dayananda should be both positive and negative. While on the one hand efforts should be made to develop in him such qualities as truthfulness, heroism, patience and cheerfulncss, thc parents should also see that the children avoid useless playing, crying, laughing and wrangling and may not develop evil qualities such as jealousy and malice, etc. They should be taught not to have superstitions. They should develop a scientific outlook towards the world. Depicting the humanistic element in his philosophy of education Dayananda wanted to develop rationalism and scientific outlook in males and females right from the childhood. He was a most vehement Critic of all superstitions, beliefs in ghosts and witches etc. He even condemned astrology and accepted only that part of it which is known as astronomy.

Moral Education

Thus, Dayananda clearly laid down the means for the moral education of the children. Moral education involves the encouragement of virtues on the one hand and the discouragement of vices on the other. The parents and the teacher should themselves present high Ideals. Unless they do so they will not be able to create respect for their advices in the children. The children should be taught to speak the truth and observe their words. They should never be vain. They should avoid deceitfulness, hypocracy and ingratitude. The child should not lose his temper nor use rough language. He should avoid useless talking and speak only as much as is necessary and that too in a sweet tone. He should be taught to respect his elders, stand and salute them. He should learn to behave in society, to occupy a seat according to his rank and status. He should never have malice towards anyone. He should always speak the truth. The children should obey their parents and tutors. In the matter of dress and diet they should conduct in such a way as to gain in health, strength and knowledge. Thus, in brief the child, "Should try to acquire virtues and shun vices; associate with the good and avoid the wicked."

Scheme of Studies

Swami Dayananda suggests a scheme of studies through which one can be master of the Vedas, the Upavedas, and other sciences within twenty or twenty one years. The following subjects have to be studied in the order given below:

1. Phonetics (Shiksha) by Panini.
2. Grammar.
3. Nighantu and Nirukta.
4. Chhandograntha.
5. Manusmriti, Valmiki Ramayana, Vidur Niti etc.
6. Six Shastras.
7. Four Vedas with their four Brahmanas.
8. Upvedas-which are four in number:
    (a) Ayurveda.
    (b) Dhanur Veda.
    (c) Gandharva Veda.
    (d) Artha Veda also called Shilpa Vidya.
9. Jyotisha Shastra which includes Arithmetic, Algebra, Geometry, Geography, Geology and Astronomy also practical training in these sciences.

In conclusion with this scheme Swami Dayananda mentions those books which should not be studied as they are written by atheists, because, once caught in them a student can never know the truth.

Medium of Education

In the ancient Indian tradition Dayananda favoured mother tongue and the Sanskrit language. He strongly pleaded the causes of Sanskrit as medium of all higher education. He wrote in details about the curriculum and teaching methods for learning and mastering Sanskrit. He was vehemently critical of using foreign language such as English as medium of education not only in primary but also at the highest stage. This seriously hampers any original and creative thinking. This tradition of regard for mother tongue and Sanskrit was supported by all the Indian educational philosophers after Dayanad.

Qualification of the Teacher

Elaborating the qualifications of teachers, whether male or female, Dayananda referred to sayings of Mahabharata. He supported the idea that, "He alone is a wise man who is never idle nor lazy, nor effected by pleasure or pain, profit or loss, honours or dishonour, public applause or censure, has always a firm faith in Dharma, and cannot be tempted by sensual objects". Thus the wise teacher should practice virtue and avoid sin. He should abstain from abusing Gods, the *Vedas* or the Virtuous people. He should have unbounded faith in God. He should be able to grasp the most difficult subject in a very short time. He should devote years after years in the pursuit of knowledge and use it for the good of mankind. He should not give opinion un-asked for nor should he interrupt another in his speech. He should not brood over his loses. He should be well versed in all kinds of knowledge. He should be a clever debater, able to speak on any subject. He should have a good memory and a sound logic. He should be able to give a true exposition of scriptures. His intellect should be in conformity with truth. When the teachers possess the above mentioned qualities then alone they will be able to fulfill the aims of education. Dayananda not only elaborated the qualities of a good teacher but also pointed out characteristics of undesirable teachers so that one may be able to compare between the two and gain by distinction.

Qualification of Students

Dayananda accepted the view mentioned by Mahabharata where it has been said, "Physical mental inertia, use of intoxicants, infatutation, idle gossip, neglect of studies, vanity, and want of Brahrmacharya, these seven vices are not to be found among students." Such students can never acquire knowledge. About the qualifications of good students again, Dayananda accepted the viewpoint expressed in Vidur niti of Mahabharata, "They alone practice virtue, subjugate their passions and never lose their reproductive element, are true Brahmacharis and become learned men." Thus, according to Dayanad, both the teachers and the students should possess high qualities.

Teacher-Taught Interaction

The high qualities can be developed through mutual inspiration. The teachers inculcate truthfulness, self-control, gentleness and physical and mental development on the educands. They should also try to eradicate evil habits of the students. The students, on the other hand, themselves try to develop self-control, mental tranquility, thoughtfulness, diligence and love for their teachers. They should try to attain physical and mental perfections. Emphasising the aim of education as perfection of man, Dayananda wrote, "They should so exert themselves as to acquire perfect knowledge, perfect dharma, perfect development of body and learn to labour." The above mentioned discussion upon the qualifications of good teachers and good scholars supply criteria for the selection of suitable teachers and suitable students in educational institutions.

Education for Different Sections of Society

While defining education as the means of individual's salvation, Dayananda also laid emphasis on its social aspect. Education aims not only on development of the personality of the educand, but also on creating such man and woman in society. Dayananda did not restrict education to a certain class. He pleaded for universal education. He elaborately discussed the education of the backward classes and women. It is significant to note that according to some Vedic scholars the Shudras and then women have no right to same type of education which is given to the higher classes of males. As a true humanist, Dayananda contradicted this interpretation of Vedic education and strongly emphasised that education must be given to every one without distinction of class or sex. He argued in details in favour of the female education and emphasised its need right from the beginning. According to Dayananda the women should be educated not only in home science but also in grammar, religion, medicine, mathematics and even in technology. Like the boys the girls also should be sent to residential educational institutions at the early age of eight.

Gurukula or Acharyakula

At the age of eight after Upanayana ceremony has been performed boys and girls should be sent to their respective schools. The schools should be situated in a lonely place and must not be within five miles of a town or village. The boys' school should be at least three miles away from that of the girls'. The tutors and other employees in the boys' schools should be all of the male sex and in girls of the female sex. Not even a child of five years of one sex be allowed to enter the school of the other sex. Tutors should see that the students perfect their knowledge, cultivate amiable dispositions and manners, and gain in strength; both of body and mind thereby grow in happiness. All the scholars should be treated alike in matters of food, drink, dress and seats. Be they princes and princesses or the children of beggars all should practice asceticism severe bodily and mental discipline. Simple living and high thinking should be the motto of the students. They should not be allowed to see their parents or hold any communication whatever with them. Being thus freed from all worldy worries and cares, they should devote themselves heart and soul to their studies. Their tutors should accompany them in all their recreations, so that they may not fall into any mischief, get indolent or naughty.

Period of Studentship

Twenty-five years is the minimum period for the observance of Brahmacharya. If anyone wants to remain celebrate till death, he may do so, but this is possible to those whose knowledge is perfect, who have full control over their minds and senses, and who are perfect yogis, free from all vices.

"After their entrance into school, the second Upanayana ceremony should be performence" and Gaitri Mantra, though given at the first Upanayana ceremony at home, should be taught to the children along with its meanings. After that Sandhyopasana long with its accessories and the techniques of Yajna performance should be taught to him. This forms part of daily worship.

Views about Women Education

Dayananda gives equal right to women and championed the cause of women's education. In this regards Dayananda cites a verse of the Atharvaveda: Just as boys acquire sound knowledge and culture by the practice of Brahamcharya and then marry girls of their own choice, who are young, well-educated, loving and of like temperament, so should a girl practice Brahamcharya, study the Veda, and other sciences and thereby perfect her knowledge, refine her character, give her hand to a man of her own choice, who is young, learned and loving. Swami Dayananda has all praise for those parents who treat their children alike and provide opportunities for education to their sons and daughters. He asserted that girls should also practice Brahamcharya. He recommends for them Grammar, Dharma, Medical Science, Mathematics and Practical Arts. Since, the main sphere of duty for women is the home its management, reproducing, bringing up and instruction of their children, he prescribes different curriculum for them with special reference to home management so as to prove good wives and mothers. Thus, he was the champion of women's education and became the first Indian social reformer who vehemently pleaded for their education.

CONCLUSION

Swami Dayananda was mainly a social reformer. He was a Sanyasi, a Brahmachari, a Scholar and an Educationist. His mission was to revive the ancient Vedic Indian Wisdom and Spirit. In his quest to regenerate the society, he established the Arya Samaj and advocated certain principles of education which became the guidelines for various institutions. It is true that Swami Dayananda did not give any technical system of education or a science of education. But it is also true that he saved the country at a critical juncture and fought for national solidarity and international understanding. His emphasis on moral values, purity of thoughts and deeds, character and righteousness of life, and above all his plea for democratic concept of education are some of the significant and remarkable contributions which have had a far reaching effect on Indian life and culture and the system of education.

19

Swami Vivekananda (1863-1902)

Swami Vivekananda was a practical saint of modern India, who wanted to revive the ancient wisdom of India, especially Vedic wisdom and succeeded in re-establishing the glorious traditions of great India. Throughout his life he preached and practised the gospels of truth, righteousness, renunciation, and brotherhood of man and the realisation of God. He had immense faith in the dignity of man and his well-being. He wanted to see India transformed—the same India which could conquer the world spiritually and show light to mankind as a whole. His voice echoed throughout the world and he enthused a new life among the masses of India. His mission was to strike a balance between the spirituality of the East and the materialism of the West. He was a world teacher and a great educationist.

A BRIEF LIFE SKETCH OF SWAMI VIVEKANANDA

Swami Vivekananda was born in 1863 in Calcutta. Right from his childhood, he was curious to explore things and find out the realities. His original name was Narendra Dutta. During his college life, he came under the influence of Sri Ramakrishna Pararmahansa. There, he was transformed and realised his self as a part of the

Higher Self—Atman. He was enlightened and got Viveka i.e. knowledge which was eternal.

Vivekananda was a great scholar and studied philosophy an poetry. He also studied all the systems of Western Philosophy and soon became an authority on the subject. He was unique in all respects. He impressed everybody. His Principal remarked, "Narendranath is really a genius... He is, bound to make his mark in life."

Vivekananda did for the gospel of Sri Ramakrishna what St. Paul did for the gospel of Christ. He broadcasted the truths of *Vedanta* in India, Europe and America, as, realised in the experience of Sri Ramakrishna. . . Vivekananda demonstrated to the world that the great Indian spiritual tradition was still alive and vigorous. He showed both by precept and example that, if the ancient *Vedanta* were reinterpreted in the light of Sri Ramakrishna's spiritual experience as applied to modern life, India would be able to solve many of her problems and would rise once again to deliver a message to humanity.

Vivekananda was the fore-runner of Gandhi and many more. He was not a politician but he wanted to establish a society of strong and self-reliant Indians. Penetrating his way though, he rendered meritorious services to the motherland and left for his heavenly abode in 1902 at the age of thirty-nine only.

VIVEKANANDA'S PHILOSOPHY

Swami Vivekananda's Philosophy is discussed below:

A True Vedanist

Vivekananda was true Vedantist, a true follower of Ramakrishna Paramhansa. According to him, Vedanta is eternal. He regards the Dvaita, the Visistadvaita and the Advaita as the different expressions of the Vedanta. To him these are merely the stages for helping the individual to proceed towards the realisation of higher and higher ideals. The ultimate goal of human life is to attain wonderful unity with the creator.

Swami Vivekananda regards the Vedanta as perfectly impersonal. To him the Vedanta philosophy, as it is known today, includes the various sects that are found in India. Consequently, various interpretations of the Vedanta philosophy have been forwarded, from the dualistic (or Dvaita) to the non-dualistic (or Advaita). Swami Vivekananda considers all these interpretrations progressive. The Vedanta is eternal. It is not originated by any person or prophet. So it is not built around any particular individual as the centre. But it does not criticise those philosophies which have been propounded by certain individuals. Swami Vivekananda regards the Dvaita, the Visistavaita and the Advaita as the different expressions of the Vedanta. So to him they are not opposed to each other. He does not consider them as absolute systems. To him these are merely the stages for helping the individual to proceed progressively towards the realisation of higher and higher ideals till everything is merged in that wonderful unity which is reached in the Advaita system.

Concept of God

As a staunch Vedantist Swami Vivekananda gives only three attribute to God. He is Infinite Existence, Infinite Knowledge and Infinite Bliss. He believes that these three are one. He says, "Existence without knowledge and love cannot be; knowledge without love, and love without knowledge cannot be. What we want is the harmony of Existence, Knowledge and Bliss Infinite. For that is our goal. We want harmony, not one-sided development and it is possible to have the intellect of a Sankara with the heart of a Buddha. I hope we shall all struggle to attain that blessed combination."

Concept of Religion

He had a very liberal conception of religion. His contention is, "Religions are different forces in the economy of God, working for the good of mankind." They are not contradictory. He thinks that every religion is progressive and has many good points. He however emphasised universalism in religions and human religion. Through religion he advocated spiritualism and brotherhood.

In brief Vivekananda strongly advocated :

(i) That no religion is inferior to any other. All religions lead to the same goal.

(ii) That God is Omnipresent and Impersonal. He is manifested in all the creatures on earth.

(iii) That the Hindu nation will again teach the whole world, as it had taught in the past, in the realm of spiritualism.

(iv) That the Hindus (Indians) must not try to imitate the European nations and Western civilisations blindly.

(v) That the Indians must stand on their own legs for improving their lot.

Synthesis between Science and Spirituality

It may be mentioned that Swami Vivekananda interpretation of the Vedanta is based upon a scientific analysis. Both the Vedanta and science maintain common principles. He stood for harmony between science and spiritualy.

Swami Vivekananda's interpretation of the Vedanta is based upon a scientific analysis. He says, "When the scientific teacher asserts that all things are the manifestation of one force, does it not remind you of the God of whom you hear in the Upanishads? As the one fire entering into the universe expresses itself in various forms, even so that one Soul is expressing itself in every soul and yet is infinitely more besides." Thus, the Swami sees that both the Vedanta and science maintain common principles.

Swami Vivekananda believed that the same methods of investigation that are applied to sciences and knowledge outside should be applied to the science of religion, because thereby it will become as scientific, at least, as any of the conclusions of physics or chemistry, and will have greater strength because physics or chemistry do not have that internal mandate to vouch for its truth, which religion has. Therefore, one must not deny the efficiency of any rational investigation into religion.

Concept of Humanism

Swami Vivekananda thinks that the same omnipresent and omniscient soul resides in every man and in every animal however, weak, small or great. He believes. "The difference is not the soul, but in the manifestation. Between me and the smallest animal, the difference is only in manifestation, but as a principle he is the same as I am, he is my brother, he has the same soul as I have."

Thus, Swami Vivekananda believes in universalism and spiritual brotherhood. He asserts that the Vedanta as the religion must be intensely practical. He urges people to apply it to every aspect of their lives. He regards the difference between various religions as fictitious and says that they must vanish. Such is his conviction about the universalism he preaches.

Swami Vivekananda has intense faith in man and he realised the dignity and diversity of human beings. In fact, he finds the manifestation of God in man. He say, "The only God to worship is the human soul, in the human body. Of course, all animals are temples too, but man is the highest, the Taj Mahal of temples. If I cannot worship in that no other temple will be of any advantage.

The moment I have realised God sitting in the temple of every human body, the moment I stand in reverence before every human being and see God in him that moment I am free from bondage, everything that binds vanishes, and I am free.

"To him the ideal of the Vedanta is to know man as he really is. This is the message of the Vedanta. He asks, "If you cannot worship your brother man, the manifestation of God, how can you worship a God who is unmanifested?.... If you cannot see God in the human face, how can you see him in the clouds, or in images made of dull, dead matter, or in mere fictitious stories of your brain? I shall call you religious from the day you begin to see God in men and women."

Swamiji Patriotism

The Swamiji, himself a patriot of the first order, advocated a deep spirit of patriotism in every Indian. He felt the pulse of the times, the communal discord, the strain of untouchability, the linguistic and provincial and caste differences, the lacks of vision, and a sort of indolence and inertia cutting through each and every call of India's life blood. So he took the whip of reprimand and hit out through his speeches. He asked all the communities to forger the points of difference, disharmony and strife, and to hear, instead, the gentle voice of the motherland. He further asked them to remove all the weaknesses to root out priest craft and orthodoxy, and to work for the economic uplift of the country through trade, commerce and agriculture.

Thus, the Swamiji teaches the eternal communion of man with the infinite through a religion of universal oneness and cosmopolitanism. He was completely consistent when he urges people to believe in a universal religion. He does not regard the various religions as contradictory. To him the various "Religions are different forces in the economy of God, working for the good of mankind." He thinks that every religion is progressive. He believes that universal religion is existing in the same way as the universal oneness between man and man already exists. He regards the realisation of Divinity, or the knowledge of *Brahman* as the ultimate goal for man, and that man cannot remain absorbed in Brahman all the time. The absorption in the *Brahman* can be only for some exceptional moments which do not last long. That is why the saint after having realised the Selfless, sees the Self in all creatures. Therefore, he devotes himself entirely to the service of all beings. It is because of this that Swami Vivekananda has emphasised universalism and spiritual brotherhood.

Swami Vivekananda believes that perfection is one's heritage. He declares, "Perfection is not to be attained, it is already within us. Immortality and bliss are not to be acquired, we possess them already; they have been ours all the time." All through his life the Swami strove whole-heartedly to make his fellow-beings realise this truth.

VIVEKANANDA'S EDUCATIONAL PHILOSOPHY

Swami Vivekananda's educational philosophy is a reflection of his general philosophy of life. His main contention is that education is the manifestation of divinity already existing in man. He believes that knowledge resides within the individual himself. He simply discovers or realise'; it. "Perfection is already inherent in man and education is the manifestation of the same." In fact, his educational philosophy is built upon the bed-rocks of Vedanta. He was revolutionary in the field of education and touched every aspect of it. Vivekananda criticised existing system of education.

Concept of Education

As we have already noted above, Vivekananda believes that education is the manifestation of the perfection already existing in man. "To him, education is not the amount of information, put into one's brain, which may be there undigested all one's life. It is rather a life-building assimilation of ideas". He says, "If you have assimilated five ideas and made them as your character you have more education than any man who has got by heart the whole library. If education were identical with information, the libraries would be the greatest sages in the world and encyclopedias, the greatest Rishis."

Vivekananda considers education as a part of human life. On one side he interprets education as the manifestation of the perfection and on the other side the essence of education, as he contends is concentration of mind, not the collection of facts. His greatest concern is the common masses and he wants to equip them for the struggle for life. He observes, "The education which does not help the common masses of people to equip themselves for life, which does not bring out strength of character, a spirit of philanthropy, and the courage of a lion is it worth the name? Real education is that which enables one to stand on one's own legs."

Accordingly, Vivekananda gives a very practical concept of education in these lines. "We want that education by which character is formed, strength of mind is increased, the intellect is expanded and by which one can stand on one's own feet."

Aims of Education

Vivekananda has summed up the aims of education in one sentence "The end of all education, all training, should be man making." He further says, "The training by which the current and expression of will are brought under control and become fruitful is called education." He however recommends the following aims of education:

Creation of self-confidence and self-realisation: Education must make a man conscious of his hidden powers. Man must know that he is neither the perishable bodily frame nor the changing mind. He is the immortal soul which is the treasure house of infinite power. All knowledge he discovers within him self. With this knowledge or divine light, he can work wonders. Man should, therefore, have full confidence in himself and strive to reach the highest goal of his life. Self-confidence leads to self-realisation. In Swamiji's—own words, "Faith in ourself and faith in God—this is the secret of greatness." A person who possesses self-confidence, can do much, individually as well as socially. We fail only when we do not strive sufficiently to manifest the infinite power within ourselves. Education of the right type should aim at removing the veil of ignorance from our mind and make us understand what we actually are and what we should ultimately be. It is only through self-reliance and self-realisation that a person can attain perfection and achieve the glory of life.

Formation of character: Character is the aggregate of a man's tendencies, the sum-total of the bent of his mind. We are what our thoughts have made us. Good and evil thoughts have an equal share in moulding character. It is, therefore, that education should aim at sublimating the evil tendencies of our mind. It should give us life-building and character-making assimilation of ideas. Swamiji says, "We want that education by which character is formed, strength of mind is increased intellect is expanded and by which one can stand on one's own feet." Education must build up character and manifest our real nature.

Development of personality: Personality is the influence, the impression, one creates on the others. It is the personality of a man that counts. "According to Vivekananda, personality is two third and his intellect and words are only one third in making the real man." The ideal of all education and all trainings should be the man-making. The man who influences, who throws his magic upon his fellow beings, is a dynamo of power. When that man is ready he can do anything and everything that he likes. That personality, put upon anything, will make it work.

Service of mankind: Another important aim of education is serving the God in man. It is not the God in symbols and images that we generally find in temples. It is the God in the sick, the poor, the miserable, the ignorant and the down-trodden that we should worship. In Swamiji own words, "If you want to find God, serve man." He was pained to see the wretched poverty of his countrymen. He, therefore, wanted that education must enable everyone to stand on his own feet and satisfy his own primary needs. Here he suggested a system of education through work experience and workshops.

Promotion of universal brotherhood: While Swami Vivekananda was a patriot and a nationalist to the core of his heart, he was also a great internationalist. His love for mankind knew no geographical boundaries. He always pleaded for the harmony and good relationship of all nations. He says "Through education, we should gradually reach the idea of universal brotherhood by flinging down the walls of separation and inequality. In every man, in every animal, however, weak or miserable, great or small, resides the same omnipresent and omniscient soul. The difference is not in the soul, but in manifestation." Thus, his internationalism is spiritual, based on the Vedantic principle of universality of self. He insists that education must call forth this power in every person and broaden it to such an extent that it may cover the whole world. Such a programme will annihilate all misery and discomfort from this earth. He declared, "I am thoroughly convinced that no individual or nation can live by holding itself apart from the community of others."

Whenever such an attempt will be made, under the false idea of greatness or policy of holiness, the result will always be disastrous. Our isolation from all the other nations of the world has been the cause of our degradation and its only remedy is getting back into the current of the rest of the world. "Thus, Swami Vivekananda advocated internationalism of world society into a compact union of hearts and souls".

Concept of Carriculum

Below are given Vivekananda's views about carriculum.

Synthesis between Science and Vedanta: Vivekananda did not prescribe any typical curriculum to be followed rigidly. He however, emphasised a curriculum based on concept of all-round development of child's personality. On one side, he recommended the study of Vedanta, Religion, Philosophy and Theology. On the other side, he favoured western science, engineering and other modern subjects. He thus wanted to synthesise these two trends which is the burning need of the day.

Stress on study of the following Subjects: Vivekananda had a comprehensive view of education and its contents. He recommended the study of languages especially regional languages, *Sanskrit*, link language and English. He also stressed subjects like history, geography, economics and other social sciences. Even home science and psychology were recommended by him.

Vocationalisation of Education: Vivekananda wanted to make education self-supporting in all respects. Economic independence should be an important aspect of education. For this he favoured agriculture, technical education and physical education. He clearly said, "Make your nerve strong. What' we want is muscles of iron and nerves of steel."

He himself was an embodiment of all these virtues and qualities. Certain it is that Vivekananda was very keen in the spiritual development of the masses as well as their economic and material prosperity.

Method of Teaching

Vivekananda also expressed his views on the methods of education. His views are given below:

Concentration of Mind: Vivekananda laid emphasis on concentration as a method of attaining knowledge. Concentration is the sole key to the treasure of knowledge. Vivekananda considers the concentration of mind as the essence of education. The literary figures and the scientists have to concentrate their attention on their subjects for a long time, and only then they can hope to discover something new in the field. Greater attention always helps in working more.

Brahmacharya for concentration: Vivekananda believes that Brahmacharya is necessary for developing the power of concentration. By observing strict Brahmacharya, all learning can be mastered within a very short time. Brahmacharya improves the power of mind and helps power of retention. Without Brahmacharya one cannot possibly have any spiritual power. Brahmacharya gives mental and spiritual power of the highest kind.

Discussion and Contemplation: In addition to concentration, Vivekananda lays emphasis on the importance of discussion and contemplation as methods of education. The pupil can remove the difficulties in his path by discussing them with his teacher in an informal atmosphere.

Faith and Reverence: The educand must have reverence for his educator. The progress of any kind is impossible in the absence of reverence. Faith in one's own-self is the first step towards advancement. One finds people commit suicide when they have no faith and devotion of the highest order. The foundation of this faith and devotion is man's own soul, but the educator inspires this devotion.

Individual Guidance and Counselling: Pupils can be kept on the right path through the method of individual guidance and counselling.

Freedom in Education: Vivekananda is a strong supporter of freedom in Education, because he believes that it is the first requisite of development. Hence no teacher should exert any kind of pressure on his pupils.

The Role of Teacher

Swami Vivekananda discusses the role of teacher as given below:

Impact of his Personality: Vivekananda attaches great importance to the personal life and character of the teacher. He thinks, that only; A Tyagi can be a good teacher.' A teacher must be dedicated to his profession and teach with devotion with purity of mind and heart.

Love for the Students: The teacher must have love for his pupils. Love is the best medium to transmit the spiritual force. The teacher must work for his pupils only out of love.

Sympathy for the Pupils: A teacher can never teach without sympathy. Vivekananda says, "The true teacher is one who can throw his whole force into the tendency of the taught. Without real sympathy we can never teach well." -

Regarding the role of teacher Vivekananda himself says, the only true teacher is he who can immediately come down to the level of the student, and transfer his soul to the student's soul and see through the student eyes and hear through his ears and understand through his mind. Such a teacher can really teach and none else.'

Place of the Child: Like Froebel and Vivekananda regards child as the pivotal point of education. The child is the store house of knowledge. Knowledge resides with in him. Vivekananda lays emphasis on the discovery of inner knowledge and says "Go into your own and get the Upanishads out of yourself. You are the greatest book that ever was or will be. Until the inner teacher opens, all outside teaching is vain."

Universal Education (Mass Education)

According to Vivekananda, education is the birth right of every human being. It is a biological, social and spiritual necessity. He was very much distressed at the pitiable condition of the common man in India. He says, "So long as the millions live in hunger and ignorance, I hold every man a traitor who, having been educated at their expense, pays not the least heed to them."

These views have been incorporated in the Indian Constitution. The root cause of all our ills is the poverty of the people. Education is the sole remedy for improving the condition of the poor in the country. Vivekananda wanted to develop their lost individuality through education. He was in favour of secular education and he felt the need of a proper organisation. He says, "If the poor boy cannot come to education, education must go to him."

To achieve this objective he recommends that self-sacrificing Sanyasins whose number is much higher in our country, should work as teachers of secular things. They will go from place to place, from door to door, not only preaching but teaching also. Vivekananda is an ardent lover of the masses who represent India in the true sense of the term. Thus, he was a staunch nationalist, great sadhu, a spiritualist, a practical saint and a world teacher who showed light to the world and showered wisdom upon all the people alike.

With such a noble ideal, pure thoughts, revolutionary command and eternal faith in the goodness of man, Vivekananda went forward throughout his life and steered a path of greatness and nobility which are the bases of a progressive society and the nation. He is great and great is his mission. He laid stress on love, sincerity and patience which are the pillars of a modern democratic secular society. Thus, he favoured a casteless society—a society where people must learn to be servants first and masters afterwards.

Religious Education

Swami Vivekananda was a great teacher. He even had the experience of being a classroom teacher. The supreme mission of his life was to spread the gospel of Vedas and Upanishads, "Arise awake and stop not till the goal is reached." He wanted to make this as the guiding-stone of education. For this he laid stress on religious education, saying, "I look upon religion as the innermost core of education—Mind. I do not mean my own, or anyone else's opinion about religion."

In this context he recommends that children should be taught lives of great saints of all lands. "One must enter into the heart of religion, that is, one must realise it in his own life."

According to Swamiji, religion must be a living experience with oneself. "Teaching of doctrines and creeds of particular religions should not form part of religious education in schools. All religions must be accepted, and only their essential spirits should constitute the religious education to be given to children."

Women Education

Vivekananda was a great champion of women education. He was highly impressed to see the women of the West working with their husbands shoulder to shoulder. Vivekananda was greatly pained at the miserable condition of women in India. He was conscious that a nation could rise only by paying proper respect to women. Vivekananda says, "There is no hope of rise for that family or country where there is no education of women, where they live in sadness. For this, reason they have to be raised first."

He recommends the ideal of chastity for women. This will help them to attain perfect womenhood. To him Sita is a symbol of purity. Indian women therefore, must be taught to follow the ideal of Sita. Vivekananda is against child marriage. He feels that there can be no hope of well-being of the country unless the condition of the women is improved. He has full faith in the Indian culture and virtues of our domestic living—an Ideal arrangement. He observes ... "To the women of this country I would say exactly what I say to the men. Believe in India and in our Indian faith. Be strong and hopeful and unashamed."

He had immense faith in our women. He put forth the ideal lives of great Indian women, such as Sita, Ahilya Bai and Mira Bai etc. He wanted to give a type of education that may make "Women fearless and brave, which may form character and enable them to face the realities of life boldly. He recommends the spirit of valour and heroism for them. Here he points out the heroic deeds of Rani of Jhansi. He also recommends the study of history, puranas, housekeeping and the arts. Ideal women must learn the duties of home-life and principles that make for the development of an ideal character. He even favoured science education and training in ethical and spiritual life.

It was his conviction that the uplift of the women must come first and then only can any real good come about for the country, for India. Thus, like Swami Dayananda he championed the cause of women education.

CONTRIBUTION OF VIVEKANANDA'S EDUCATIONAL PHILOSOPHY

It is needless to point out that Vivekananda was a great educationist and he revolutionised the entire thinking of Indian educationists. No doubt, he has not given a particular scheme of education to be implemented in our schools, yet it is a reality that Vivekananda set the Indian Youth right and inspired millions of people to receive and provide right kind of education fitted to their needs, their cultural background and their national traditions.

His greatest contributions are his emphasis on self-knowledge. Self-reliance, faith in one's self, concentration and attaining perfection. He was a great lover of masses and their education and correlated their betterment with the betterment of the country. He actually sounded a warning to the contemporary regime and laid the foundations of independent India.

By advocating women education he visualised better homes, better people. better society and a prosperous nation.

Vivekananda was a great teacher and he therefore, called upon the teachers to be Karamyogis, men of character, wit and wisdom and ideal in all respects. Any selfish motive on the part of the teacher will destroy the whole spirit of teaching and love which is the best medium to transmit the spiritual force.

Establishment of Ramakrishna Mission Ashrams is the most remarkable contribution of Vivekananda. Through their establishment throught the world, he perpetuated the memory of his master and spread the gospels of Vedas.

Vivekananda was in favour of indigenous education. Time and again he emphasised Indiananess in education. The greatest need today, therefore, is to Indianise Indian education and incorporates the suggestions given by Swami Vivekananda. This will certainly help in the reorganisation of our system of education.

CONCLUSION

The Swamiji spoke the language of practical spirituality. He emphasised man-making and nation-building education. In man making education, he further emphasised character-building selfless service to the nation, freedom and equality. He was a revivalist of Indian culture. From him preceded a wave of national consciousness and patriotism. He taught humanitarianism and his dynamic philosophy flowed into an ocean of compassion and love for the suffering millions, of the country. True education, to him, was not for personal career but for contribution to the nation. His Vedantic philosophy gave a new interpretention to the goal of life and that of education Renunciation' to him meant not renunciation of the household and social obligation, but renunciation of selfish and narrow ends. "He became a teacher of love: the love of God flowing into service of man, of faith flowing into works and both forging character, which is manliness, and manliness which is spirituality."

Swami Vivekananda continued the tradition of 'saints and sages of the land, but he was a saint with a difference. He was not a forest recluse, but a dynamic society-mover say, a world-mover. He was a modern Rishi, who spoke on all aspects of life including Sociology, Culture, History. Political Science, Philosophy and Education. And he spoke with the Authentic voice of the spirit in man in a language which at once goes to the recesses of heart. His voice is eternal and his teachings are an inspiration.

We may sum up in the words of Romain Rolland: "In the two words 'equilibrium and synthesis'. Vivekananda constructive genius may be summed up. He embraced all the paths of the spirit. The four yoga's in their entirety, comprehends renunciation and service, art and science religion and action from the most spiritual to the most practical. Each of the way that he taught had it own limits, but he himself had been through them all, and embraced them all. As in a quadriga, he held the reins of all four ways of truth and he travelled towards Unity among them all simultaneously. He was the personification of the harmony of all human energy."

20

Aurobindo Ghosh (1872-1950)

Sri Aurobindo came from a respectable Bengali family. He was born in 1872. He was educated in England from the age of seven. On returning to India he joined the Baroda State Service. The resigning his post, he joined the political struggle in Bengal, suffered imprisonment for some time, and in 1919, retired to Pondicherry to devote himself to philosophy. He died in 1950. Two of his important works are *The Life Divine* and *The Synthesis of Yoga*.

AUROBINDO'S PHILOSOPHY

Aurobindo's Idealistic philosophy of life is based upon Vedantic philosophy of Upnishads, i.e. Spiritual penance, Yoga practice and Brahmacharya for the development of human soul. He exhorts that the sole aim of the principle of growth should be to achieve all pervading Divine Power. During cultural growth, a stage arrives whereby virtue of this supreme development of mental power, a man attains the status of Supreman himself. Then he experiences the supreme happiness and divine bliss and gains the insight into all creation and the inner spirit of cosmos, which pervades the whole creation of God.

The basis of his entire thought is his stress on the 'Life Divine'; which can be realised through Integral Yoga. Aurobindo believes that while philosophy is a quest for the truth of things by the human intellect—the endeavour to realise the truth in the inner-self and in outer-life is 'Dharma'. Aurobindo immersed himself in Vedanta and Yoga. Instead of seeing conflict or finding inconsistencies between the East and the West, he evolved a synthesis of both. He also evolved a synthesis of spirit and matter, of science and Vedanta. According to Aurobindo, everyone has in him something divine, something his own, a chance of perfection and strength in him however small in measure. The task is to find it, develop it and use it. His life is based on spiritual discipline and the one end ardently sought after everything done is the attainment of the 'Life Divine' while living in the world.

Aurobindo considers all forms in the universe as multiple cells of One Consciousness and Yoga as the means through which one can come in contact with the true self and unite the separate parts of oneself and can also see the same divine in others. In his Yoga work is as important as meditation. His Yoga is not that of a 'Sanyasi' who turns away from life in order to turn towards God. On the other hand his Yoga is of the ordinary man, who has put God on shelf while he carries on his worldly pursuits. The seeker must experience the 'Ananda,' love, consciousness and energy of the 'Supreme' Trust must be lived. Work done in full concentration and in the Spirit of surrender takes one's consciousness nearer to the Divine. Knowledge, work, devotion and meditation are all integrated in his Yoga. The most important thing is to have an inner urge for the Divine. As Sri Aurobindo says, "One who chooses the Divine is chosen by the Divine. As the call for the Divine grows more intense, so does His help come more readily."

Aurobindo says that we must aim not only at an inner realisation but an outer realisation also—the establishment of the kingdom of God not only within the heart but also in the world of human affairs—in economics and politics. And he assures us that this is possible.

Yoga can be practiced in ordinary life. If a merchant wishes to follow this yoga, his business itself is regarded as work divine and he cannot practise corruption or do black-marketing. In the same way a student would look for higher values and will be saved from many useless and harmful activities. Brahmacharya (self-control) is the most important thing in a student's life. Sri Aurobindo says, "The practice of Brahmacharyai's is the first and most necessary condition of increasing the force within and turning it to such uses as may benefit the possessor or mankind. All human energy has a physical basis. The source of life and energy is not material but spiritual. But the basis, the foundation on which the life; and energy stand and work is physical. The ancient Hindus clearly recognised this distinction between Karan and pratishtha, the north pole and the south pole of being. Earth or gross matter is the 'pratishtha', the Brahman or the spirit is the Karan. To raise up the physical to the spiritual is Brahmacharya, for by the meeting of the two the energy which starts from one and produces the other is enhanced and fulfils itself. The more we can, by Brahmacharya, increase the store of tapas (heat), tejas (light), vidyut (electricity) and ojas (life-force), the more we shall fill ourselves with utter energy for the works of the body, heart mind and spirit."

PHILOSOPHY OF EDUCATION

Aurobindo was an eminent educationist also. He showed to mankind the way to the highest spiritual growth i.e. real solace giver of the people. Shri Aurobindo expressed that the main aid of a teacher is his conscience. This conscience has four stages namely: (1) Consciousness, (2) Mind, (3) Intellegence and, (4) Knowledge. Education should develop all these four stages as much as possible. He held the view that any education involving all the factors spiritual penance, practice of Yoga and Brahmcharya, will definitely develop man to the fullest extent. According to Aurobindo a man does not possess a physical spirit only, he is endowed with higher mental, godly intelligence and a very high spiritual soul element also. He has a capacity to recognise and realise God. To realise this great aim, he has to develop his powers of thinking, concentration and deep meditation together with other divine faculties to the fullest. According to Aurobindo, real education is that which provides a free and creative environment to the child and by developing his interests, creatively, mental, moral and aesthetic senses finally leads to the development of his spiritual powers. Aurbindo writes, "That alone would be true and living education which helps to bring out to full advantage all that is in an individual man."

Basic Principles of his Education at Philosophy

Below are given basic principles of Aurbindo's Educational Philosophy:

1. Education should be imparted through the medium of mother tongue.

2. Education should be child-centered.

3. Education should be according to the menal aptitudes and psychological needs of the child.

4. Education should develop to the full the latent powers of the child.

5. Education should achieve the physical purification of child.

6. Education should develop consciousness.

7. Education should train the senses of child.

8. Education should develop the soul substance of individual.

9. Brahamcharya should be the basic foundation of education.

10. Subjects of education should be interesting.

11. Education should develop all the faculties of child to make him a complete man.

12. There should be religious tinge in education otherwise it will spread corruption.

Concept of Education

Shri Aurobindo was deadly against the prevalent education of his times. According to him our education should be in accordance with the needs of our real modern life. In other words, education should create dynamic citizens so that they are able to meet the real needs of modern complex life. Shri Aurobindo thus writes, "Education to be true must not be a machine-made fabric. But a true building or living evocation of the power of the mind and spirit of human being".

Shri Aurobindo realised that Indians were gradually drifting from Idealism towards Materialism with the result that the inherent divine light in them, was gradually on the wane. He vehemently condemned the western materialistic education as it could not sustain and develop Indian ideals, values and culture. According to Aurobindo, we Indians need an education which develops the powers of our mind and should achieve our fullest growth. With these ends in view, he opened an Ashram at Pondichery and established and International University and provided over there an education suited to the ideals and values of Indian culture, bases upon Brahamcharya, yoga, concentration and meditation through which an individual could develop to the full in body, mind and soul in a harmonious way. Dr. R.S. Mani has rightly described. "Aurobindo's philosophy of education is based on the principle of evocation of potentialities of the individual in all its entirety and full development of as many sides as possible". His views on education reveal that Shri Aurobindo was one of the most eminent and distinguished educationists of our country.

Aims of Education

Shri Aurobindo Ghosh was deadly against the prevalent education of his times. He has admitted that after the attainment of independence, changes have occurred in our system of education, but it is not in on conformity with the mental and spiritual needs of children and demands of the nation. According to him our education should be in accordance with the needs of our real modern life. Sri Aurobindo writes, "Education to be true must not be a machine-made fabric, but a true building or living evocation of the powers of the mind and spirit of human being."

Some specific aims of Education advocated by Aurobindo are gven below:

1. Physical Development and Purity: The first aim of education is to achieve complete physical and pure development of a child. According to Aurobindo, it is the body which performs all religious obligations. Physical development and purification are the two basis on which the edifice of spiritual development is built.

2. Development of Senses: The second aim of education is to train all the senses namely hearing, speaking, listening, touching, smelling and tasting. According to Aurobindo these senses can be fully trained when nerve, chitta and manas are pure.

3. Mental Development: The third aim of education is to achieve mental development of the child. This mental development means the development of all mental faculties namely memory, thinking, reasoning, imagination and discrimination etc.

4. Development of Morality: Aurobindo has emphasised that without moral and emotional development mental development becomes harmful to human progress. For the moral development of child emotions, ingressions or habits and nature are the three essential factors. Thus, the ideals of a teacher should be so high that the child, by mere imitation, is able to reach higher and higher stages of development.

5. Development of Conscience: Another important aim of education is to develop the conscience. According to him, it has four levels namely: (1) Chitta, (2) Manas, (3) Intelligence, (4) Knowledge. A teacher should develop all these four levels harmoniously. This will promote the development of conscience.

6. Spiritual Development: Shri Aurobindo emphasised that the main aim of education is to promote spiritual development. According to him every human being has some element of divinity in him, he says, "The chief aim of education should be to help the growing soul to draw out that in itself which is best and make it perfect for a noble use."

The Curriculum

Aurobindo prescribed free environment for the child to develop all his latent faculties to the maximum and suggested all those subjects and activities which should possess elements of creativity and educational expression. He wished to infuse a new life and spirit into each subject and activity through which the development of super human-being could becomes possible. He laid down the following principle for curriculum:

1. Curriculum should be in such a way which child find as interesting.

2. It should include all those subjects which promote mental and spiritual development.

3. It should motivate children towards the attainment of knowledge of the whole world.

4. It should contain creativity of life and constructive capacities. Aurobindo describes curriculum for different stages of education.

(i) Mother Tongue, English, French, Literature, National History, Art, Painting, General Science, Social Studies and Arithmetic should be taught at primary stage.

(ii) Mother Tongue, English, French, Literature, Arithmetic, Art, Chemistry, Physics, Botany, Physiology, Health Education, Social Studies at secondary stage.

(iii) Indian and Western Philosophy, History of Civilisation, English Literature, French, Sociology, Psychology, History, Chemistry, Physics, Botany at university level.

(iv) Art, Painting, Photography, Sculptural, Drawing, Typing, Cottage-Industries, Mechanical and Electrical Engineering, Nursing etc. at vocational level.

Teacher-Taught Relationship

Aurobirndo enunciates certain sound principles of good teaching, which have to be kept in mind when actually engaged in the process of learning. According to Aurobindo, the first principle of true teaching is "That nothing can be taught." He explains that the knowledge is already dormant within the child and for this reason, the teacher is not an instructor or task-master; "He is a helper and a guide." The role of the teacher "is to suggest and not to impose". He does not actually train the pupil's mind, he only shows him how to perfect the instruments of knowledge and helps him and encourages him in the process. He does not impart knowledge to him; he shows him how to acquire knowledge for himself. He does not call forth the knowledge that is within; he only shows him where it lies and how it can be habituated to rise to the surface.

The Concept of School

Aurobindo's philosophy of education aims at modifying the school curricula, maximising the learning modalities, helping the child to achieve his potentiality at his own pace and level and devote his time to discover himself. This kind of schooling is seen as an anti-thesis of an imposed uniformity of prescribed courses and teaching which the traditional schools purport to do and can be linked to what was taught in schools under the colonial rule. The type of schooling visualised by Sri Aurobindo is seen as aiming to bridge the gap between the child's life at school and that at home.

In contrast to the educational ideas of Aurobindo, the present day education system in India is purely an instruction-of-information enterprise, supported by a subject-time-bound curriculum, which neither relates to the needs or abilities of the learner nor takes into consideration the way children learn successfully. Instead of being child-oriented it is subject-oriented. The schools focus on competition with others, mastery of subject matter for getting better marks or grades than on learning in cooperation with and from one another for personal growth and for welfare of others.

This is not exclusive to Indian phenomenon, rather all over the world education is largely reductionist, materialist, ego-enforcing, and devoid of the joys of the spirit. It is in this context that there is a need to examine initiatives which are rooted in Indian tradition, seek alternatives in curriculum, teaching and learning for measuring success, involve children in the process of learning and focus on learning from the another and not from an authoritative pedagogue.

Concept of Discipline

Children should be provided with a free environment so that they are able to gain more and more knowledge by their own efforts. According to him, any retrained and imposed environment stunt the growth and natural development. Aurobindo propagated the concept of self-discipline which was the cure of impressionistic discipline.

AUROBINDO'S CONCEPT OF INTEGRAL-EDUCATION

'Integral Education' is the vision of Sri Aurobindo, who first put his views on this topic in various newspapers and magazines in between 1904-08. According to him, the pattern of education should be liberal enough and a student should have fulfill freedom to choose whatever he likes. The main aim of integral-education is: student will be guided by his/her psychic-being. The teache duty is to inculcate this quality in the student's mind. Examination system will not put any pressure on the students; depression never comes to a student's mind. And evaluation process will be in such a way to influence the students instead of being frustrated.

These thoughts were brought to action when "The Mother" of Sir Aurobindo Ashram, Pondicherry stepped forward to start such dream institute in the name of 'Sri Aurobindo Integral-Edcuation Centre' in the year 1943. Till date the institute is running under the special guidance of Sri Aurobindo Trust.

True education, according to Sri Aurobindo, is not only spiritual but also rational, vital and physical. In other words it is integral-education. This integral-education has been explained by Aurobindo's closest collaborator, the Mother in these words. "Education to be complete must have five principal aspects relating to the five principal activities of human being: the physical, the vital, the mental, the psychic and the spiritual. This education is complete, complimentary to each other and continued till the end of life. Aurobindo's scheme of education is integral in two senses. Firstly, it is integral in the sense inculcating all the five aspects of the individual being. Secondly, it is integral in the sense of being an education not only for the evolution of the individual alone, but also of the nation and finally of the humanity. The ultimate aim of education is the evolution of total humanity. In this scheme of evolution, the principle of growth is unity in diversity. This unity again, maintains and helps the evolution of Diversity.

The Integral School

The circles of moral responsibility and loyalties proceed from wider to narrower and vice-versa. The man has to develop first as a human being then as a citizen and finally as an individual:

NATIONAL SYSTEM OF EDUCATION

Aurobindo strongly argued for national system of education. He put forward the following elements.

- Education does not become national by tagging the word 'national' to the system.
- Education should pay due attention to sacrifice, progress and increasing knowledge.
- Mere knowledge of science doesn't make us educated in the true sense. This must be related to powers of the human mind and spirit.
- There should be a balanced understanding of the national and international relationship of universal relationship.

CONCLUSION

The synthesis of the great philosophy of Sri Aurobindo can be summed up in one phrase: "Realisation of the sublime 'Truth' which can be achieved through the integral view of life, being a superman and the Gnostic individual, Descent of Divine Power, intuition, yoga and super mind. By integral view of life, he implied "a healthy integration of God and Man". Aurobindo placed premium on intuition and not on logical reasoning and preached the gospel of 'intuition and more perfect intuition'. His idea on yoga was aimed at divinising the whole man and for this he advised the education of the mind. To Aurobindo only such education was true and living which helped one to develop his latent powers and enabled him to enter into the right relationship with life, mind, soul of his nations well as with the total life, mind and soul of humanity. Information cannot be the foundation of intelligence, but can help build knowledge, the starting point of further discovery and creation of fresh knowledge. An education that confines itself to imparting knowledge is no education. Education must be based on the psychology of the child's nature. Parents and teachers must enable the child to educate himself, to develop his own practical, intellectual, moral and aesthetic capacities and to grow independently as an organic being.

Bibliography

Adams, Sir John : *Modern Developments in Educational Practice*. University of London Press, London, 1928.

Allen, E.A. : *Existentialism From Within*, R and K Paul, London, 1953.

Ayer, A.J. : *Philosophical Essays*, MacMillan and Co. Ltd., London 1959.

Blackham, H.J. : *Six Existentialist Thinkers*, MacMillan & Co., London, 1951.

Brubacher, J.S.: *Modern Philosophies of Education*. McGraw Hill, New Delhi, 1969.

Brubacher, J.S.: 'Education for Death' School and Society, LVI, Aug. 22, 1942, pp. 137-141.

Butler, Donald: *Four Philosophies and their practice in Education and Religion*, Harper and Row, New York, 1968.

Childs, J.L. : *Education and the Philosophy of Experimentalism*. Appleton Century, New York, 1931.

Connord, J.O. : *An Introduction to the Philosophy of Education*, Routledge and Kegan Paul, London, 1966.

Dewey, John : *Democracy and Education*, The MacMillan & Co., New York, 1944.

______, *Child and the Curriculum*, Phenix Books, University of Chicago Press, Chicago, 1956.

______, *School and Society*, Phenix Books, University of Chicago Press, Chicago, 1956.

______, *Problems of Men*, Philosophical Library, New York, 1946.

______, *Creative Intelligence*. Holt Rinehart, Winston, New York, 1917.

Dickens, Charles : *Hard times*.

Froebel : *A Selection from his Writings by Irene M. Lilly*, Cambridge University Press, Cambridge, 1967.

Dhiman, O.P : *Gandhian Philosophy Acritical and comprehension study the Indian Publications*, Ambala Cantt. 1971.

______, *Betrayal Gandhi*, Kalpaz Publications, New Delhi, 2010.

______, *Principles and Teacniques of Education*, Kalpaz Publications, New Delhi, 2007.

Dhiman, O.P : *Understauding Education*, Kalpaz Publications, New Delhi, 2008.

Gurudutt, K. : *Existentialism and Indian Thought*, Philosophical Library, New York, 1960.

Heidegger : *'Existence and Recognition in NSSE 54th Year Book*, Public School Pub. Co., Bloonington III.

______, *Existence and Being*, Vision Press, London, 1949.

Henderson, S.V.P. : *Introduction to the Philosophy of Education*, University of Chicago Press, Chicago, 1947.

Hiriyanna, M. : *Outlines of Indian Philosophy*, Allen and Unwin, London, 1932.

Hocking, W.E. : *Types of Philosophy*, Charles Scribrers and Sons, New York, 1937.

Horne, H.H. : *This New Education*. Abingdon Press, New York, 1931.

______, *This Philosophy of Education*, MacMillan & Co., New York, 1937.

James, William : *Pragmatism,* Longmans Greens & Co., New York, 1941.

Kilpatrick : *Philosophy of Education*, MacMillan & Co., New York, 1936.

Kneller : *Existentialism and Education*, Philosophical Library, New York, 1958.

______, (ed.) : *'Contemporary Educational Theory' in foundations of Education*, John Wiley and Sons, New York, 1967.

King and Brownell : *The Curriculum and the Disciplines of Knowledge*, JohnWiley and Sons, New York, 1966.

Longford, Glenn and O'connor, D.J. (ed.) : *New Essays in the Philosophy of Education,* Routledge and Kegan Paul, London, 1973.

Montessori: *A Text in the History of Education*, (educational series), Norwood Edns., 1905.

______, *Montessori Method*. Vols. I & II, William Heinemann, London, 1918.

Munshi, K.M. : *Foundations of Indian Culture*, Bhavan's Publications.

Niblett, W.R. : *'On Existentialism and Education in British Journal of Educational Studies*. Vol. II, No. 2, May 1954.

Nunn, T.P. : *Education its Data and First Principles*. The Modern Educators Library Series, Edward Arnold and Co., London, 1920

Park, Joe : *Selected Readings in the Philosophy of Education*, MacMillan & Co., New York, 1968.

Patrick, G.T.W. : *Introduction to Philosophy*, Allen and Unwin, London, 1951.

Peters, R.S. : *'Must an Educator have an Aim?' in Authority, Responsibility and Education*. Allen and Unwin, London, 1959.

Phenix : *Philosophy of Education*, holt and Rinehart, New York, 1958.

Reid, Lewis, Arnold : *Philosophy and Education*. Helnemann, London, 1961.

______, *Philosophy and the Theory and Practice of Education*. Evans Brothers Ltd., London, 1965.

Ross : *Ground Work of Educational Theory*. George G. Harrap and Co. Ltd., London, 1958.

Rousseau, J.J. : *Emile* (tr.) Barbara Foxley Everyman's Library, Dent, London, 1911.

Ruggeiro : *Existentialism* (ed.) Happen Stall, Seeker and Warburg, London, 1946.

Russell, Bertrand : *History of Western Philosophy,* Unwin University books, Aleen and Unwin, London, 1969.

Sartre, Jean Paul : *Existentialism and Humanism,* (tr.) Co., London, 1948.

______, *Existentialism.* The Philosophical Library, New York, 1952.

______, *Being and Nothingness.* (ed.) Dr. H.E. Barnes Philosophical Library, New York, 1956.

______, *Of Human Freedom,* (tr.) W. Baskin Philosophical Library, New York, 1966.

______, *Condemned to Freedom* (ed.), Jusus Streller Philosophical Library, New 1960.

Report of the Secondary Education Commission, 1952.

Report of the Indian Education Commission, 1966.

Report of the University Education Commission, 1948.

Challenge of Education – A Policy Perspective, 1985.

The Ram Murti refont 1990 .

Smith, P.G. : *Philosophy of Education,* Harper & Row, New York, 1965.

Spencer, Herbert : *On Education* (ed.) Andreas M. Kazamias, Classics in Education, Series No. 30, Teachers College Press, Columbia University, New York, 1966.

Srinivasan, G. : *Existentialist Concepts and the Hindu Philosophical Systems,* Udayana Publications, Allahabad, 1967.

Wahl, Jean : *A Short History of Existentialism, Philosophical Library,* New York, 1949.

Index

E

T